A FEW GOOD WOMEN

To John + Stella
Semper Fi' !
Sarga Ferris

A FEW GOOD WOMEN

Memoirs of a World War II Marine

Inga Fredriksen Ferris

To order additional copies of this book, contact:
Xlibris Corporation
1-888-795-4274
www.Xlibris.com
Orders@Xlibris.com
14685

A FEW GOOD WOMEN is dedicated to all of the women who served the cause of freedom in the greatest war the world has ever known. And to Mary Gertrude Kilgallen Crowley, who inspired me to record some of the events that took place in our little corner of that war.

SPECIAL THANKS TO:

My late husband, Milt Ferris, who, early in our marriage, introduced me to the joys of writing while I worked with him, publishing his weekly newspaper in Joshua Tree, California.

And to my first born, the late Kirk Ferris, for helping me select my first computer, son Lloyd Ferris for teaching me how to use it, and daughter Vikke Phalen, who interested Curtis Corlew, her gifted friend, in designing the cover. Curtis, you were an inspiration!

Thanks also to the writers in my critique group, who taught me the meaning of the word "cut":

Dorothy Bodwell, Dottie Brendlen, Virginia Crill, Jacque Hall, Laura Leonard, and Fran Wojnar.

And most especially to my friends, Nat and Kay Carleton, for that meaningful final edit.

*   *   *

Front cover photo taken by Sgt. Anna Tierney (Williams) on a hitchhiking trip through Boulder City, Colorado following author's discharge.

BACKGROUND

Tuesday, September 5,1939
John Marshall High School
Chicago, Illinois

"You boys, here in this classroom, will be called to fight in the greatest, most devastating war the world has ever known."

That's how Mrs. Busby began our senior World History course at Marshall High. She had just returned from sabbatical leave in Europe, where she witnessed the mounting tension.

I glanced around the room at the boys, eagerly raising their hands with questions. Who, among them, would have to go?

The following spring I covered my yearbook with the front page of a newspaper. The headlines read, "PARIS FALLS." The boys in that history class would soon register for the draft.

After graduating I found work with Burny Brothers Bakeries and assumed support of my widowed mother. A year later she inherited a home in Portland, Oregon and in October, 1941, I joined her there.

On the morning of December 7th I was working in the bakery section of a Fred Meyers department store when a customer came in with the news. Japan had bombed Pearl Harbor.

A woman working across the aisle from me had a son stationed there. She fled to the women's locker room and cried. She returned later, red-eyed, and finished her day.

As Portland prepared for war, I applied at the employment office for defense work. They gave me a letter of introduction, and sent me to a place called Radio Specialty Mfg. Co. They knew how to grind radio crystals that were desperately needed in walkie talkies to communicate with our men on the fighting fronts. During the next two years it grew, and in December of 1943 we earned the Army Navy E for our contribution to the war effort.

INTRODUCTION

There's A War Going On

Portland, Oregon. One Sunday in February, 1944

My mother motioned Tom, her gentleman friend, to follow her outside. "Come see how my victory garden is growing."

Instead, he came into the dining room and watched as I stitched the long leg seam of a pair of work pants. Leaning his large frame against the bookcase, he said, "Inga, we have to talk."

I removed my feet from the treadle and turned to him. "Sure Tom. What's on your mind?"

"I'd like to marry Sadie." Raising his voice, he added, "I want to ask your mother to marry me."

I had been wondering when he was going to get around to it. "That's wonderful, Tom. She's very fond of you."

"But something bothers me." He scratched his head, rearranging a thick growth of gray hair. "You have a very good job. I'm just a night watchman at Kaiser Shipyards. I couldn't do for her the same way you do."

I was the first woman my company had hired for work in a field vital to the war effort. It paid well, but I knew the job would last only for the duration of the war. Before I could protest, my mother came in waving a fistful of radishes.

"Look at the size of these!"

Tom followed her to the kitchen sink. A tall, portly gentleman with a kind face, he towered over my mother, who was shorter, soft and round. She put an apron on him to protect his suit. Then she stood back and they laughed.

I got the machine humming again, but my mind was not on the work pants. Why did Tom feel he had to compete with me? While it was true I was well paid, and supported my mother, I couldn't fill the empty place in her life, my father's death had left.

I stitched the waistband on backwards.

"Dinner's ready. Come and get it."

The meatloaf looked like it had taken our whole week's meat ration. Tom relished every bite of it and took seconds of everything. That seemed to please my mother.

When we had finished eating he said, "Sadie, I'll help you with the dishes so we can get an early start." Turning to me he added, "We're going to the dance at the Lonesome Club tonight."

"I'll get these," I assured them. "You two run along."

My mother had said that to me many times when my date had come to dinner. Had we switched roles? The thought sent me flying through the dishes so that I, too, could "run along."

Leaving the waistband problem for another day, I hurried down the hill to catch the Foster bus. There would be juke box dancing at the USO, where I was a junior hostess.

The next morning it was raining hard when I left for work. Leaving my hair in pin curls, I stuffed a couple layers of waxed paper under my babushka and headed out into the wet darkness.

We were near the end of the line so the 5:15 bus was almost empty. The ride would take forty-five minutes. More if the bridge was up. I settled into a window seat in the back.

As more workers entered, the smell of wet wool, mingling with rubber raincoats and old leather work boots, soon filled the air. Before I had time to think about what Tom had said yesterday, a large, buxom woman took the seat beside me.

"You with Kaiser Shipyards?"

"No, I work at Radio Specialty."

"You're not working for the war?"

"Oh yes. I am."

She nodded approval. "I'm a welder at the shipyards," she began, and talked for the rest of the trip. By the time we reached her stop, just over the bridge, I had heard the story of her life, and had no time to think about my own. I transferred to a Powell bus for the short ride to Glisan.

Due to coffee rationing, and my mother's dependency on it, I had my first cup at Marie's, a cafe near the plant. At that hour it was always filled with Coast Guards who preferred Marie's aromatic brew to the "mud" served in the galley. Their station was directly across the street from us. They called it "The USS Ninth and Glisan."

An incident had occurred shortly after we moved in. It was summer and all of our windows, as well as theirs, were left wide open. The women on my crew got the giggles every time they saw a Coast Guard walk past in shorts, or wrapped in a towel. The day a towel dropped they let out a scream that was heard across the street. That afternoon their windows were nailed shut and painted battleship gray.

I entered Marie's and took an empty stool at the counter to the right of Petty Officer 1st Class Merriweather. His wife worked in the cutting room at the plant.

Marie poured me a cup of coffee. I really needed that.

A female Coast Guard strutted in and took the stool on the other side of me. These women were called SPARS. The name is taken from the Coast Guard motto, Semper Paratus—Always Ready. She looked sharp and trim in her Navy blue uniform. I had wanted a suit that color, but couldn't get the material. All available blue dye was needed now for military uniforms.

The mirror behind the counter reflected a depressing contrast between us. My orange plaid babushka had slipped back, exposing layers of waxed paper over dishwater blonde pin curls. I yanked it forward.

Merriweather noticed that I was watching her. "Inga," he grinned, "when are you going to join us?"

How I wished that I could! I now felt my mother would be cared for if I enlisted, but I had been trained in vital defense work, so I was trapped. They called it "frozen on the job."

"Merri, this morning I'm ready to sign up, but it wouldn't be right. Besides, Ken probably wouldn't let me.

"Who's Ken? Your boy friend?"

"No. I don't have a boy friend. One date with me and they ship out. But I've got the longest list of pen pals in town."

To answer his question I added, "Ken Johnson is the plant manager. Maybe you've seen him in here. He's that tall slim blond, wears glasses. I don't know what he'd do without me."

"Simple. He'd hire somebody else."

"It's not that easy, Merri. I was the first woman he hired. He spent a lot of time training me, and now I train the crews. By the time he had someone else knowing everything he's taught me, this war could be over."

He burst into a loud guffaw. "War? What war? You mean there's a war going on?"

Every Coast Guard in Marie's heard that remark. They joined in the laughter and added a few remarks of their own.

"Do you see a war?"

"No, I don't see a war."

This was a sensitive subject for them. It was their job to protect the coast from invasion, but so far it had been quiet.

It was beginning to get light. My coffee finished, I took one last envious look at the SPAR. Then, checking to make sure my babushka hid the pin curls, I headed for the plant.

I found Ken upstairs at my desk, reading *The Oregonian*. I glanced at the headlines: FIRST MARINE DIVISION TAKES TALASEA.

He looked up. "Inga," he began in his quiet way, "as soon as you have your girls set up, come to my office. We need to talk."

After the talk with Tom yesterday, I thought I was ready for anything. "I'll be there," I said, and he left.

I hung my wet coat on a hook in the cloak room and let my hair down quickly, anxious to know what was on Ken's mind. I sensed, by his manner, it was important.

When the seven o'clock whistle blew, my crew had their schedules and they were working. I hurried downstairs to Ken's office. He was studying a number of papers spread over his desk. The forms were not familiar to me.

"These reports came in from St. Louis late Saturday, right after you left," he began. "They're going to completely change our method of finishing crystals."

The plant in St. Louis was the only other manufacturer of radio crystals used by the Army Signal Corps. It was not as large as ours, but it met the same high standards of performance. I listened intently.

"They've found a way to etch the crystals down to frequency in acid. It will give them a stronger, more stable activity with much less hand work than we're having to do now. I've already talked to them this morning."

I looked at my watch.

"It's two hours later there," he said.

"We're switching over to this new method as soon as we can. You'll need to retrain the crew to an entirely new system. They're sending their man out to explain it and help us get started. Any questions?"

"Yes. Does this mean everything you've taught me about finishing radio crystals is now obsolete?"

"Well, most of it." Ken paused thoughtfully. "It's like the finishing crew is starting over again. What's on your mind?"

"May I have some time off later this morning?"

By ten o'clock I was in the Coast Guard recruiting office. While I tried to imagine how it would feel to wear her uniform, the SPAR recruiter raved on about the great life I would have as one of them.

"They try to station you near your home," she said. "I'm from Eugene, so I get down there every weekend. There's so few of us, they put us up in apartments and give us subsistence pay to cover the cost of our food. You'll probably get stationed here in Portland, so you can continue to live at home."

She handed me an application.

"And you can be thankful you're not joining the Marines. When

I took basic training at Hunter College, we drilled the same time they did, with just a chain link fence between us. Every once in a while we'd take a break and rest, you know? But those Marine DIs wouldn't let their girls relax for a minute. They had to drill the full hour, nonstop.

"And those Women Marines never know where they're going to go. They get sent all over the country."

I put my pen down. "May I use your phone book?"

"Oh sure," she said. Turning smartly to reach for it, she added, "You need a phone number for one of your references?"

"No." I shook my head. "I want to locate the Women Marine's recruiting office."

*   *   *

FREDRIKSEN, Inga V. (771814)
Taken: 18May44
Enl: 14Mar44

Boot camp mug shot

Sadie and Tom

Saying goodbye to Mom

A FEW GOOD WOMEN

By Inga Fredriksen Ferris

CHAPTERS

CHAPTER 1.
MAKING CAMP

May 4, 1944. New River, North Carolina

The troop train lurched to a stop. It was time, now, to leave the Pullman car that had been my home for six days. I really needed a bath.

"New River, North Carolina," the porter's voice rang out in rich baritone. "End of the line for you Marines. Watch your step, ladies."

Margaret Elder had taken the berth below me when we boarded in Portland, Oregon. An attractive girl, she was about my age and almost as tall. Sitting across from me now, she ran a comb through her auburn locks one more time and glanced out the window.

"The station's empty. Nothing here but a few stray pigeons."

When the porter opened the door I knew she was wrong. A woman was out there, and she was shouting at us. "All right you boots, step out. STEP . . . OUT!"

I jumped up and edged a long, lean leg into an already crowded aisle. Elder was close behind.

"I said step out. STEP OUT! On the double now!"

That wasn't a very friendly way for her to greet us. Recruits up ahead were tripping over each other trying to get out. Nearing the door, I saw her. That had to be the biggest, meanest looking woman Marine sergeant they could find. Elder shook her head. "I sure wouldn't want to tangle with her."

Elder was so gentle, she couldn't tangle with anyone. We had become close friends during the trip. I hoped we would not be separated.

"Come on boots, move. MOVE!"

"Freddy, she's ugly."

Elder insisted on calling me Freddy after the sergeant on the train told us we would use our last names in the service. "Fredriksen's too long," she said.

I took another look at the sergeant. While certainly authoritative, she was far from ugly. Tall, with a firm jaw and high cheekbones, her face reflected the classic type of beauty I had seen on recruiting posters. Honey blonde hair a bit lighter than mine was cropped and trained to look as if it was growing up instead of down, curling over the brim of a spruce green bowler hat. It matched the stripes in her seersucker uniform.

She gripped a baton firmly in her right hand. Aiming it toward a flat paved surface nearby, she shouted, "Over there. Line up OVER THERE. Hey, let's look alive!"

Moving out from the darkness of the Pullman car, I was blinded by the brilliance of midday sun. As I paused to get my bearings, she came at me. "Come on, get out. GET OUT! What's the matter with you civilians?"

I thought I was a Marine.

As I stepped down she yelled, "Thirty-five. One more, that's all." She motioned to her companion, nearby. "Sgt Sullivan, the next one's yours."

I turned to make sure Elder was still behind me. Perhaps we should not have been in such a hurry to leave the train. Better to have taken our chances with Sullivan.

"I'm Sergeant Booth," she began. "You'll be assigned to my platoon. I only have six weeks to try to make Marines out of you." She shook her head. "From the looks of you that's going to be an impossible job."

Turning, she led us to a waiting bus and tapped the door of the vehicle with her stick. It opened. The woman behind the wheel was dressed in men's dungarees and overseas cap. Admiring that heavy cotton twill, I hoped I'd get a job where I could dress like that. Stockings and garter belts were just too much trouble.

After we climbed aboard and found seats together, we were quiet for a while, each deep in our own thoughts. I wondered what was waiting ahead for us. Considering the reception we just had, it seemed that we were going into enemy territory.

The silence was broken when we stopped at the gate to Camp Lejeune. When our driver presented papers to the guard, Elder remarked, "Wow, it looks like they're taking us to prison. How much time do we have to serve?"

She made it sound like this would be punishment for doing something wrong. I reminded her we were freeing a Marine to fight, having enlisted for the duration of the war, plus six months.

She twisted the diamond ring on her finger and sighed. "That could be a very long time."

I didn't want to think about it.

When the bus moved on, I looked out the window. The base seemed to have endless rows of identical two-story red brick buildings, all of recent construction. They looked like they had been built to last a long time. It made me feel uneasy. How long did they expect this war to go on?

Most of the grounds were cleared, save for patches of grass and some newly planted shrubbery. But here and there a pine tree had escaped the axe and at a distance, virgin forests of them stood tall, undisturbed by military encroachment.

We stopped at an open area where Sgt. Charlotte Plummer, director of the Marine Corps Women Reserve's band, greeted us with music from one of the songs we had been taught on the train. Stepping out, I began to sing along.

"Marines, we serve that men may fight in air on land and sea . . ."

Sgt Booth frowned at me with disapproval. "Pile your luggage on that flat-bed," she said, pointing to it with her club. "Then fall into platoon formation over here." She gestured toward a wide asphalt path. "That's three rows of twelve."

Marching to the mess hall for lunch, I kept checking with the others to make sure I was in step. I always had trouble telling left from right.

Sgt. Booth gave us the rules before entering. "These mess girls are not boots," she began. "They have completed their training, and are now full-fledged Marines. You will give them your total respect and do everything they ask of you, without question." She added, "Take only as much food as you will eat, and eat everything you take."

That would be no problem for me. I was starved.

One chow line had been left open for us. The mess girls were dressed in dungaree pants with white skivvy shirts, aprons, and turbans. They seemed anxious to heap food on my tray. They must have known I was hungry. There was mashed potatoes, gravy, and roast beef any civilian would die for. I took it all.

At the table Elder passed me a large stainless steel pitcher of milk. As I filled my glass, three mess girls came over. To the tune of "Bring Back my Bonnie" they sang: "Stand up, stand up, stand up you boots stand up stand up.."

We did as we were told. They grinned. We smiled back. Before we could sit down, the singing began again.

"For she's a jolly good fellow . . ."

At the end of that song, I had just hit the bench when they repeated, "Stand up, stand up . . ."

It got pretty ridiculous. They kept us bouncing up and down with no chance to take even a bite of food until Sgt. Booth came in and ordered us out on the double.

I gulped some milk while I stood in line to empty my tray. A mess girl watched and scolded as I scraped off the food. "Why did you take so much, Boot? Look! You didn't eat any of it. If you want to be a Marine, you can't waste food like that, BOOT!"

If the depression taught me anything, it was not to waste food. I bit my lip, placed the tray on a rack, and moved on to dump milk in front of another mess girl. This one must have been six feet tall.

"Don't take more milk than you will drink, BOOT. And wipe your lipstick off that glass, BOOT."

I couldn't do anything right.

I tried not to think of my empty stomach on the march back. We passed through wooded areas and crossed little bridges over the streams that ran through camp on their way to the sea.

At our first stop we were issued supplies. When Elder went for the closest, longest line, the sergeant yelled, "take any line, and keep them all moving."

Not wanting to annoy the sergeant any further, I headed for a shorter line. Elder pulled me back. "We have to stick together," she said.

When we fell into formation again, each with a laundry bag full of necessities flung over our shoulder, we were marched to the women's barracks area. Recruits from earlier battalions stood at their windows calling to us as we passed. "You'll be sorry! You'll be sorry!"

They could be right.

The luggage was waiting for us, in front of Bldg. 24. Grabbing my suitcase, I followed the sergeant inside and up the stairs, where she gave us a tour of the upper deck.

The barracks were H shaped. Each of the squad rooms that would make up the two long sides would sleep eighty-eight women. The center crossbar held our shower room, basins, and toilets, which we would learn to call heads. There were closets with utility tubs, cleaning equipment and supplies, and a storage room for our luggage. The sergeant told us the office was at the foot of the stairs, and the laundry was in a separate building behind the barracks.

She didn't show us the bathtubs.

As we entered the squad room Sgt. Booth announced, "You have been assigned to Company E, platoon 5, of the 32nd Battalion. When I call 'E-5' I'm talking to you, and you had better listen up."

The squad room was immaculate. I didn't know anything could

smell so clean. It was a relief to know we wouldn't have to do any scrubbing around here for a while.

It was time to be billeted (assigned our bunks.) Elder and I hurried to an empty set, second from the end. "I'll take the top bunk," I said. "I got used to it on the train. Besides, my legs are longer."

That was a mistake. Oddly, my mattress was different from the rest. It was much older, showing yellow between the blue stripes on the ticking instead of white like the others. It sagged in the middle, and the corners were round. But I could sleep anywhere, and we were only going to be here six weeks. Why would I need square corners?

I was about to find out. Sgt. Booth ordered, "My platoon will follow me to the linen closet."

That line really moved. We were soon back with our sheets. The sergeant selected a top bunk about the middle of the platoon and we gathered around her to watch some lucky boot get her bed made. "I'm only going to show you once, so you had better pay attention."

She reached for a sheet and in one quick move centered it atop the mattress. "Square those corners," she began, "and pull hard on your sheets. I want to see all four corners perfectly squared, with the blanket on top pulled so tight that when you finish you can bounce a dime off of it."

Glancing back at my mattress, I felt a little sick.

"And when you fold that extra blanket at the foot of your bunk, I want those edges to look like they've been cut with scissors."

When she had finished she took a dime from her pocket and dropped it on the blanket. It bounced up and she caught it.

The boot whose bunk she made smiled shyly. "Thank you, Sergeant."

"Don't thank me, Boot. There are no favors in the Marine Corps, BOOT!" She stripped the bed and left.

I threw a sheet over my bunk and started in. The sergeant had made it look easy, but it wasn't. To make matters worse, I kept bumping into Elder.

I was still working on the blanket, pulling the ends tighter from between the coils underneath, when Sgt. Booth returned. She walked down the aisle pausing at each bunk to make a nasty remark. When she got to mine she stopped. "This one is a disgrace. Do it over, and do it right next time. I want to see SQUARE CORNERS."

"But . . ."

"And I will accept no excuses. There are no excuses in the Marine Corps!" She tore it apart and moved on.

Thompson had the top bunk on the end next to mine. She was tall enough to get a good look at the problem. "Your mattress looks like it's left over from the Civil War."

"I know. But what can I do?"

"Maybe if we pull hard on those sheets and blankets we can make them tight enough to get by."

Thompson was athletic. She was a lot of help. Together we tackled my mattress with a vengeance, pulling and tugging until it was as tight as we could get it.

Elder looked on sadly. "Poor Freddy," she said.

But when Sgt. Booth returned she had lost interest in my bunk. She had come to explain the cleaning procedures. She called it "policing the area."

"Every morning before chow," she began, "you will scrub everything until it shines. Special details will be assigned each week according to your bunk numbers, so that one of you will be policing around the area of your bunk while your bunkmate works on the detail. These will include the heads, showers, gear closets, Venetian blinds and the open common area here at the entrance to the squad room.

"While you are at the chow hall I will conduct an inspection to make sure everything is in place and spotless. If it isn't, the responsible boot will receive an hour or more of EPD, or extra

police duty. A typical EPD assignment might be to scrub the stairway corners with a toothbrush.

"And every Friday night we have a party."

Great!

"It's called a GI party, because that's when you GI everything,
moving the bunks and clothes poles to swab and wax the entire
deck. Make sure you put it all back exactly as before, bunks and
center clothes poles lined up perfectly down the center of the squad
room, from one end to the other."

Fortunately, it was only Thursday.

"Another thing," she continued. "From now on you boots will
move on military time. One A.M. is 0100, two A.M. 0200, and
so on. You will add 1200 to every hour past noon, each hour
followed by the minutes."

She looked at the clock over the door. "It's 3:57 P.M. civilian
time. In the military, that's 1557. All schedules are posted on
military time. Get used to it."

There seemed to be a lot of things we had to get used to.
When would I get to take a bath? I was beginning to itch.

"You will unpack now."

As I set my suitcase on the foot locker, I heard a boot off to my
right moan, "Oh, no!" I looked up and saw a short, rather chubby
figure. It was Gordy, and she was waving a Teddy bear. "Where am
I supposed to put Junior?"

Rudkin, Thompson's bunkmate on the other side, was studying the plan for displaying articles in the foot locker. "Stuffed animals aren't mentioned in here," she said. "Why don't you just
drop him in your laundry bag?"

Rudkin was a bit taller than Gordy. She had bright red hair,
delicate features, and an amused expression, as if she thought this
boot camp business was really very funny.

I wished that I could see the humor in it.

"Poor Junior," said Gordy. "I should have left him home. I
didn't know it was going to be like this." She gave the bear a hug
and pushed him down into the bag.

Before I finished unpacking, a boot by the door yelled "AT-TENTION!" and I knew the sergeant was back. I was glad we were in the far corner. If I had been the first to see Sgt. Booth, I probably couldn't make any sound at all.

She yelled, "E-5 will fall out for chow."

Great! We had been issued green bowler hats and told we must be "covered" whenever we went outside. Grabbing mine, I headed out, hoping they would let us eat this time. I was already well below the minimum weight requirement for my height. The civilian doctor who gave me my physical in Portland had let me put my heavy Chesterfield coat back on before weighing me, then "forgot" to deduct for clothing. It was not likely I would get that cooperation here.

We gathered outside and the sergeant arranged us in our permanent marching positions, so that we were graduated in height. "I want to see three rows, or squads, of twelve with the tallest in the lead. They will be your squad leaders." She paused. "Those in the rear are called feather merchants."

Thompson, the tallest of the squad leaders, would march on the right as right guide. At five feet six and a half, I was third from the front in the middle row, behind Murdock.

Gordy was a feather merchant.

"Remember your position, and when you hear 'E-5, FALL OUT!' you get down here on the double and arrange yourselves exactly as you are now. Any questions?

"All right." She taught us right face. "You will sing as you march to chow. Forward, march!" and we were on our way, singing "We're Lady Leathernecks."

They let us eat this time, but I still didn't trust them. I kept that milk pitcher close by and poured just a little at a time. That Amazon wasn't going to yell at me again for wasting milk.

When we got back to the squad room, I was looking forward to a bath, but first I would finish unpacking. We had to be careful to tie, button, and buckle everything.

Having tied the last shoelace, I was reaching for my bar of

Lifebuoy when I heard "ATTENTION!" Sgt. Booth had come to tell us about quiet hour, a ninety-minute period when we would remain in the squad room in total silence. "So if you need to go to the head, go now."

I grabbed stationery and climbed up on my bunk. Would there ever be time for a bath? I hadn't even had a chance to locate the tubs.

I wrote short notes to my mother in Portland and to my brother and sister in Chicago, before tackling the long list of servicemen I had been writing to in the Pacific Theater. I had met most of them at dances, some at the USO where I was a junior hostess. One date with me and they got their orders. I was a sucker for any service-man who said, "Will you write to me?"

"Of course." It was the patriotic thing to do.

I used the brief V-mail forms. That sent it on something new called microfilm, getting there faster and taking less space. I hadn't told them I was joining the Marines, wanting to make sure they accepted me first. No doubt they would be pleased to know that I, too, would be taking a more active part in this war.

Meanwhile, below me, my bunky Elder had only one service-man to write to. Charles Woods, her fiance, was an Army Air Corps cadet pilot.

We could write "FREE" in the place where the three-cent stamp would go. With everything given to us, we probably wouldn't need any money at all.

I was almost finished when I heard Sgt. Booth call, "End of quiet hour." Leaping to the floor, I reached for my robe, grabbed soap and towel, and headed out. Nothing was going to stop me from getting that bath now. Everyone else had the same idea, and they were closer to the door. I noticed they were all turning in at the showers. Evidently there were no bathtubs in this place, just one big community showering room. It was open on one side, with showerheads lining the other three walls.

Several naked boots were already crowded under every spray. This might take some getting used to. I stripped and waded in, pretending it didn't bother me. As I soaped down, a full figured boot, wrapped in a towel, entered from a head and moved swiftly toward the light switch.

CLICK!

Suddenly we were all in total darkness. The soap slipped from my hands. I bent down and felt around for it, but there were naked bodies getting in my way everywhere.

A voice called, "Who turned off the lights?"

Somebody had to turn them back on. I couldn't shower without my soap. I waded over to where I remembered seeing the switch, found it, and flipped it up.

Fortunately, I was not electrocuted.

Valdez was caught in the middle of the showers, trying to conceal her nakedness. She covered her ample breasts and screamed, "Oh! Oh! I don't have any clothes on!"

Crouching, she turned and ran, grabbing her robe from the bench on her way to the privacy of an empty head.

Seeing her terrified reaction to total exposure, I knew I wasn't the only boot who was scared, confused, and thoroughly overwhelmed by this intimidating lifestyle called Boot Camp.

The Marine Corps was trying to mold a group of naive young women into what had always been a very macho all-male organization.

Maybe some of us wouldn't make it.

*　　*　　*

CHAPTER 2.
DAY ONE

Reveille came with a brilliant flash when the lights came on directly above my bunk. The sergeant yelled, "Hit the deck. HIT THE DECK . . . come on, LOOK ALIVE!"

My first full day as a boot had begun. I wasn't too thrilled about it. My watch read 5:45AM. No, make that 0545. Better get used to it.

I slithered out of the sack, being careful not to disturb it. Dangling my legs off the side, I flipped over on my stomach and let my toes search for the rail below. Soon I was standing on the deck, wondering what I got myself into.

There was a loud thud a few bunks down. Thompson called out, "When the sergeant yells 'Hit the deck,' you don't have to hit it that hard." I noticed she had almost finished making her bunk in the time it took me to just get out of mine.

We had a lot of work to do. I glanced at my bunkmate. A late sleeper, Elder had not been disturbed by the lights, and she didn't hear the sergeant. She had to wake up fast.

Bending down to her, I called, "Elder, it's time to get up."

There was no response.

I nudged her shoulder and pleaded, "Come on, wake up."

She rolled over, away from me.

Thompson noticed I was having trouble. "Elder," she spoke softly, "If you don't get up right now, we're going to tear your bed apart."

She rolled back fast and lifted her head. "Don't do that. I'll get up."

I glanced at Thompson. "Thanks."

"No problem," she answered. "I had one like that in my room at the college dorm, but she came around."

Policing the area was a lot of trouble, especially on an empty stomach. Finishing late, I grabbed my toothbrush and made a run for the head. There was only one toilet and one basin still available. The rest had all been polished and roped off with toilet paper.

Due to a dental problem diagnosed as malocclusion, I had been fitted with a bite bar to pass the dental requirements for enlistment. It clamped down on my lower teeth so I could chew. I took it from my mouth, wrapped it in tissue, and placed it on the shelf above the basin. As I reached for my toothbrush a voice behind me yelled, "Last call for the head."

I left to take care of a more urgent problem.

When I returned my toothbrush and toothpaste had been dumped in the basin, and my bite bar was missing. The big GI (galvanized iron) trash can was gone, and so was the boot who had been cleaning. I ran back to the squad room. Stopping at the entrance, I yelled, "Who took my bite bar?"

A boot nearby asked, "What's a bite bar?"

"Who cleaned the basins this morning?"

No one was listening. Without my dental appliance I was 4F, physically unfit for military duty. I ran down to the NCO office and blurted out my story to Sergeant Booth. She was not sympathetic. "Can't you hold on to your gear, Boot?"

She followed me up the stairs. The first recruit to see her yelled, "ATTENTION!"

The sergeant asked, "Who cleaned the basins?"

"I did," came a voice from the back of the squad room.

"Front and center."

She came quickly, looking scared.

"Did you take something wrapped in tissue from the shelf?"

"Yes, Sergeant."

"Where did you put it?"

"In the GI can."

I interrupted. "The GI can in the head is gone."

"Who took the GI can in the head?"

Another frightened boot admitted to that.

"Where did you dump it?"

"In the other can that was here in the common area."

Two boots entered the squad room, each holding a handle of that can. It was empty.

"Where did you dump it? My bite bar was in there!"

One asked, "What's a bite bar?" She caught a glance from the sergeant. "Come on, we'll show you."

All five of us took off down a back stairway and headed outside to the dumping area. It looked hopeless. Since it had been on the top of the can, it was now at the bottom and contents of still another had been piled on top of it.

Overcome with anxiety, I began pawing frantically at the heap, like a dog digging for a bone. The others joined in, and we squeezed every fragment of tissue that looked like it might hold a dental appliance. Someone yelled, "Hey, the basins are secured. How are we going to wash our hands?"

My whole future was at stake, and she was concerned about her dirty hands?

I pawed desperately through the heap for what seemed a very long time before I heard a boot yell, "I found it!" Holding it out from her body as if it were a filthy thing, she begged me to take it. I grabbed it fast.

When we returned, my platoon was falling out for chow and I was faced with another problem. Where can I put the bite bar? Certainly not in my mouth, after it had been in two GI cans and the trash bin out back. The footlocker had to be left open for inspection. Spotting my laundry bag hanging on the corner of my bunk, I tucked it under a dirty sock and rushed out to muster.

Sgt. Booth called, "ATTENTION!" Even though we were running late, she took the time to add, "You are each responsible for your own gear. Don't ever leave anything of any value where it can be thrown out by the cleaning detail.

"Right face, forward march."

Would I ever learn to stay out of trouble? Everything always seemed to be my fault. I was too upset to break out in song as we marched, but I moved my lips. She wasn't going to yell at me for not singing.

In the chow hall I sat at the same table as the boot that found my bite bar. I noticed she was cutting her toast and eating it with a fork. Good idea.

Passing the pitcher of coffee to Elder, I heard singing nearby. The mess hall choir was serenading some boots who had just arrived. "Stand up, stand up . . ."

"Look at how pleased they are," said Elder. "They don't know they won't eat any breakfast."

We watched with sadistic fascination as they stood up, sat down, and stood up again and again. Later, we could hear the mess girls yelling at them as they left.

"Don't waste food, BOOT!"

"Wipe that lipstick off your cup, BOOT!"

Elder smiled. "You know, that routine is pretty funny when it happens to somebody else."

As we gathered outside to wait for our last recruits to finish eating, earlier platoons, in uniform, were waiting too. Some were singing, to the tune of "The Old Grey Mare,"

"Here we stand like birds in the wilderness,

"Birds in the wilderness, birds in the wilderness,

"Here we stand like birds in the wilderness

"Waiting for our chow hound."

We would join in the singing another time. Today that was not possible. Easy to spot in our civilian clothes, we were being invaded by a number of homesick boots.

"Anybody here from Syracuse?"

"Nebraska?"

"Arizona?"

Thompson saved them further questions. "We're mostly from Oregon, and some from Washington, with one Texan left over from the train ahead of us."

One asked, "What paht of Texas? Honey, tell me which one she is."

Thompson seemed amused at being called "Honey." Smiling, she nodded toward the path. "That's her coming up now."

The Texan waited for Valdez. Then she grabbed her arm aggressively, spinning her around so that they faced each other. "What paht of Texas ah ya'll from, Honey?"

"El Paso. Why?"

The other boot looked disappointed. "Glory be, that's about as far from Beaumont as you can get, and still be in Texas." She left quickly.

Valdez turned to Thompson. "Why did that boot want to know where I was from?"

"She probably just wanted to talk to someone from home."

In a couple of weeks, when the next battalion of recruits arrived, we would surround them outside the chow hall the same way, asking, "Anybody from Oregon?" because two weeks seems like a long time when you're so far away from home.

But today the whole procedure seemed pointless. I was relieved when Sgt. Booth called us to attention and marched us back to the barracks. She followed us up the stairs with a report on the morning's inspection. Valdez had "kittens" under her bed. They were little balls of fuzz that rolled around on the floor. The boot with the bunk they happened to be under for inspection would get an hour of EPD. Valdez had to clean the Venetian blinds in the NCO office. I was admonished for a sloppy bunk, but it was only a warning.

Since classes wouldn't start until Monday, I expected to have the day free. I had clothes to launder, letters to write, and I needed to wash my hair. But the sergeant wouldn't leave us alone. She gathered us outside in platoon formation to teach us things the DI would expect us to know.

We learned to do a "Column left, (or right) march." That was simple. We just followed the squad leaders and let them decide which way to go. But when she taught us "Left (or right) flank march," we all changed direction at once. I needed more time to decide which way to turn. I had to do something fast. I dug my nails into my left palm till it hurt and repeated to myself, "Feel that? That's left." Being dyslexic wasn't easy before I knew they had a name for it.

She taught us "About face" and told us to practice until we could do it perfectly. It was difficult. We had to place the right toe to the left of the left heel and spin on them so that we ended facing the opposite direction with our feet positioned the same as before.

When she dismissed us she cautioned, "Be ready to fall out in five minutes, dressed for physical training."

We jumped into our high school gym suits brought from home and got a softball game going. It was Thompson's team against Murdock's. I was on Murdock's team. We lost.

We got back a while before lunch. I had so many things to do, I didn't know where to start. But before she dismissed us, the sergeant ordered, "You have five minutes to get showered and dressed."

What now?

She was back in exactly five minutes. We sat on the floor in the open common area by the entrance to the squad room while she briefed us on military conduct until it was time to fall out for noon chow.

The food here was always good, and we had almost enough time to eat it. But there was no free time after lunch either. Sgt. Booth ordered us to the PX to get "things you will need for the time you are here."

I thought I would get stationery, a bottle of ink, toenail clippers . . .

"And make sure you have plenty of sanitary napkins."

I was shocked. I hadn't heard those words spoken out loud

since my sister explained the facts of life to me. Wasn't anything personal here?

The PX was like a small variety store, as immaculate and orderly as if ready for inspection. There were civilian women working behind the counter. They treated us decently and never once called us Boot.

On the march back I had so much to carry it was hard to maintain a military manner. Gordy, in the rear, was having more trouble. She bought a pillow with the Marine Corps emblem on it. When we got back, she said, "It's for my parents." She tried to stuff it in her laundry bag on top of Junior, but it stuck out.

"Hey, where can I put this?" She turned to her bunky, Murdock. "Can I slip this in your laundry bag?"

Murdock shook her head. "Not a chance."

Elder frowned at Murdock. "You can use mine," she said.

Sgt. Booth was soon back. We gathered around her in the common area again, sitting on the floor to get instructions for the GI Party that evening.

"Everything must shine," she warned, "because WOMEN OFFICERS will be here tomorrow morning to conduct a white glove inspection. They run those gloves over everything looking for dust, and they had better not find any."

I had yet to meet my first Woman Marine officer, and already I was frightened of her.

"Are there any questions?"

I couldn't remember enough of what she had said to ask an intelligent question, and anyway, I didn't want to call attention to myself. That always got me in trouble.

I figured everybody else understood, because no hands went up, but after the sergeant left, Elder seemed to be as confused as I was. She asked, "What did she say we use to wipe the heel marks off the floor?"

"Steel wool," said Thompson, as she left for the head.

"Where do we get that?" asked Valdez.

Nobody seemed to remember. Elder plopped down heavily

on her bunk. "This is one party I wish I hadn't been invited to. Do we RSVP?"

Murdock, in the next bunk above Gordy, sneered. "Hah! You're not going to get out of this one."

I studied her. She was large and muscular, with coarse features and flashing eyes. I figured she would make a good sergeant.

"Maybe," I suggested, "while it's still fresh in our minds, we ought to write down everything we remember."

Elder looked out from her bunk. "Freddy, I wouldn't know where to start. She makes me so nervous I can't remember anything."

Murdock sneered again. "What's the matter with you girls? Didn't you listen?"

I could see we'd get no cooperation from her. I left to iron a skirt and blouse for tomorrow.

Just before we went to chow that evening, Thompson offered some advice. "We'd better not eat too much because we're going to be getting a lot of exercise when we get back."

I felt like we were training for the Olympics.

After chow we put on our gym suits. Thompson found the steel wool and Gordy started rubbing out the heel marks on the floor.

Murdock, working on the Venetian blind, yelled, "You're doing it wrong! When you take off marks with the toe of one shoe, you make new ones with the heel of the other. Don't be so stupid!"

Gordy threw her arms out helplessly. "What am I supposed to do?"

"Use your hands!"

Elder said, "Steel wool can ruin your fingernails." She took off her tennis shoes. Grabbing some steel wool with her toes, she began rubbing off marks around our bunk in her stocking feet. Then we all took off our shoes.

Later Thompson brought in two full buckets and a couple of swabs. She shared one of each with a boot on the other side, warning, "Remember, Sgt. Booth said to wring those swabs as dry as you can. She doesn't want the floor wet."

Thompson and I each took an end of our clothes rack and moved it from the center to swab beneath it. Down the line, one by one, the other racks were shoved out of place. The bunks went next. Some boot on the other side of the racks knocked over a bucket, spilling the soapy water out on the floor.

"Wait 'till the sergeant sees that," said Murdock.

The two boots holding swabs rushed over to sop it up, but it was still wet when the wax was passed down. Valdez took a towel from her laundry bag and finished drying it.

The squad room was in complete disorder. Clothes racks, bunks, and footlockers were running every which way.

Murdock kept picking on Gordy until Thompson yelled, "Knock it off!"

Thompson and I started lining up the clothes racks. It was getting close to quiet hour so we had to work fast. With cooperation from the other end of the room and everybody in between, we arranged them so that they came down the exact center, the full length of the room, in one straight line on either side of the open common area.

The bunks were next, and time was running out. They must be placed twelve inches from the wall. The tape measure I brought from home to lengthen my uniform skirts came in handy. When I had finished with it, I passed it down and the place began to look like a squad room again.

Thompson was carrying out the wax when Sgt. Booth came to announce the beginning of quiet hour. Totally exhausted, I climbed up on my bunk to rest for a moment before starting a letter to my mother.

Ninety minutes later I was awakened by the sergeant's call. "End of quiet hour."

I hadn't even removed the cap from my fountain pen.

If all the days here were going to be as exhausting as this one, I might not even make it through the first week.

*   *   *

CHAPTER 3.
WEARING DOWN THE BOOTS

After surviving a Friday night GI Party and our first white glove inspection, I felt we had come a long way. We could line up our clothes poles straight down the center of the squad room and fold our blankets so that the edges looked like they had been cut with scissors. We had memorized exactly where everything was to be displayed in the footlocker, and learned to walk carefully indoors to avoid scuff marks.

Toilet habits needed discipline to conform to head inspection. Fortunately, stewed prunes were always available at morning chow.

When we heard "E-5 FALL OUT," we all ran like hell. We never went anywhere without our platoon, and as we marched, eyes must be focused on the back of the head in front of us. Consequently, only the squad leaders had any idea where we were going.

Saturday we had hair inspection. When Sgt. Booth said hair may touch but must not cover the collar, she meant with collar pulled up, hair pulled down, and head bent way back. Thompson was the only one who passed. Hers had been shingled up the back for her college swim team. Elder tried piling her curls on top of her head, but wisps of it kept falling down. We paired off, snipping and cutting on each other until there was nothing left at the nape of the neck. When we finished, anything still hanging beneath our bowler caps looked like the rats had been gnawing at it, but it passed inspection.

Sunday, after church services, everybody headed for the laundry. We had a limited number of stationary tubs, each equipped with washboard, hand-cranked wringer, and a line of boots waiting their turn. And the Catholics got there first.

When I finished my wash, all the dryers were full. They were long metal racks on rollers. We pulled them out from the large drying ovens to drape our wash on them. Once a boot found room for her clothes on the rack, she rolled it back into the oven and headed for the cooler squad room.

The clothes dried fast, but no one came to get them. Anything dry that didn't have a name tag on it got tossed out. The rest got thrown in the lucky box. The owner had to do an hour of EPD to get it back, whether she wanted it or not. I learned to be careful what I put my name on.

By Monday I was anxious to get started. I wanted to get this boot camp business over with. Our itinerary was posted weekly on the bulletin board. We were each responsible for knowing everything that was there. Glancing at it that first Monday morning, I could see that we would be on the run all week, rushing to physical training, obstacle course, classes, drill, orientation, assemblies, demonstrations, and dispensary.

Then on Saturday we march in review. What's a review?

We sometimes had Alice Marble, the tennis champion, for physical training. She joined The American Movement and had been loaned to the Marine Corps to help whip us into shape. She was a sweetheart and we loved her.

The obstacle course, easier for us long legged ones at the front of the platoon, was a challenge to feather merchants in the rear. Everyone in our platoon made it through except Gordy. Her legs wouldn't get her over the tallest hurdle. She returned to the squad room crestfallen, certain that she would be sent home. But Alice Marble took her back down to the course that evening and worked with her until she made it over the top.

Once, in the middle of a snappy game of volleyball, Elder stepped in a hole, twisted her ankle, and went to sick bay. She was put on "light duty," meaning she didn't have to march to classes for a few days. She just limped along beside us.

They gave us three minutes to shower and change after every workout. That was hardly enough time to get wet.

In the class for Military Customs and Courtesies we learned how to spot an officer and when to salute. "And any of you caught fraternizing or spending time with an officer for any reason other than to carry out your military duties will be punished severely. Don't even think of doing it."

Of course, I would never think of doing that.

Marine Corps History covered important battles our Marines had bravely fought and won. I thought of the men on the front lines now, making new history for the Corps.

In Naval Law we were reminded that we are part of the Navy, subject to Naval Law. Minor infractions could be handled by our NCO, (non-commissioned officer, an enlisted person with the rate of corporal or above) at something called office hours. Worse violations like fraternizing got a deck court, where you would face an officer. Courts-martial were saved for more serious crimes like murder or being absent without leave (AWOL).

We got our first case of office hours at the end of the second week when the new boots were coming in. Valdez, having quickly overcome her modesty, had showered after physical training and was returning to the squad room stark naked when she noticed some of us standing at the window yelling, "You'll be sorry!"

We had thrown on our uniforms and were calling to them as we fastened garter belts and pulled cotton lisle hose up over damp legs. Valdez maneuvered her way past us to stand at the window, still naked, and yell, "You'll be sorry! You'll be sorry!"

Thompson said, "Valdez, you'd better get dressed."

She ignored her.

Murdock yelled, "Valdez, put some clothes on. You're going to get in trouble!"

There was no response until Sgt. Booth called up the stairway, "E-5, FALL OUT!" Then Valdez ran for her clothes while the rest of us headed out. When the sergeant asked Thompson for the muster report, she replied, "All but Valdez present and accounted for."

Valdez burst out the door, hat askew, trying to hang on to her books while she buttoned her blouse. The sergeant sent her inside to finish dressing. When she came back out she was told to report at 1900 for office hours. She got two hours of EPD. Borrowing my extra toothbrush, she scrubbed all of the stairway corners twice. There wasn't much left of the toothbrush.

At the War Bond assembly we were told we would buy war bonds. I had always bought them. It was the patriotic thing to do. However, they were already taking $28.00 from my $50 monthly stipend for my dependent mother, plus life insurance and an assortment of other deductions. After adding war bonds to that, I feared I might end up owing them.

We attended a lecture early one afternoon on moral behavior, followed by a graphic film on venereal disease. Valdez got sick and vomited her lunch.

In an effort to build esprit de corps, we attended another assembly with a panel of Women Marines. There were two sergeants and a first lieutenant.

The staff sergeant began. "When a sailor tells you that you are just a small part of the Navy, you tell him yes, but we're the best part. And if he says the Marines have to come to the Navy to take care of them when they get sick, you say the reason the Marine Corps doesn't have medics is because we don't get sick."

Maybe not, I thought, but we do get awfully tired.

The tech sergeant added, "And when the old-timers tell you the Marine Corps isn't what it used to be, tell them that's right. It's better now. It's got WOMEN."

The lieutenant finished with, "Always remember you are a Marine. When you walk into a room, walk in like you own that room and everyone in it."

That would be hard to do on what they were paying me.

When we studied chemical warfare, they led us into a big tent and handed out gas masks. "A dangerous gas is about to be released into this tent," said the instructor. "At that time you will put on your mask, take three deep breaths, and leave."

I didn't trust it. I put on my mask, held my breath a very long time, and was first out. Elder was close behind.

At one demonstration we watched male recruits perform some of the agonizing physical training necessary to prepare them for combat. As one lifted a heavy weight, sweating profusely, we exchanged glances. At that moment, I longed for assurance that he would return safely. For me, no news report could have brought the war closer.

Shortly after we got our uniforms we spent a night in the guardhouse, each taking a turn at guard duty. We took two-hour shifts and walked in pairs.

We had each been issued a copy of THE MARINE'S HAND-BOOK. On page 224 were listed the eleven general orders for a sentinel on post. We had to memorize them all so well that if the sergeant were to ask one of us, "What is the second order of guard duty?" the boot would immediately reply, "The second order of guard duty is: 'To walk my post in a military manner, keeping always on the alert and observing everything that takes place within sight or hearing.'"

The bunks at the guardhouse were single. I bunked next to Rudkin. We walked guard duty together from 0200 to 0400. About half way through the first hour I asked, "Rudkin, are you observing everything?"

"Heck no. I thought you were."

Some time later, we had just come back from evening chow when Sgt. Booth entered the squad room and yelled, "Private Fredriksen, FRONT AND CENTER."

What have I done now? I hurried to the common area.

"Private Fredriksen reporting, Sergeant."

"You will report to the dispensary tomorrow morning at 0800. There is something wrong with your x-rays."

That was devastating news. My grandmother and two aunts

had died at a young age, all of tuberculosis. Was I to be next? I
stayed awake throughout the night, worrying.

The next morning I was stumbling down the stairs to get a
pass for the dispensary when I met Rudkin coming up.

"I'm going with you, Freddy. I just got my pass."

"Aren't you feeling well?"

"I feel all right," she said, scratching her head. "I just have a
scalp irritation, but it's getting worse."

I was relieved that I didn't have to venture out alone. As we left
together I asked, "Do you know where the dispensary is?"

"No, don't you?"

"I have no idea."

"I thought you would know. You're up there close to the front,
but I'm stuck in the back with the feather merchants. I can't see
anything."

We got directions from a mess girl. As we entered the dispensary I braced myself for the bad news. Approaching the desk I said,
"I'm Private Fred . . ."

Before I could finish, the pharmacist mate stuck a thermom-
eter in my mouth. Handing me a pencil and some forms on a
clipboard, she said, "Sit down on that bench and fill these out."

Rudkin got the same treatment. Several boots ahead of us were
already filling out forms and sucking thermometers. When my
turn came she looked at my paper and said, "You're Fredriksen?
Why didn't you say so? They're waiting for you. C'mon."

She led me down a very long hall. My mouth was dry when
she ushered me into the x-ray room. The technician asked me to
remove my clothing and slip on a gown she called an angel robe.
"I'm sorry," she said. "Someone must have opened a door while
your x-rays were being developed."

I was surprised to find that the relief I felt was more from the
fear of being discharged than of being seriously ill. As miserable as
this Boot Camp experience was, I really wanted to be a part of the
Marine Corps.

I finished first and waited for Rudkin. She came out wearing a white turban. I asked, "What did they do to you?"

"I have to wear this. I have lice."

My scalp began to itch. "I wonder if I got 'em."

She stepped closer. "Want me to take a look?"

I drew back. "No. Don't touch me!"

"The nurse said anybody can get them."

"Rudkin, you can't go outside dressed like that. You're out of uniform. Don't you need a note from the doctor, or something? What if we meet an officer?"

"Let's just hope we don't."

But we did. About half way back, an officer crossed the street to confront us. Giving our first salute, in shaky chorus we said, "Good morning, Lieutenant."

She returned the salute and stopped us. Addressing Rudkin she said, "Private, you are out of uniform. Do you have anything to say in your defense?"

"Yes, Lieutenant. I have bugs, Lieutenant."

The officer looked shocked, but her voice remained calm. "Carry on."

They found lice in the guardhouse. Every platoon that spent a night there went in for scalp inspection, and the guardhouse was deloused. Rudkin wore her turban for a while, and everybody gave her plenty of room.

On our next trip to the dispensary we lined up for shots. I was behind Thompson, who acted like she got a shot every day, laughing and joking with the boots in front of her. All I could think of was that needle. I brushed my shoulder against her back, hoping some of her courage would rub off on me. It didn't work. My breakfast was not settling well.

The line moved quickly. It was soon Thompson's turn. When the nurse reached for her arm she passed out and fell to the floor, her head landing at my feet. Two WAVEs were called in. They dragged her to a cot nearby, and a nurse hurried over to attend her.

As I watched them, I heard a pharmacist mate say, "Move on, Fredriksen." I hadn't even felt the shot.

When we lined up outside, our right guide was still missing. Sgt. Booth asked, "Where's Private Thompson?"

She appeared a moment later, seeming only slightly embarrassed. "They couldn't give me the shot while I was out," she said. "They had to bring me around first!"

That evening, before lights out, Sgt. Booth talked to us in the squad room. "Some of you may have a reaction to the shot," she said. "If you do, come down to the office and report to the NCO on duty. There's always someone there, any hour of the day or night."

With no explanation of what a reaction might be, we had no idea what to expect. I didn't plan to lose any sleep over it.

About 0200 I heard a deafening shriek. Someone turned on the lights, and I could see it was Valdez, two bunks down.

She was still screaming hysterically when Sgt. Sullivan entered the squad room in her pajamas. Murdock suggested, "I think she's having a reaction to the shot."

The sergeant left to call for an ambulance. Then she rushed back upstairs and sent Thompson down to show them in.

The Navy medics didn't need any help to locate the source of the screams. They bolted in before anybody could yell "Man aboard," and Valdez was already on the stretcher when Thompson returned.

I was so worried about Valdez I couldn't go back to sleep. She came in about an hour later, managing to make it up the stairs on her own. She tried to slip into bed unnoticed, but Murdock wouldn't let her get away with it.

"What was that all about?"

"It was nothing," she whispered. "I just slept on my arm a funny way and it went to sleep. I hope I didn't wake anybody up."

*   *   *

CHAPTER 4.
TAILOR SHOP

E-5 was the last platoon in our battalion to get our uniforms. Except for those green bowler hats, we had worn only civilian clothes brought from home for two weeks. The new recruits were arriving. We feared we might be mistaken for them. Finally, on Friday afternoon of the second week, we were scheduled one hour at the tailor shop.

I had spent more time than that just buying a scarf.

The sun hid behind a dark cloud as we marched over. It gave welcome relief from the heat. While we waited our turn to enter, Sgt. Booth briefed us on how to conduct ourselves once inside, stressing the importance of keeping the line moving.

I was barely through the door when a loud voice on my left asked, "What size uniform, BOOT?" Her brisk attitude demanded a fast answer, but I needed time to think about it. I had hoped we could try them on first.

Then, louder, "WHAT SIZE UNIFORM?"

She was obviously getting impatient. I wasn't used to ready made clothes. With my measurements, I had learned to make them myself. "I might try a twelve."

She handed me the top to our winter service.

"Put on this blouse."

"You mean jacket."

"I mean blouse, BOOT. You WILL call this a BLOUSE."

It looked like a jacket to me. I put it on and went to the mirrors. It was a little short in the waist, but the fourteen Thompson was trying on would have hung like a sack on me. The skirt needed to be lengthened, but it had a good hem. I took the twelve.

Summer seersuckers were next. Another twelve. There were tailors to make alterations, but I heard one say, "We don't do hems. That's your job."

I wondered what they told the men when they made the pants too long.

We had to carry back our entire wardrobe. Along with summer and winter uniforms, there was an assortment of heavy rayon underwear, six pairs of cotton lisle hose, laced oxfords, (a bit tight, she insisted they would "loosen up") and beige seersucker exercise outfits with elastic at the legs, that we would call "peanut suits."

When Sgt. Booth ordered, "Wrap everything in your trench coat and fall out," I tightened the belt around all of it and hurried outside.

Plop. A big drop of rain hit my nose, quickly followed by more . . . much more. We were trapped in a sudden downpour. The sergeant yelled, "Right face forward MARCH . . . DOUBLE TIME!" and we raced for home.

While Sgt. Booth ran along beside Thompson urging her to speed up, Gordy, our feather merchant in the rear, tripped on the belt to her trench coat. We covered some distance before the sergeant noticed she was missing.

"Platoon, HALT!"

It was like standing at attention fully dressed in the shower room with all the sprays turned on. The sergeant ran back yelling, "Pick up your gear, BOOT! On the double, BOOT!"

By the time we reached the barracks I felt like I had fallen into a swimming pool fully dressed. A trail of water followed me up the stairs and into the squad room. I tried not to think about the GI party scheduled for that evening.

My uniforms were dry, but when I hung my trench coat it dripped puddles on the floor and into my shoes below. I would have to deal with that later.

As soon as we changed into dry clothes, Sgt. Booth came in to teach us how to dress. "When you put on this uniform you become one of the best dressed women in America," she began. "In March the Fashion Academy's list of the best dressed women put the WACS, WAVES, SPARS, and Women Marines first, to share top billing. Our uniform is something to be proud of. Make sure you always wear it correctly."

She held up a winter service hat. "These were designed by Knox of New York. Notice the cord that ties in front, over the visor. It's the same shade of red as your muffler. Elizabeth Arden has created a color to match it, especially for us. It's called Montezuma Red, and that is the only shade of lipstick and nail polish you will wear."

I hadn't worn lipstick since the mess girl yelled at me for leaving some on my glass, and I certainly had no time for nail polish. I didn't care what I looked like anymore as long as I passed inspection and the sergeant didn't yell at me.

"The handbag," she went on, "is made of elephant hide. That's the toughest leather they could get. You will hang it from your left shoulder, and adjust the strap until it rests just below your waist. Make sure you secure it beneath the flap at your shoulder.

"There is cordovan brown Dyanshine in the assortment of things that were issued to you in your laundry bag. Keep applying it to your shoes until they are so dark they look black. To get the best shine, you will mix spit with your Kiwi shoe polish. If your mouth goes dry, think of lemons.

"The emblems are an important part of your uniform," she continued. "The eagle, globe and anchor is the symbol of the Marine Corps. The eagle represents our obligation to our country, the globe our obligation to the world, and the anchor reminds us we are a part of the Navy.

"Those eagles must fly high at all times. If you don't screw them down tight they can slip, and the eagle will tilt. Make sure you put them on straight and screw them down tight." Emphasizing, she twisted her wrist.

"Take a close look at those emblems. Notice they have a dark coating. In the course of time it wears off, revealing the bronze metal beneath. That makes you look salty, like you've been a Marine for a while."

She pointed to the salty emblems on her lapel. "Rub some of that off with steel wool so you won't look like you just joined up. Now, are there any questions?"

Valdez raised her hand.

"Yes private?"

"Well, Sergeant, the women in the Army are called WACS, in the Navy they're WAVES, and the Coast Guard women are SPARS. So what do they call us?"

Sergeant Booth frowned. "We don't have a nickname. We are Marine Reserves, and we are called Women Reserves, or WRs. People who are not familiar with that term simply call us Women Marines." She paused. Then, lowering her voice, she added, "And don't ever let anyone call you anything else."

She seemed angry. I wondered what that was all about.

After the sergeant left I drained water from my shoes and wiped up the spill. Gordy tried on a summer seersucker skirt and it hung to mid-calf.

Murdock shook her head. "You can't wear it like that. It's down around your ankles. You look terrible."

"I can't sew. What'll I do?"

"I'll hem it for you," I said. "Let's see how much you need it shortened. It should hit just below the knee."

Thompson showed interest. "I'll give you a dollar each if you'll let down the hems in mine."

Gordy heard that. "I'll pay too."

"I can't take your money, Gordy. I offered to do it."

By now Thompson was going through her wardrobe picking out the skirts. "Here's two winters and three summers, and there's five dollars paid in advance."

She plunked the skirts on my bunk, and placed a five-dollar bill on top of them. Because of my dependent, I had received nothing at our first pay call. it looked good to me. I took it.

Word got around that some boot up at the north end of the squad room was hemming skirts for a dollar and I had more business than I could handle. I had to set some rules.

"I won't take any skirts that don't have name tags in them."

Gordy asked, "Freddy, will you sew in my name tags?"

"No."

Reluctantly, she brought out her sewing kit. "Then will you thread my needle?"

I picked up speed as I lengthened the stitches and by Monday I was the richest boot in the squad room. My fingertips were ragged, but I had money.

With so many skirts to hem, there was barely time to wash my civilian clothing before sending it home. The sergeant gave us boxes for mailing. I thought about my mother as I packed. When I enlisted she was about to marry Tom Olson, her gentleman friend, so I felt free to leave, listing her as a dependent, temporarily. But in her last letter she mentioned that Tom had become quite ill with " . . . something that was going around." Their marriage would have to be postponed until he recovered.

I was concerned that my mother was still alone. I liked Tom, and hoped he would soon be well so they could be married. Perhaps I had enlisted too hastily.

Finishing, I folded down the flaps on the box. As soon as Elder was through with the string, I tied it up. What's done is done, I thought.

Elder took her winter hat from its box. Carefully, she fastened the emblem, screwing it down tight with the eagle flying high. She placed it on her head and asked, "Freddy, is my hat on straight?"

I was shocked. I had become accustomed to seeing her in the summer bowler. "Why, Elder, you look like a Marine!"

"Of course. I am a Marine. We're all Marines. Is it on straight?"

"Yes. It's on straight."

I got out my winter hat and affixed the emblem. Then I took

it down the hall to the mirrors that were over the basins. Carefully, I placed it on my head, then stepped back for a larger overall view.

To my surprise, a Woman Marine reflected back at me. And she was wearing my face.

*   *   *

CHAPTER 5.
GETTING THE DI

The Marine Corps boot camp drill instructor, the DI, shows his boots no mercy. We got off on the wrong foot with ours the first day Sgt. Booth marched us to his drill area. We found him standing in the middle of the road, hands on hips, waiting impatiently.

"Platoon," she said, "this is Sergeant Gunn. He is going to try to teach you drill."

He eyed us critically. "Is this the best they can send us? Do they expect us to make Marines out of these?"

Sgt. Booth shook her head. "They're getting worse all the time." She walked away, leaving us to face him alone.

His first order was, "Fall out and stow your gear under that tree. Then fall in again."

He sounded like he was scolding us, and we hadn't done anything wrong yet. I got my gear over there fast.

In formation again, he folded his arms across his chest and strutted back and forth in front of us. An imposing figure just short of six feet tall, his trim waist and broad, muscular shoulders were outlined beneath a closely tailored khaki shirt. He looked fighting ready. The sergeant's stripes on his sleeve and the pronounced scar dangerously close to his left eye suggested he had already seen action in this war. And the expression of disdain on an otherwise handsome face implied that he was thoroughly bored with his present assignment.

There was something in the way he held his body, the way he walked, and the inflection in his voice that let us know he was a

symbol of everything the Marine Corps stood for, everything we
wanted to become a part of. There was also the inference that we
could never attain it.

"ATTENTION!" he commanded. "So yew women think you
want to be Marines. Well, you're nothing more than a sorry looking bunch of civilians, but let's see if I can teach you how Marines
drill."

Obviously we weren't supposed to like him. I had no problem
with that.

"Now. Yew women will march in review Saturday, and you
had better not embarrass me." He stared at us for a moment. "Suck
in those guts! Further! FURTHER! Come on, you can do better
than that!"

That was the best I could do. I'd already sucked them in as far
as they would go on the first command, but I tried to make it look
like I was "doing better."

"Throw back those shoulders! I said back, not up! What's the
matter with you people?"

I dropped my shoulders way down and pushed them back as
far as they would go, certain that he was looking directly at me in
the middle row.

"Get those heads back. Get those chins up. Don't you lame-
brains know how you're supposed to hold your head? When I order you to attention, this is how you will stand. I hope there will
be some improvement in the next six weeks.

"Dress right . . . DRESS!"

Sgt. Booth taught us that one. I threw my left arm straight
out to the side and whipped my head to the right so we could
straighten our lines and space ourselves uniformly.

"Ready . . . FRONT!" He shook his head. "That was awful.
When I say 'Dress right', I want you to be ready to snap those
heads right the moment I repeat 'Dress,' and I want all of you to
do it as one. That arm goes up the same instant the head turns.
Now, dress right . . . DRESS!

"That's not fast enough. We'll keep trying.

"Now, yew women do not carry weapons, so when you are given the order to present arms, you will salute instead. When I say, 'Present . . .' you be ready to bring that arm up fast, and when I say 'ARMS' all of those arms go up as one unit. All right, let's try it. Present . . . ARMS!"

He shook his head. "That was terrible."

We gave him one disappointment after another that first day. When he taught us parade rest, our left foot didn't rock the deck loud enough, and we didn't clasp the left thumb behind us fast enough. There was no pleasing him.

He gave us right face forward march, and growled, "Step out further! I want to see a thirty inch regulation step." He moved along beside the platoon, keeping just ahead of Thompson. "It's up to the right guide to set the pace." Turning his attention to Burnside and Callahan he added, "You other squad leaders, LINE UP WITH HER!

"Come on, right guide. Step out! STEP OUT! Awn awp reep. Reep fawya laf." He counted cadence with a nasal twang. It sounded like he was yelling through a bullhorn.

Thompson was stepping out as far as she could, but he kept repeating, "Step out! STEP . . . OUT! Fawya laf . . . ya laf . . ."

Just before we reached the bend in the road he ordered, "To the rear, HARCH!" Spinning on the ball of my left foot, I headed back.

Something had gone wrong. The shorter boots, or feather merchants in the rear couldn't keep up. They had fallen far behind, more than doubling the length of the platoon. But now they were in the lead. Gordy was acting right guide, and she would not be rushed.

We closed rank fast. I soon felt Murdock at my heels while I tried to avoid scraping Valdez. In an attempt to get some distance between us, we slowed down until we were hardly moving. All the way back the DI yelled at Gordy to "Step out. Come on, STEP OUT!"

Eventually we heard, "Platoon, HALT! Right, FACE!" Now we were crammed together, rubbing shoulders.

"How did you jugheads get yourselves into this mess? Can't you numbskulls do anything right?"

He was distracted when a shapely little mess cook sashayed up to him. He lifted his overseas cap for a moment, revealing a close crop of black curls.

"Hi Pieface, what did you bring me today?"

She wore white pants and skivvy shirt, her hair bound in a white turban. After fingering something wrapped in a napkin, she presented it to him. "This is for you."

He peeked inside. "Chocolate cake! I love it!"

Still standing at attention, I heard someone snicker.

He looked up. Changing back to his voice of disdain, he ordered, "Dress right, Dress." We needed to make a lot of space between us. "Ready, front! Right face. Forward HARCH! Yeow laf... laf..." He turned his attention back to Pieface while we continued the march. We were almost at the bend in the road when he yelled, "To the rear, HARCH!"

When we returned Pieface was sitting under our tree, holding the cake. She watched with an amused smile while he put on a good show for her. In rapid succession he shouted "To the rear HARCH! Right flank HARCH! Laf flank HARCH! To the rear HARCH! Rear HARCH! Rear HARCH!"

He kept it up. I was getting dizzy, bumping into Valdez, then Murdock, until Sgt. Booth came back to take us to chow.

"Platoon HALT!" He waited until we caught up with his last command. "Fall out and get your gear and fall in again."

Pieface giggled. I hated when she did that.

When we were back in formation he sneered. "That was the most disgusting display of bungling I have ever seen. Unfortunately, our time is up, but we will go at it again tomorrow. Platoon dismissed."

The DI was the main subject of conversation that evening, right up to quiet hour. We were angry, and we needed to talk about it. Valdez sat on her bunk, shaking her head. "I wish we could get him. I wish we could really get him."

Gordy began taking it out on Thompson. "You shouldn't take such big steps. The short ones in the rear can't keep up."

Thompson frowned. "Sorry, Gordy. That thought never occurred to me. He kept saying to step out. I'll try to be more considerate of you feather merchants from now on."

I stopped practicing about faces and sat on the bunk beside Elder. "He probably pulls those tricks on all the platoons the first day," I said. "It's like the way they treated us at our first meal in the chow hall. He'll be more friendly tomorrow."

Gordy puzzled. "Do you think so, Freddy?"

"Sure. He can't keep yelling at us like that for six weeks."

He could, and he did. He taught us new drill commands every day, then ridiculed our attempts, even when we got it right. And always he took time to review everything we had previously learned, until it became a part of our nervous system.

Every day, near the end of the hour, Pieface arrived with a treat for our DI. She sat under the tree, in the midst of our gear, and giggled tactlessly as she watched him humiliate us. And every evening Valdez would say, "I wish there was some way we could get him."

While his insults continued, I never stopped believing that on the last day he would admit we were not just a bunch of stupid knuckleheads. I hoped he would even admit he was proud of us.

At the beginning of our final week he taught us "To the winds, march." It was a complicated series of maneuvers. Upon command, each squad began to function independently, literally taking off in three different directions. The DI counted cadence while each row carried out its own routine until we were back together again, marching in platoon formation, exactly where we had begun.

Once mastered, "To the winds march" was fun. More like dancing than drill, I was able to forget, for the moment, how much I resented the DI's attitude.

As we marched to our last period of drill, I knew this was the day he would break down and congratulate us on how well we had performed. Actually, we were pretty good. When he called us to attention you could hear our heels click down the road and across the street. We carried out orders as fast as he called them, and we were willing to march into a brick wall if he didn't stop us. We were getting excellent ratings for Saturday review. Surely he would give us credit for that.

But the last day started out like all the rest. By the time Pieface showed up he had called us knuckleheads, lame brains, fools, numb-skulls and jugheads several times each. He switched to his sweet voice when he turned to her with the usual "What did you bring me today, Pieface?"

She opened the napkin slowly. "I baked this myself, just for you."

"A strawberry tart! My very favorite. You made it just for me?"

He sent us marching toward the bend in the road and turned his attention to Pieface. Their conversation grew faint. Then a headwind came up, and we couldn't hear them at all. We continued the march, listening for our next order, but it never reached us.

As we neared the grove of trees where the path turned, I heard another DI shout, "To the winds, HARCH!" and I knew we were heading into trouble.

Behind me, Valdez muttered, "Keep going! Keep going! We're gonna get him!"

We had no choice. We marched straight into the other platoon. One of their feather merchants changed direction in front of Thompson and they both went down. The rest of us moved on, continuing to invade their ranks.

Some boots in the other platoon, totally confused by this un-expected assault, abandoned the routine and fled in panic. But Thompson, our right guide, rose quickly to her feet and led us on. We battered their lines unmercifully. I was thankful for Murdock, in front of me, running interference.

The other DI, at a loss for words, brought both hands up to cover his face in disbelief. There was nothing he could do.

Meanwhile, back at the tree, our DI was becoming upset with us. He abandoned Pieface and charged up from behind, repeating "To the rear harch . . . to the rear HARCH!" By the time his voice reached us, we had marched through more than half of the other platoon and he gave the command on the wrong foot, giving us an extra step forward before retreating.

The other DI smiled. "You'd climb trees for him, wouldn't you?"

Sgt. Gunn was furious. Heading back, he scolded, "Of all the dumb, idiotic tricks!"

Now I could see Gordy in the distance, standing alone by the tree. She was the only one who had heard his first command.

He shouted indignities all the way back. When he stopped us, his face took on a sadistic expression. Lowering his voice, he ordered, "Fall out and get your gear and fall in again."

I looked at my watch. We had fifteen minutes of drill instruction left. Why would we need our gear?

When we were back in formation, my bag hung from my left shoulder and I held the books down at my right side.

"Ten HUT!" We came to attention. "Dress right, DRESS! . . . Ready, FRONT!" Then, with a satisfied smirk, he ordered, "Present, ARMS!"

I didn't think that was very smart. We had to transfer the books from the right hand to the left before we could salute.

"What's the matter there? What's all that fussing with your gear about? Can't you carry out a simple order? You've given me plenty of sloppy salutes, but this is the worst. Ready, DOWN!"

He folded his arms across his chest and eyed us with contempt. "You fools are going to do this until you get it right. Dress right, DRESS!"

Now we had to bring the books back to the right hand to dress right. More insults. Giggles from Pieface were getting louder and more annoying.

"Ready, FRONT! . . . Present, ARMS!"

We fumbled with books again.

"What's the matter with yew people? Can't you do anything right? What's all the fussing with your gear about? Ready, DOWN! . . . Dress right, DRESS!"

He kept that up for the rest of the hour. I thought Sgt. Booth would never come for us. When she did, it was the first time she ever looked good to me.

We waited for the DI to dismiss us. I had heard they broke down and became friendly at the very end, telling us we had done a good job. But Sgt Gunn was not smiling.

Slowly he walked the length of the platoon with his arms crossed over his chest. Then he came back to the center and faced us. This would be his last chance to congratulate us on a job well done. But his face still wore that expression of contempt.

"Yew women are stupid," he said. "DISMISSED!"

*   *   *

CHAPTER 6.
FIRST CHOICE

I didn't join the Marines to be a boot. The six weeks dragged on, and there seemed no end to the misery. It was all I could do just to get through each day, look alive, and try to stay out of trouble.

Radios were forbidden. Except for letters, we seldom heard news from the outside. Once Barthelomew, on the other side of the clothes rack, had a phone call. When she came back upstairs, she announced her father had just been elected coroner of Lane County, Oregon. But there was no time for celebration. Sgt. Booth followed her in with other plans she had for us.

There were two other, more solemn, occasions for news. The first came on Sunday morning, June 4th. Sgt. Booth had asked the entire squad room to be seated in the common area. I lowered myself to the floor beside Elder and waited.

She faced us solemnly. "There was a tragic fire at Cherry Point yesterday. Five Marines died, including two WRs, Lt. Mary Rita Palowitch and Corp. Germaine Laville. They are the first WRs to be killed in line of duty."

Flags were flown at half-staff in their memory. I felt I had lost two sisters and three brothers.

Two days later, on June 6th, Sgt. Booth called us together again, this time to brief us on the invasion of Normandy. It was a reminder to me that while I was learning to do an about face and salute officers, brave men were fighting and dying in this war. I grieved for the lives being lost in the conflict.

Yet, here at Camp Lejeune, life continued on schedule. Our

last week's agenda listed "Assembly, Aptitude Testing" for Monday afternoon. Perhaps our next assignments would be determined by our performance on those tests.

Right after noon chow the entire battalion was marched to the assembly hall. Once seated, the booklets were passed out and testing began quickly. It wasn't going well for me. I was just getting started on page one of clerical aptitude when I heard Murdock turn to page two.

The tests that followed went no better. The only one I felt comfortable with was math. Not too many jobs in that field. There didn't seem to be anything I might qualify for until we started the last test, on mechanical aptitude.

It was a snap. Fun, like figuring out a Rube Goldberg cartoon of weird inventions, it showed wheels, cogs, and belts of varying sizes running all over the page. We were to figure the direction and speed each gear would turn. It went fast. I was almost finished when I heard "STOP."

The back page listed job placement opportunities open to our battalion. We could select our first and second choices from that list. I picked Aviation Machinist training in Norman, Oklahoma as my first choice. I wanted to work on airplanes. I listed Aviation Precision Instrument School in Chicago second. It sounded like interesting work. I had a sister and brother in Chicago, and friends I had gone to school with. I would enjoy spending time with them again.

I left the auditorium confident that I would get one or the other of my choices, because I had done so poorly in all the other tests, and "forgot" to list typing as a skill.

When we returned to the squad room we talked about our options. Thompson said, "I asked for motor transport. I'd like to be a grease monkey, and work on those jeeps."

Gordy smiled. "I put down motor transport too, but I'd rather chauffeur the officers around. I just love to drive."

Women driving cars? I thought. What next?

"I asked for cooking school," said Valdez. "I can make tortillas and burritos like you never tasted."

"You're right," said Elder, "on account of I've never tasted tortillas or burritos. Never even heard of 'em."

Valdez nodded. "You will, you will."

Callahan heard us talking and came around from the other side of the clothes racks. "I want to go to parachute rigging school."

If any woman could rig a parachute, it was Callahan. She was almost as tall as Thompson, and plenty strong.

I asked Elder what she chose.

"I put down secretarial work in Washington, D.C. I think it would be interesting to be there now." She frowned. "What did you put down, Freddy?"

"Aviation Machinist training, in Norman, Oklahoma."

"Me too," said Rudkin. "Maybe we'll go there together."

"I'd like that." Rudkin was O.K., now that she had been deloused.

Later Elder seemed pensive. "Freddy, do you think we'll be ready to go out into the world? I'm so used to being a boot I'd probably get lost without the platoon, and I'm really scared of meeting an officer."

"Elder," I answered, "if we can get used to boot camp, we can get used to anything."

She had changed. There was little resemblance to the civilian I arrived with six weeks earlier. She had come in with rather long auburn curls, silky white complexion, and an annoying habit of sleeping late. On the train she always put on lipstick before leaving the dining car and often checked her hair. But she stopped wearing make-up the day I whacked off her curls. Her skin was now tanned, her hair closely cropped.

Had I changed that much? I didn't feel like I knew my self anymore.

Standing at parade rest that last Saturday morning, waiting to pass in review, I had more on my mind than white glove inspection. When we returned to our barracks, our orders would be posted on the board.

As soon as we were dismissed, Thompson took the stairs three at a time. First boot topside, she headed straight for the bulletin board. We heard a whoop and a holler as she spotted her orders. "I got it! I got it! I got motor transport school," she shouted. "So did you, Gordy."

So did Barthelomew.

As Thompson left, Rudkin jumped in. "I have Aviation Machinist Mate! I'm going to Oklahoma!"

Up ahead of me, Callahan yelled, "I got parachute rigging school!"

Such a crowd was gathered around the board now, with the tallest in front, I couldn't see a thing, but I wasn't worried. Everyone seemed to be getting their first choice. I edged my way to the front and found my name. There it was: "Fredriksen: Battalion Area."

"What's Battalion Area?"

Valdez answered, "It's over on the other side of the base."

"Yes I know, but what does it mean?"

Murdock smiled. "It means you'll be picking up cigarette butts."

I was devastated. I had left a defense job to join the Corps. I thought I was going to free a Marine to fight. Instead, it looked like I would spend the duration of the war picking up trash here in Camp Lejeune.

Murdock was going to Chicago for Precision Instrument Training. "Don't feel bad Freddy," she said. "Some people just don't have the qualifications to go to school."

Now I was really upset. I headed for my bunk. Burying my face in the pillow, I began repeating to myself, "Don't cry. Don't cry. Please, don't cry."

There was no way to be alone in this outfit.

When Elder found out what happened, she tried to cheer me. "Freddy, what are you wearing to the dance?"

I had forgotten about that. Tonight a group on the base from Radio Operator's School was hosting a dance for us.

"And what will you do with your hair?"

"What hair? Elder, I don't have any. I think I'll skip it. I don't feel much like dancing."

"You have to go. It's an order."

Sgt. Booth entered the squad room. I jumped down from my bunk and stood at attention until she put us at ease and we gathered on the floor in the common area.

"Congratulations on successful completion of your six weeks of boot camp. All of you made it." She was friendly now, actually smiling. "However, you will remain boots until you arrive at the dance. Therefore, you will march over in platoon formation and proceed home independently."

I hadn't been out alone in six weeks, and except for the two Navy corpsmen who hauled Valdez out on a stretcher, the only man I had seen during this time was the DI. I'd forgotten how to talk to a man, and the thought of proceeding anywhere independently was frightening.

Later, Elder started in on me again. "You need to shave your legs. Do you have a razor?"

"Yes, I have a razor."

"And tweeze your eyebrows."

"Why are you picking on me?"

"Because I'm going to miss you, Freddy." Suddenly she hugged me and said, "You must feel terrible. Picking up cigarette butts!"

Elder's outburst brought me close to tears again, but it was comforting to know she understood how I felt. "I'll never forget you, Elder."

Rudkin walked by on her way to the showers. "Can I borrow somebody's baby oil?"

Life would go on, and there was much to be done. I shaved my legs, tweezed my eyebrows, and did something with my hair. Then I marched to the dance. It was held in a gymnasium with a five-piece band of Marines supplying the music. They played a lot of Glenn Miller favorites, starting with "Juke Box Saturday Night."

Soon I was out on the floor, amazed that I hadn't forgotten how to dance. The first Marine I danced with asked, "You BAMS get your orders yet?"

"I have Battalion Area. What's a BAM?"

"You mean you haven't heard our name for you? That's what we call ya. BAMS. You gonna be in Battalion Area? Swell. Maybe we can get together."

I remembered something Sgt. Booth had said. "We are WRs. We have no nickname, and don't ever let anybody call you anything else."

"Just a minute," I said. "What does BAM mean?"

"Well . . ." he thought a moment. "It stands for Beautiful American Marine. Yeah, that's it," he chuckled. "Beautiful American Marine."

I was suspicious. When the music stopped, I found my bunkmate by the coke machine. "Elder, do you know what BAM means?"

"I just found out but I can't tell you. It's too dirty."

"Could you give me a hint?"

"Well, the B stands for broad, the M is for Marine, and the A, uh, it's a three letter word that means donkey."

"So that's it!" I was furious. "How dare they?"

We were soon dancing again. I only heard the word BAM once more that night. I stepped on his foot.

As the evening passed, I began to wonder how I would find my barracks. I had no idea where we were and I didn't see any of our squad leaders who could show me the way. I confided my problem to a sympathetic corporal as we danced.

"Do you want to go back now?" he asked.

"Yes."

We waited until they finished playing "I've Got a Gal in Kalamazoo." It was one of my Tex Beneke favorites. Then he said, "Come on, I'll take you home."

He had to leave me at the edge of Area 1, but I managed to find barracks 124 by myself. I was not the first one back. I found Thompson sitting on a bench by the showers, where lights had been left on. She was finishing a letter.

"I was anxious to write my folks the good news," she said, "so I didn't stay long."

I sat down beside her. She was sharing parts of her letter with me when Elder came in. "Do you know, I couldn't find my way home? I had to ask a nice Marine if he'd show me where I live."

By Monday morning Elder was gone. I stripped my sack. When I turned my linen in to Sgt. Booth she was actually friendly. Smiling, she said, "You had that top bunk second from the end on the north side, the one with the substitute mattress. I've been waiting for you to check out. The replacement has come in."

She had known about my mattress from the beginning.

I was at the curb with my sea bag when the bus came to pick up the cigarette butt brigade. There were a quite a few waiting. I spotted Abramovitz, Ferris, Hoover, and Wood from my platoon. I found some comfort in knowing I wasn't the only one among us assigned to trash detail.

I climbed aboard and took a window seat. A sultry looking blonde sat beside me. Her hair fell in large curls, almost touching her collar, and her exotic eyes fascinated me, but I tried not to stare.

"I'm Fredriksen," I said. "They call me Freddy."

"I'm Lawson. Freddy, do you know what we'll be doing?"

"Yeah. We're going to be picking up cigarette butts."

"But I don't smoke."

"Neither do I."

Once I got used to Lawson's very natural, unaffected glamour, I liked her. She didn't seem aware of the feelings she must have stirred in every man who looked at her.

"I'm from Missouri," she said. "A little farming community a ways outside St. Louis. We have 120 acres in corn. They wouldn't take my brother in the Army. They said they needed farmers worse than soldiers, so I signed up. I figured one of us ought to go and serve our country. But picking up cigarette butts? I would have been more help on the farm."

It was a short trip. The driver pulled up to a brick building much like the one we had just left. "This is it gals," she said. Lifting her overseas cap, she wiped the sweat from beneath it before opening the door. "I hear there's a bathtub in there."

A bathtub! How I had wished for a long, leisurely bath during those weeks of quick showers. I was determined to have one now, no matter how long I had to wait in line for it.

A corporal met our bus. The driver reported to her, "I only counted thirty-five, but that's all there is on the roster. Do you know anything about it?"

The corporal nodded. "They told us there'd only be thirty-five this time. Nobody knows why." Turning to us she added, "I'm Corporal Dean. I'll be your NCO while you're here. As soon as you find your sea bags I'll show you to your quarters."

The bags had already arrived. While we scampered about searching for the one with our name on it, a single figure sauntered off and leaned against a tree.

The corporal asked her, "Do you have a sea bag?"

"Oh yeah, sure," she said. "I figure after all these guys find theirs, the one that's left will be mine."

The one that was left was stamped WHALEN.

Our squad room was on the main deck. The bunks were single. It seemed to add light to the room. The atmosphere was more relaxed than it had been at boot camp, and the corporal treated us as if we had some intelligence.

It was hard to get used to that.

We were billeted as we came in. I bunked next to Lawson, with Whalen on the other side. I was unpacking my sea bag when the corporal came back. "They need two volunteers to work in the art department."

That was for me! I put my hand up fast. So did Lawson. No-

body else had a chance. We were to report to the recreation building after lunch.

"The rest of you will meet out in front of the barracks at 1300
to police the area." She added, "The women's chow hall will open
their lines in about twenty minutes for lunch. A map of the base is
on the bulletin board, in case you need help finding it. Be back
here in plenty time to report for duty."

I had eaten every meal in that chow hall for the last six weeks,
but I had no idea where it was. When Lawson and I headed for the
map, a voice behind us called, "Hey, wait up."

It was Whalen. She was about my height, but heavier with
broad shoulders. Her pixie features were tanned and freckled, and
her short black hair hung in loose bangs. There was a relaxed roll
in her walk, but she moved quickly.

"Hey," she said as she came near, "you guys are lucky, getting
out of policing the area. I would have raised my hand, but my
uncle Harry told me never to volunteer for anything. I guess it's
just as well, because I flunked art." She shook her head slowly.
"But now I have to write and tell him I got a job picking up trash.
How's that going to help win the war?"

Later, after chow, we passed our barracks on the way to the
recreation building. The group was already gathering. Lawson and
I stopped with Whalen for a few minutes.

Cpl. Dean was issuing dungarees. She gave each WR two pairs
of pants with matching jacket, a cap, and two skivvy shirts, plus a
canvas sack large enough to hold a lot of cigarette butts, and a stick
with a nail at the tip to spear them with.

Lawson and I moved on to the recreation building. It was red
brick, like everything else at Camp Lejeune. The Art Department
was in a large, otherwise empty room on the ground floor. Two
WRs were seated at a long table near the door. A corporal looked
up when we came in.

"You must be the two from boot camp. Take a chair," she said.
"We're making posters for the dance next week. Here's the information we'll need on each poster. You can lay it out any way you

want, but use this thicker paper, and the show card colors. You'll find brushes in the sink."

I felt like I was back in the art department at John Marshall High School in Chicago.

Lawson seemed to be familiar with the material. Sitting down, she studied the information to be put on the poster. "Freddy," she said, "this dance looks like fun."

The corporal shook her head. "Too bad you can't go."

Lawson protested. "Why not? Why can't we go? We're not boots anymore."

"Well, look at that date. It's not until the end of next week. You'll be in Oklahoma by then."

*   *   *

CHAPTER 7.
ON THAT TRAIN AND GONE

I couldn't believe we were going to Oklahoma. As soon as we got back to the barracks, I checked with Cpl Dean.

"That's right," she said. "New classes start in Norman every week. We only graduate boots every two weeks, so we keep you busy here until the next class starts. I thought you knew that."

"No," I said. "We were never told."

Lawson let out a yell and we headed for the squad room to share the good news. Morale shot up fast and life took on a new meaning for us all. I started packing my sea bag again. I would just leave out a couple of summer seersuckers, pajamas, and a toothbrush. No use making myself at home here.

I heard a husky voice from a few bunks down, on the other side of Whalen. "Let's have a big fat pahdy!"

Whalen, relaxing on her bunk, raised her head. "I hear Brooklyn," she called. "Where are you, Brooklyn?"

"Bongiorni here. You from New Yahk?"

"Yeah, Queens."

Bongiorni sat up to see where the voice was coming from. Four bunks down, she was shorter, softer, and rounder than Whalen. Her straight black hair curled under in a short pageboy, and she wore glasses as thick as the Marine Corps would accept. Her wide, toothy smile and infectious laugh would make her the life of any party, if we were to have a party.

Bongiorni was just what Whalen needed to motivate her out of the sack. She jumped to her feet and dashed down to investigate. From that moment, they were best buddies.

When Cpl. Dean came in I was glad we didn't have to hop to attention anymore. "Maybe some of you have noticed the bathtub down by the showers," she said. "There's a sign-up sheet for it on the bulletin board."

Great. I would certainly sign up, but not tonight. Lawson had heard of a place called the slop chute, where we could go for a beer. A quick shower would have to do for now. The showers here were single, with canvas curtains and individual dressing areas. It gave us more privacy than we had at boot camp.

Tuesday night there was a movie we wanted to see, so I put off the bath and showered instead.

Wednesday Lawson and I went bowling. We showered to get an early start. I would have signed up for a bath Thursday, but we had met a couple guys at the bowling alley who said they'd meet us at the slop chute that night.

Friday morning I thought of putting my name down for the bath tub at 1800, but no one had used the tub all week. Surely there would be no problem getting it. About 1800 that evening I was reaching for my towel when we heard a strange noise coming from down the hall.

Lawson said, "That sounds like a seal."

"Yeah, and I hear splashing. It must be taking a bath."

I found Bongiorni in the tub, up to her neck in suds, flipping about and making seal noises. When she finished, she left it so clean it was ready for Saturday's inspection. I wasn't about to mess it up. I felt relieved. Baths were just too much trouble.

Monday morning we were back on the curb with our sea bags. The same driver who brought us to Battalion Area came back to take us away. Opening the door for us she asked, "How was that bathtub?"

"Great!" said Bongiorni, and that settled it.

As we filed into the bus, we seated ourselves in the order we had been trained to do in boot camp, filling the back seats first. Lawson, ahead of me, took an aisle seat, I sat by the window in front of her, and so on. A sergeant came in last and settled behind the driver. Then Cpl Dean stepped in to take a final count.

"It's still only thirty-five," the driver assured her. "This is the first time they've been short one. Any idea what happened?"

"No idea." The corporal shrugged. "But everything seems to be in order." She handed her clipboard to the sergeant. "You can leave now."

The door closed. As the bus pulled away from the curb I felt a sense of loss. Where was the girl who had so willingly abandoned the comforts of civilian life at the Portland recruiting office? I could find no trace of her in the Woman Marine now occupying my seat.

Only two months ago I painted flowers on my fingernails to go dancing. My legs were painted too, with a line drawn up the back to make it look like I was wearing the nylon stockings that were no longer available. My seams were always straight. And my entire wardrobe was hand tailored originals. I had made them myself.

I looked at my nails. They were bare now and filed close. I wore cotton lisle hose no civilian would be seen in, and I was surrounded by women dressed exactly as I was. My old set of priorities didn't work anymore. I had a new sense of what was really important.

What would my friends back in Portland say if they could see me now? No doubt they would laugh. Never mind, let them laugh. They were no longer part of my life. From now on the Marine Corps would decide what I eat, clothing I wear, work I do, and even when I will or will not be free to go out.

I had separated from my friends, and replaced them with buddies. I thought of Elder, my boot camp bunky, and wondered if I'd ever see her again. I must write her when we get our new address in Norman.

The WR at my side pulled me from my reverie. "It's a lovely day to start on a trip. Everything is so green and bright after yesterday's shower. Oklahoma summers can get pretty dry."

"You've lived there?" I asked.

Her smile revealed a wide row of straight teeth. "No, I'm from Vermont. But I have read about it. I'm Pellier. Call me Pelly."

"I'm Fredriksen . . . Freddy."

"Scandinavian."

I nodded.

"My father was French. I got my blue eyes and light brown hair from my mother. I suppose you would call her Early American Quaker. Her nationality was mixed, but her religion was not. It must have been difficult for her, being married to an irrepressible Frenchman."

"And which do you favor?" I asked.

"Both, each at different times." She smiled again. "I try always to be like my mother. But of course, she would have been a conscientious objector in this war.

"When I was fourteen, both my parents were killed in an accident. My brother and I went to live with a dear friend of my father's. He was a retired Marine brigadier general, and a fine gentleman. He was a strong influence on me."

There was a sense of peace about her. She could speak of death as easily as she spoke of life, and she seemed to have no fear of either.

Our train was waiting for us at the New River station. The sergeant stood and asked us to remain in our seats. "I'm Sergeant Jackson," she said. "I will accompany you on this trip. See me if you have any problems."

While her attitude was official, she seemed friendly. She nodded to the driver and the doors were opened. When we filed out of the bus I got a good look at the train. It was so old, it looked like it belonged in a museum. It creaked as we entered. Evidently they were putting the older, retired cars back in service for the duration of the war.

Lawson and I chose a compartment and settled in. White curtains, not much heavier than bed sheets, replaced the familiar green canvas drapes that had been pulled across at night on my earlier trip east to Camp Lejeune.

I thought of a commercial on the radio introducing the new white packaging for Lucky Strike cigarettes. "Lucky Strike green has gone to war . . ." It looked like Pullman car green had gone the same way. I glanced down at my uniform and vowed never to take the color of it for granted.

From the seat behind us I heard, "Golly, where'd they get this ole' crate?"

That was Jeter. Lawson had sat with her on the bus. Now she and Pellier shared the compartment next to us. The train had hardly begun groaning its way out of the station when we left our seats to join them.

Jeter was sitting across from me now. Her eyes were large and penetrating, almost mystical. Slim and tense, she seemed unable to relax, even now when nothing was expected of her. She kept running her fingers through brown short-cropped curls.

"When we pull inta Birmingham tomorra mornin'," she said, "Mamma's gonna be there with fried chicken an' biscuits like they don' make up Noath. You guys 'r gonna jest love it!"

"It sounds delicious," said Pellier, "but she probably doesn't plan on feeding all of us."

"Oh sure, Mama'll have a shopping bag plum fulla good thangs to eat. Prob'ly enough to feed the whole car."

Lawson was skeptical. "Did she tell you this?"

"No, but I know my mama. She'll be there with the chow, all right."

The next morning, as the porter walked through the car, he announced, "We'll be an hour and a half late getting into Birmingham . . . We'll be an hour and a half late . . ."

Pellier turned to Jeter. "It doesn't look like you'll have much time to visit with your mother," she said. "Do you think she'll still be there?"

"She'll be there. I promise."

Later our train was sidetracked to wait for one with a higher war priority to pass. That set us back another half hour. Still, Jeter's faith was unshaken.

Sgt. Jackson came in from the other car to talk to her. "We have to stop in Birmingham to take on passengers and supplies," she said. "They might finish in as little as ten minutes, but I have talked to the porter. If your mother is there, you may step out for a brief visit by the door. No one else in your group will be allowed to leave the train."

They had almost fifteen minutes together. When the porter yelled, "All aboard!" Jeter returned with two bulging shopping bags. They filled the car with the pleasant aroma of southern fried chicken.

Pellier shook her head. "Your mother must have been up before dawn to cook all that."

Jeter gave her a cherubic Sunday school smile. "I knew she'd be there. I know my mama. She thinks I'm still her little baby."

No one in our car went to the diner for lunch that day.

There was plenty of free time on the train. I wrote several letters, leaving space at the end of each for my new address. When I got out the V-mail forms for the servicemen overseas, it occurred to me that none had answered the letters I sent them from boot camp. That was strange. In the past they had always answered promptly.

By the next day we were hours late again. They had to serve us our evening meal in the dining car and it was dark before we pulled into Oklahoma City. We transferred there to a Navy bus that took us to the Naval Air Tactical Training Center in Norman, Oklahoma.

When they dropped us off in front of our barracks, a friendly sergeant came out to greet us. "Welcome to Norman," she whispered. "I'm Sgt. Salisbury." There was a wholesomeness about her. She was my height with short light brown hair, dark brown eyes, and a pencil over one ear.

"The women's classes are on the early shift this month. They've been asleep for an hour. When you have found your sea bag, slip in quietly. I'll issue linen and show you to your bunks."

We searched through the pile of sea bags in the moonlight.

The four on the bottom read "Lawson," "Pellier," "Jeter," and "Fredriksen." Whalen took the one that was left, and we were last in.

Even in the dark, it was evident that these barracks were old. The wood had weathered a lot of dry summers. Entering the darkened squad room, I noticed the double bunks here were placed lengthwise with the room. There were three across on either side of the center aisle with three double lockers lined up at the foot of them to create a separation from the next row of bunks. This formed us into groups of six in what was called a bay.

The sergeant motioned us into the second bay on the left. Jeter took the top bunk by the window, Pellier the one below. Whalen threw her sea bag on the center bottom cot, so Lawson took the one above it. I was heading for the top bunk on the aisle when Sgt. Salisbury put her hand on it and whispered, "This one is saved."

Quietly, I spread my sheets on the mattress below. I hung my uniform on the slivered wooden bedpost and crawled into the sack, leaving the blanket folded at my feet.

In the darkness, I stared at the empty bunk above me until I fell asleep.

*   *   *

CHAPTER 8.
THE BUNK MATE

I had been asleep only a couple of hours when someone began talking in the NCO office. My bunk was close enough to the door that it woke me.

"I have to get my sea bag. It's still outside."

Sgt. Salisbury whispered, "Sit down and rest. I'll get it."

"No." The other voice was raised. "I'm under orders to accept no special favors. I must do everything for myself. I'll get it."

The front door opened, then closed. When it opened again the sergeant whispered, "That's too heavy for you."

Louder, the answer, "No. I will handle it."

"Shhhhh everyone's asleep."

You wanna bet?

The other half of the double door opened, letting more light into the squad room. Two figures came in and stopped at my bunk. Sgt. Salisbury patted the bare mattress above me. "This one is yours," she whispered.

I stuck my head out into the aisle for a better look. The sergeant stood nearby in her nightgown while a corporal, bent over as if in pain, tugged at her sea bag with one hand while she held her side with the other. "Can you make it up there?"

"I have to!"

There was a problem. "Sergeant, I can take the top bunk," I whispered.

"No," the corporal insisted. "If that's the one that was saved for me, I'll take it."

"Hey, I like top bunks," I explained, softly. "If it's O.K. with the sergeant . . ."

"It doesn't make any difference to me. I haven't made up the billet report yet."

I got up and started tearing out my sheets.

"No," said the corporal. "The doctor made me promise that if he released me to come here now, I would ask no special favors. I'll take the bunk that was saved for me."

She talked as we helped her make it up. "They took out my appendix last week. The doctor wanted to keep me in the hospital and cancel my transfer. I had to do some fast talking."

"Shhhhh," said the sergeant.

Making the bunk was easy, but getting her up there was not. Sgt. Salisbury brought in a wooden chair from the office and Pellier came over to help. As the corporal stood on it, insisting that she do it herself, the three of us lifted her, gently, to the top. Then we covered her and went back to bed.

Things had barely quieted down when I heard a soft whisper from above. I thought it said, "I have to go to the bathroom."

I started to crawl out.

"But I'll try to wait until morning."

It was hard to go back to sleep. Her groans were disturbing, and when she rolled over the old wooden bunk swayed precariously. Eventually I dozed off, but I had a strange feeling, as if I slept at attention for the rest of the night, which, it turned out, wasn't that long. At 0445 loudspeakers over the double doors blasted out a scratchy recording of "Oklahoma," and the lights flashed on. I leaped up and began searching for my toothbrush.

Sgt. Salisbury entered the squad room fully dressed. "The new class can stay in bed."

It was too late for that. The WRs in the class ahead of us were in the same squad room, closer to the head. They were scurrying about with their voices raised, policing the area.

Their shouting did not disturb Whalen. She slept on.

I glanced at my bunkmate and our eyes met. "Hi. I'm Freddy."

"Kilgallen" seemed to be all that she could manage.

Her face was ashen but the features were strong and above them, the brilliance of copper red hair made the pale skin seem like a mask.

It was difficult to know what to say. "Did you sleep?"

"A little. It doesn't matter, I'm here. What time is it?"

I looked at my watch. "It's 0445."

"What time is that?"

And this is a corporal?

"It's 4:45AM. Can you go back to sleep?"

"No. It hurts too much. Besides, I have to go to the bathroom."

That was the second time she had referred to the head as a bathroom. Didn't she learn anything in boot camp?

Bringing the chair back around to the center aisle, I asked, "Pelly, can you give us a hand?"

"I have to do it myself," Kilgallen insisted. First she tried going down on her back. I heard a helpless cry and she scampered back up. "I'll try it another way."

Turning over on her hands and knees, she threw one leg over the side, carefully letting it down as far as it would go. It was nowhere near the chair.

"I have a splendid idea," said Pellier.

She went to the office for another chair and put the two together. We each stood on one, made a chair with our arms, and lowered her down. She was heavier than she looked.

After Kilgallen took off for the head I started to unpack, leaving the end locker for her. As I set her sea bag on a chair beside it, I wondered how long it takes to recover from an appendectomy.

When Kilgallen returned, she looked even more ghastly than before. "As soon as I find my soap," I said, "I'm going to take a shower. Why don't you rest on my bunk?"

"No. I can't do that."

The other class was falling out for chow as I left for the showers. When I returned Whalen was still asleep and Kilgallen was sitting on a chair, looking at a snapshot. "Picture of your family?" I asked.

Glancing over her shoulder, I saw a photograph of a nun who looked a lot like Kilgallen. "Promise you won't tell anyone," she said. It seemed I had accidentally invaded her privacy. I agreed and she explained, "I was a nun for ten years. Do you know what that means?"

I shook my head.

"Evidently you're not Catholic. At the end of ten years, a nun takes her final vows. From that time on she is married to the church, and can't leave in good graces."

"Does that mean you're not Catholic anymore?"

"They made an exception in my case," she said, "because I gave them so much trouble. I kept explaining that I was emotionally unfit for life in the convent.

"I couldn't stand the cloistered life any longer, but I couldn't leave the church, either. I'm Catholic. I had to get formal dispensation from Rome. But I think they were glad to get rid of me."

It was hard to know what to say. Fortunately, Jeter came in, ending the conversation.

Having a locker was real luxury. It was old and worn, but it matched the olive drab wooden bunks. A shelf at the top held hats, with a rod beneath it for hangers. There were drawers below on one side, and a mirror and towel rack on the door. A place for everything, I thought, until I heard a voice from the next bay.

"Hey, where can I put John's picture?"

That would be Graves. John was the Air Force Major she was engaged to. We had all admired his photo.

Heavy boondocker boots hit the deck with a thud, announcing the return of the class ahead of us. They were a salty looking bunch in men's dungaree pants, secured at the waist with belts and topped with a white skivvy shirt, optional jacket, and dungaree overseas cap.

I recognized Rudkin when she stopped by my bunk. "Hi

Freddy, welcome to Oklahoma. How did you like the wake-up call?"

"'Oklahoma?' What ever happened to 'Reveille'?"

"Somebody got mad and broke the record last week. By the way, when you go to chow, don't bite down on the beans. You could break a tooth."

"Beans for breakfast?"

"Yep. You're in the Navy now. They serve beans regularly at morning chow. I think they start cooking them when they hear us coming because they're barely warm."

I cringed. "Thanks for the tip. How's the coffee?"

"Pretty bad today. They only clean the urns once a week for Saturday inspection."

Pellier and Lawson were working on Whalen, trying to wake her up. There was no response until Sgt. Salisbury called, "The new class will fall out for chow!"

Then she opened her eyes and yelled, "Hey, let's look alive!"

Already partially dressed, she slipped out of bed, threw on her skirt, stepped into her shoes and slammed on her hat. Then she grabbed her blouse and beat me out the door.

First we arranged ourselves in our permanent marching positions. Sgt. Salisbury motioned to a stately blonde who was obviously the tallest in the platoon. "The squad leader in the middle row, how tall are you?"

"I'm five feet ten and a half, Sergeant."

"And your name?"

"Private Erickson, Sergeant."

"Is anyone here taller than five ten and a half?" No one answered. "Okay Erickson, you're right guide."

She traded places with the WR standing behind her while the rest of us maneuvered about, pausing now and then to ask, "How tall are you?"

I was standing in third place in the middle row when Kilgallen tapped me on the shoulder. "How tall are you?"

"Five six and a half."

"I'm five eight."

I would never have guessed it, bent over as she was. "Are you sure?"

"Yes, I'm sure."

I yielded reluctantly. She didn't look that tall.

Now, facing the sergeant, I stood behind True. Whalen was settled into fourth position in the back row directly behind me. She bent down to tie her shoes.

"While you are here," said the sergeant, "you will be known as class 52-44. When I call you to fall out, '52' is the number that will be used to designate your class."

I heard the wooden steps behind me creak. A short, cocky WR in dungaree pants and khaki shirt came out and stood beside the sergeant.

"This is Corporal DiPalma. She's your drill instructor."

Oh no, not another DI!

Cpl. DiPalma did not smile. Just over five feet tall and trim, she stood erect, chest out, hands on hips. Her jet black hair was straight, her eyes as dark and shiny as her cordovan brown shoes.

"ATTENTION!" She roared in a deep voice. "Right, face." She paused to look us over. "Forward . . . MARCH."

Fortunately, the women's mess hall was nearby. I couldn't go much further without food. Taking a couple slices from the stack of toast, I moved on to the beans, reluctant to ask the mess girl about them. These were WAVEs, having just graduated from our school. It was difficult to tell if they were friendly.

Kilgallen, ahead of me in the chow line, was not afraid of them. She asked, "How are the beans?"

The WAVE tapped them with her spoon. It sounded like she hit a pile of rocks. I grabbed another slice of toast and skipped the beans. From now on, I would stock Baby Ruth bars in my locker to tide me over on the mornings they served them.

Class 51 was gone when we got back from chow. We had the squad room to ourselves. I noticed Sgt. Salisbury had leaned a small hooked ladder against Kilgallen's bunk.

My mattress looked like the one I had left in boot camp, but at least here it matched the others. I made up my bunk and finished unpacking. When there was nothing left in my sea bag but the winter uniforms, I locked it up.

After Sgt. Salisbury had taken us upstairs to put our bags in storage, Jeter noticed Kilgallen, sitting on a chair, ripping corporal stripes from a summer blouse.

"What happened? Did ya git busted?"

"No, I busted myself. When they said I couldn't come here to school because I was a corporal, I gave them the stripes."

Pellier asked, "Where did you come from?"

"Washington D.C., where there's four hundred women to every man, and the men are all married. They said the only way I'd get transferred out of there was to a hospital, so I convinced them I needed an appendectomy. I had to find some way to get out to California."

Lawson smiled. "Are we going to California?"

"Some of us will. I might as well be one of them. I have two sisters in Long Beach."

Pellier asked, "Are they in the service?"

"One's a WAVE. She's married to a Marine officer. The other works at the Navy base there."

"Where is your home?" I asked.

"Chicago. Oak Park really, if you know where that is."

"Oh, sure. I used to work there at Burny Brother's Bakery."

"I know that place. It's on the corner, and they have a big side window. Once when I was home I saw a papier-mache scarecrow on display there. I'll never forget the expression on its face."

I was pleased that she noticed it. "That was my Halloween decoration back in 1941, just before I moved to Portland. I can't believe you remembered it!"

"I'm glad to know there's another artist around here."

"Not really. I'm just a doodler. If you're looking for an artist, you should talk to Lawson. She turned out some great posters for a dance at Camp Lejeune."

Lawson heard that. "Freddy, that dance is tonight. I'm kinda sorry we'll miss it."

Kilgallen studied her. "You'd be popular at a dance."

Sgt. Salisbury came to the door. "Welcome to the Naval Air Tactical Training Center. You'll like Norman. It's a quiet university town, and the people are friendly. You can catch an electric car from there to Oklahoma City.

"Class 52 is free this morning to get settled. If you need anything, Ship's Service is in building 22. You go down to the main road and turn right.

"After noon chow, you will fall out at 1300 and march to the auditorium for orientation."

"What time is that?" Kilgallen again.

Salisbury continued. "You will be expected to march to the mess hall for all meals. If you want to skip one, you can get a chow cut slip from my office. You'll be allowed two chow cuts a week."

A large off-white shaggy dog of questionable ancestry trotted into the squad room. The sergeant patted his head. "This is Chow Cut, our mascot. I guess he heard his name mentioned. He was left here by the WAVEs who occupied this barracks before us."

After the sergeant left, the dog stayed to make friends.

Kilgallen needed to go to Ship's Service for aspirin and PFC stripes. Lawson was out of Lux soap flakes so she went along. When they returned, Lawson was behaving strangely. She motioned me outside. I followed her. "We have to talk," she said. "It's about your bunky."

"Kilgallen?"

"Yes. She made me promise not to tell, but I just have to tell somebody!"

"Go ahead."

"We were on our way to Ship's Service when, out of the corner of my eye, I saw this khaki uniform. Well, you know how scary it is when you're about to pass an officer."

I nodded.

"I threw my arm up fast and said 'Good morning, Sir,' so

Kilgallen did the same. Then we got a good look at him. "Freddy, we saluted the Coca Cola delivery man!"

I started to laugh, but Lawson was serious. "She said if I ever told anybody about that, she'd kill me. She said it twice. But that's not all . . ."

She lowered her voice. "Do you know what she was before she joined the Marines?"

I had promised to keep that a secret. "I can't guess."

"We stopped for a Coke, and she showed me this picture of herself. She was a nun! She made me promise not to tell anyone. But you're her bunky. I thought you should know."

"Well, I already knew. What's the problem?"

"The problem is, I don't know how to talk to a nun. What do we say to her?"

"She's sworn us both to secrecy, so let's treat her like everybody else. She'll just have to get used to it."

When we went back inside, Kilgallen was standing by the lockers, showing Whalen the picture.

It was going to be hard to keep her secret if she kept sharing it with everybody.

*   *   *

CHAPTER 9.
ORIENTATION

It was a long march to the auditorium. Kilgallen, directly in front of me, appeared to be in trouble. She walked bent over and her steps lagged behind the cadence. It was hard to avoid stepping on her heels. I felt relief for her when we finally arrived and she could rest.

There were about three hundred sailors in summer whites already seated, but we were the only group of women. I followed Kilgallen to our places and she slumped into her seat with a groan. Three Naval officers and one Marine captain were seated on the platform. The Marine officer, on the far left, had two Doberman pinschers sitting at attention by his side.

Kilgallen dozed as the talks began, but now and then something would grab her attention and she would mutter, "That's asinine," before dropping back into a semi-conscious sleep. I don't think she missed much.

As each Naval officer spoke in turn, we learned three schools were represented here. Ours, Aviation Machinist Mate (AMM), was the longest course, and the largest. There were four AMM classes starting. The other three were all sailors. One group would be on the same shift with us, and we would change shifts with the other two AMM classes every four weeks. There were also two classes each of sailors who were here for Aviation Gunner and Aviation Metalsmith, with one class on each shift.

Early classes begin at 0700. (No wonder "Oklahoma" blasted into our squad room in the middle of the night.)

Upon graduation, the top man from each of the three schools

would receive a certificate suitable for framing, and a ring from the people of Oklahoma City.

The student with the highest grade in each class would get first choice for his next assignment, going down the list from there until there were no choices left.

Kilgallen muttered, "I'm going to have to study."

On liberty, we must not travel more than fifty miles from the base. Any of us caught beyond that point would be considered out of bounds and subject to a deck court.

"For the love of Mike!" said Kilgallen.

Oklahoma City was within bounds, but they had a curfew for enlisted military personnel on the streets and it was strictly enforced.

"How asinine!"

We were to salute the base commander's car, whether he was in it or not.

"Asinine!"

We would march in review Saturday morning, followed by liberty from noon until lights out Sunday night. Liberty cards were also available Wednesday evening for those on the early shift.

When the Naval officers had finished, Captain Butler, the Marine officer, was introduced. The two Dobermans followed him to the podium and stood attentively at his side while he focused his attention on our class. He was a rugged looking man of average height, with a square jaw and piercing eyes.

"I will be in charge of discipline for you women," he began. I sensed he enjoyed his work. "Always remember you are a guest here. As a Marine, I expect each of you to make certain your conduct sets an example for the Navy personnel aboard.

"And one thing that will not be tolerated," he warned, "is fraternizing. You are enlisted Marines, and you will not speak to any officer except as it becomes necessary in order to carry out your military duties."

Kilgallen opened her eyes. "For the love of Mike, they're treating us like children."

"I have a son who is a sergeant in the Marine Corps," he went on. "When he comes home on furlough he enters and leaves by the rear door, and we do not eat together."

That brought a gasp from the entire audience.

"I warn you again, fraternizing will be punished and no excuses will be accepted.

"Now, ten percent of you women will be assigned to El Toro, California. The rest will be sent to Cherry Point, North Carolina."

Kilgallen looked up. "I'm really going to have to study."

He recited a few lines lifted from the book of Marine Regulations and ended with, "Remember, you are Marines. You must always set an example."

He was about to sit down when he thought of something else. As he came back to the podium, the dogs followed in momentary confusion. "And beginning with this class, there will be no stripes awarded to Marine graduates."

I was so fresh out of boot camp the captain's speech didn't bother me, but Kilgallen was seething. By the time we got back to the squad room she was acting more disoriented than before we attended orientation.

"The officers are like a bunch of little toy soldiers playing war," she said. "And the one in charge of us thinks his own son isn't good enough to break bread with him, because he's not an officer."

She was on a roll. "Now, these women officers with their bachelor's degrees in domestic science, they're just playing house. I have a master's degree. I requested Officer's Candidate School, but those little second lieutenants gave me two stripes and sent me to Washington to correct papers for students of the Marine Corps Institute.

"I joined the Marines to get away from correcting papers! I thought I was going to be an officer!"

Lumpkin came in as Kilgallen ended her speech and sat on her bunk, across the aisle from us. "You joined for OCS?" she asked. "So did I. I'm a school teacher. I have a bachelor's degree in home-making. But do you think they'd accept me for Officer's Candidate School?"

"I'm surprised they didn't," Kilgallen mused.

Lumpkin took that as a compliment. Smiling coyly, she fingered a strand of pale blonde hair and tucked it securely into the bun in back. "It looks like I'm going to end up fixing those dirty airplanes, no matter how much schooling I've had."

It was a warm day. She unbuttoned her blouse, revealing a rather full figure. I was wondering how she was going to fit into those men's dungarees when Sgt. Salisbury entered the squad room. "Class 52, line up alphabetically topside to get your dungarees."

That was good news. Cpl. Dean had collected the ones she issued to our group while in Battalion Area. She said they couldn't get any more of them. The summer seersuckers were a dead giveaway that we were fresh out of boot camp. Now we would look like everyone else.

At least, I thought we would.

"The new women's fatigue uniforms have just arrived." She smiled. "Your class will be the first to wear them."

Darn!

Cpl. DiPalma joined her and we followed them upstairs to the recreation room. It was large, drab, and sparsely furnished. A bookcase on one wall held a few books. Two or three old couches and overstuffed chairs were scattered about, some with floor lamps and ashtrays beside them. I saw nothing worth climbing the stairs for until, off in a corner, I spotted an electric sewing machine. Great!

Cpl. DiPalma unwrapped the uniforms quickly. I was anxious to see what we would be wearing. She held up a one-piece garment. It was of a limp, wrinkled, thin gaberdine in olive drab. Pants had an attached top with straps that crossed in the back and came over the shoulder to button in front. It was to be worn with a white skivvy shirt and optional matching jacket.

Abramovitz got hers first. She fingered them. "You take a muddy green like that, it won't show the dirt."

That was the best that could be said for our new dungarees.

We each took our turn, getting four of the overalls, two jackets, and six white skivvy shirts, plus a matching bowler hat and a pair of boondocker boots in rough leather. A green and red rayon snood called a machine operator's cap completed the outfit. We hurried downstairs to try them on.

Kilgallen didn't seem disappointed. Evidently she was used to wearing whatever was handed to her. "At least," she said, pulling a strap down over her shoulder, "there's nothing tight around my incision."

Lumpkin grumbled. "Some man must have designed this. There's not enough fullness up here for the bosom."

I had no problem with that.

Ward came up from a bay further down toward the head. A slight, frail looking girl, her dungarees hung loose. "This is the smallest size they had, and it's way too big." She pulled out the waist to show us. "I've lost a lot of weight since I left home. They just don't serve the kind of food in the mess hall that we ate back in Virginia."

When she let go, the waistline slipped back down, resting on her hips. I remembered the sewing machine upstairs. "I do alterations."

"Great! You're on."

"Did I hear someone say they do alterations?"

A crowd soon gathered around my bunk. It seemed everyone had something they wanted let out, taken in, lengthened, or shortened.

I was beginning to feel oriented.

*   *   *

Len Telfer   Edna Hamilton

Virginia Jeter Mary Young

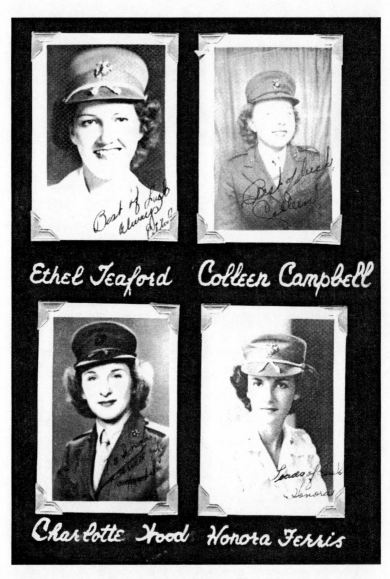

Some of my buddies

CHAPTER 10.
SATURDAY REVIEW

An area some distance from our barracks was covered with a thick growth of tall weeds. Cpl. DiPalma took us there every afternoon to drill for Saturday Review. When she brought us back on Friday she talked a while before dismissing us.

"You people are in for a real treat," she began. "Tex Beneke is stationed aboard. His band will lead you on to the field tomorrow."

What a break! I loved his "Chatanooga Choo Choo."

"He used to play with Glenn Miller's band, until Glenn joined the Air Force. Then Tex kept the group together for a while, called themselves 'Tex Beneke and the Glenn Miller boys.' Remember 'I Got a Gal in Kalamazoo,' and 'The Atchison, Topeka, and the Santa Fe'? That was Tex. Tomorrow morning his band will gather across the street, right there in front of the gymnasium."

She turned and gestured toward that area, as if it had been sanctified by his presence. For once, I was actually looking forward to review.

The next morning the musicians arrived shortly after chow. Jeter raised the Venetian blind to get a better look. "Ah think ah see 'im. There he is. See that chief? Isn't that him?"

I rushed to the window. Tex Beneke was easy to spot. Looking sharp in his white Chief Petty Officer uniform, he roamed about, twirling his baton as the musicians tuned their instruments. I got a closer look when Cpl. DiPalma called us to fall out. While my body stood at attention, my eyes followed Tex. It was hard to concentrate on her instructions.

Eventually the band fell into formation and began to play. I watched Tex lead them on to the parade ground beside our barracks. Over three thousand sailors followed the band, marching past us on the street, in order of seniority. I couldn't see the band anymore, but I could hear the beat and feel the splendor of the Sousa marches. Waves of white uniforms moved in unison as class after class of men paraded past us to the rhythm of its cadence.

The ground had been cleared of vegetation, leaving the red earth bare. As the sailors marched on to the field, disturbing the soil, a cloud of pink dust rose from it.

When all of the men had passed, WAVEs in the AMM classes ahead of us followed. Then it was our turn. Several earlier classes of WRs led the way, and we followed behind class 51-44. We were the last on the field.

It smelled of hot dry dust. Already the sun had been beating down for hours and it felt oppressive. A row of ambulances parked behind the women's platoons caught my eye. We never had those at our reviews in Camp Lejeune. I wondered why they were here.

As soon as we were in position, the music stopped and all were given parade rest. The deck rocked as we stomped out in unison, sending up another wave of pink dust. At the same instant arms whisked back, right hand clasping left thumb. There it would stay throughout the duration of lengthy speeches, until it was time to pass in review.

July in Oklahoma felt even hotter than June in North Carolina. The heat built up under my hat until sweat ran down my face. I couldn't wipe it off. I clung to that thumb and tried to remember if I had taken my salt pill.

An ambulance started up and drove away. I turned my eyes in the direction of Kilgallen, and was relieved to see she was still standing at my side.

Later another ambulance left, and yet another. There was some commotion behind me to my left before a fourth vehicle drove off. I couldn't turn to see who it was.

It seemed an eternity before I heard, "Pass in review." The

ordeal would soon be over. Tex Beneke raised his baton and the military music began to thrill me again. As the sailors moved past the reviewing stand and off the field, I noticed their white uniforms had turned a pastel dusty pink.

Our class was the last to leave. When Cpl. DiPalma gave the command, "Eyes . . . RIGHT!" we straightened our lines to move as one past the reviewing stand. Then "Ready . . . FRONT!" and we followed class 51 off the field. As soon as we were dismissed, I hurried into the barracks to escape the sun's relentless heat.

Lumpkin was already there, relaxing on her bunk. Bongiorni remarked, "What happened to you, Lump? Can't you take a little heat?"

"Oh, I could, I guess, but why bother?" She giggled shamelessly. "I noticed that some of the sailors were dropping, and an ambulance just came and took them away.

"I was getting warm and uncomfortable, so I decided to drop too. They took me to sickbay to check my heart. Then they let me come home. Was it hot enough out there?"

Lumpkin recovered quickly for the march to chow and seemed to suffer no loss of appetite. I wasn't the only one disgusted with her for what she had pulled.

But she had missed an important notice on the bulletin board. Later when she lined up outside the NCO office for her liberty card, just ahead of Kilgallen and me, Sgt. Salisbury let her stand in line until it was her turn. Then she said, "Lumpkin, you don't get liberty this weekend."

"Why not?"

"Anyone who passes out on the parade ground is considered physically unfit for liberty."

"Well," she answered, "if I had known that, I certainly wouldn't have passed out."

*   *   *

CHAPTER 11.
WE HAD CLASS

We were soon hitting the deck and going to chow with class 51. We shared cleaning details and followed them to the chow hall and classes, but socially we remained separate. Somehow, they made us feel like the new recruits, even though both classes were from the 32nd boot camp battalion.

Maybe it was those silly outfits we had to wear. Class 51 already had their men's dungarees so faded they looked like they had been washed a dozen times in Fels Naptha.

It didn't help that they had something they called a Dzus key hanging on their belts. It jangled as they tramped down the center of the squad room, so that I knew they were class 51 without looking up.

And they had McGinnis. She wrote great words to familiar tunes. They sang them in the squad room and in the showers. From Bing Crosby's holiday hit we heard:

Christmas Eve will find me,
At my favorite bar.
I'll be home for Christmas,
No matter where I are.

When McGinnis needed money, she didn't have to take in sewing. She just wrote a few clever lines, sent them off to her greeting card company, and the check was in the mail.

While class 51 was singing, class 52 was hitting the books. We all wanted to be among the top three in our class so we could go to El Toro. Even Campbell studied hard, and she wanted Cherry Point. Kilgallen could never understand that.

Not that she was worried about her own grades. "I have a master's degree," she explained. "I should make the top ten percent easily."

The first half of every day was spent in the classroom. We started on simple math. After chow we had shop time, where we began making our Dzus keys. They were handy little tools used to open the Dzus fasteners that held the cowling fast against the engine enclosure.

The first week we cut the key into shape and bored a hole in one end to attach it to the key ring so we could hook it on our belts. But the new women's dungarees had no belts. We had to stuff the key, with its ring, in our rear pocket. It was uncomfortable when we sat down, and we had to be careful that it didn't fall in the toilet when we undressed to use the head.

We took a written test at the end of each week on subjects that were in our manual. It counted for half of our grade. The shop instructor based the other half on his observations as we worked on our assignments.

When our first week's grades were posted, True came in first. A slim, thoughtful girl in thick glasses, she once confessed to me that her family doctor helped her memorize the eye charts to pass the physical exam for the Marine Corps.

True and I were the only ones who got 100 on the math. My shop grade was lower so I came in second. Not a bad start, I thought. Maybe this would be easy. Erickson was third. She had missed one problem.

"I should have double checked that last one," she said. "I know better than that." It was the only time any of us beat out Erickson for first place on our grades list.

Jeter was fourth, and Campbell came in fifth.

Kilgallen scanned the list with grim determination. Her name was a bit further down. "I'm not a mathematician," she said, "and they'll never make one out of me."

Class work the second week was nomenclature. I studied hard all week, memorizing the names of all of the parts of a plane that might be on the test. Meanwhile, in shop we had to finish our Dzus key. I never got to the front of the line at the machine that smoothed off the edges. The instructor marked me way down for that, plummeting my shop grade for the week.

Kilgallen didn't finish hers either. She stuffed the manual in the back of her locker and began hanging out at the slop chute with Lawson.

When my grades were no better the third week, I figured I, too, would be headed for Cherry Point. I let Kilgallen convince me that spending every evening in the squad room brooding over the manual was wasted time. "We won't need that stuff," she said. "They're going to stick us all in some office, shuffling papers."

I began to join Kilgallen and Lawson occasionally on their trips to the slop chute. The sailors here were very friendly, and they never referred to us as BAMs.

As the weeks passed, the grades list settled into a pattern. Erickson's position at the top was never challenged. Evenings we could always find her sitting on her bunk, facing the center aisle, memorizing the manual. Nothing disturbed her. Jeter, with little effort, was taking turns with True, who studied a good deal, for second and third place. Campbell was usually fourth.

"I can't understand it," said Kilgallen. "If Campbell wants Cherry Point, she doesn't have to study at all."

Every Monday evening after the previous week's grades were posted, Kilgallen would retreat to her bunk with her rosary. Bongiorni, passing by, once asked, "Were your grades that bad, Kil?"

"Bonny," she replied, "I'll never make it to California on my grades, so I'm taking it to a Higher Authority."

We marched endless miles to and from class as Sousa's music, played on scratchy records, blasted out over the base public address system. I memorized every note of "Stars and Stripes Forever," "The Thunderer," and "El Capitan."

Our instructors were sailors. Most were married, in their mid thirties to early forties. Many gave the impression that they believed women were incapable of understanding what lifted a plane off the ground or moved it through the air. However, they treated us with respect and except for our consistently low shop grades, we had no complaints.

Our classroom instructor for the week of hydraulics came in looking very uncomfortable Tuesday morning. He was hesitant and red faced, blushing for no apparent reason. I had never seen a sailor blush before.

"Today I have to cover hydraulic fittings," he began. He turned his back to us and cupped his face in his hands for a moment, like something was bothering him. Facing us again, he continued. "All right, let's get it over with. These are hydraulic fittings."

He held up a pair of them. Then he started talking so fast I couldn't understand what he was saying. His face turned a deeper crimson as he finished. "There. I'm glad that's over."

He tried to move on to another subject. I was willing to let it pass, but Erickson was not. She raised her hand.

"I couldn't understand what you just said about hydraulic fittings. Would you please repeat it?"

"I'm sorry, I can't. It's too embarrassing to talk to ladies about things like that."

Whalen spoke up. "Aw, he just said they're called male and female fittings. I already knew that because I used to work with 'em." Erickson wrote that down and he went on with the lecture, apparently grateful for the help.

We worked in pairs the week we changed airplane tires. Lawson and I had removed our wheel but we were having trouble getting the tire off the rim. I had never seen such a large tire iron. I stood on the end of it, but the tire didn't budge.

"Jump on it," said the instructor.

I jumped. Still, it would not yield.

"How much do you weigh?"

"A hundred and ten."

He turned to Lawson. "How much do you weigh?"

"A hundred and twenty pounds."

"You jump on it."

A hundred and twenty didn't do it either.

"It's going to take both of you."

I began to wonder if a woman's place wasn't, after all, behind a typewriter.

We spent two weeks studying carburetors, training mostly with the Stromberg Injection model that was used in the planes we would be working on.

"One thing you should remember," the instructor emphasized, "is that the main function of the carburetor is that it atomizes, meters, and mixes." He repeated it several times, usually followed by a warning that it would be on the test.

After a few days Lumpkin asked, "I have memorized the atomizes, meters, and mixes part, and I'll get it right on the test, but could you just tell me what it is that this carburetor is supposed to do?"

He folded his arms impatiently. "I can't take the time for that now. We still have too much to cover. Just get it right on the test."

We spent three weeks studying engines. That's when Whalen began dropping her spoon in her coffee mug. "That's my cooling fin," she explained.

I found engines to be the most interesting subject of all. We learned that aluminum was used because of its strength and lighter weight. That explained why we had been asked to sacrifice our aluminum pots and pans to the war effort.

I never questioned how engines worked before. One of the first things we were taught was never, never to call an engine a motor. "An engine," said the instructor, "is a machine that creates its own power of motion through consumption of a fuel. A motor, on the other hand, takes its power from an outside source such as electricity or a battery.

"I remember one WAVE who came through here on her third week of engines. When she asked the instructor a question, she referred to the engine as a motor. He made her go back and repeat the whole three weeks of engines."

Since that day, I have never called an engine a motor.

Workshop period during those weeks was spent taking apart the various sections of the Pratt Whitney radial engine, then putting them back together. It was important that this work be completed each day, to be ready for the other shift. Kilgallen always had trouble remembering where the parts belonged. I caught her one evening emptying a collection of nuts and bolts from her pocket into her locker.

I asked, "What are you doing, Kil?"

She slammed the door shut to hide the evidence. "I don't know where all those things are supposed to go. I am a poet, a dreamer, and a lover, and they'll never make a machinist out of me."

When we came to the end of our last shop assignment in engines, we finished cleaning up early. The instructor gathered us around his workbench and opened a book.

"Would you like to hear the formula for finding the horsepower of a radial engine? It won't be on the test."

Erickson said, "Oh yes," and reached for her notebook.

I wasn't paying much attention until he said, "Now, it's worth ten points on your grade if you can figure out this next part." That's when I started listening.

"You take the total cubic inches of the cylinder head piston displacement per revolution and multiply it by two."

He stopped reading and looked up. "None of the instructors here in the department have been able to figure out why that number is multiplied by two."

I didn't hear anything else he said, but it didn't matter. Erickson was getting it all down. I pondered that ten-point question until I thought I had it figured out.

When he finished, I raised my hand. "Could the displacement per revolution be multiplied by two because it takes two complete revolutions to fire all the cylinders?"

He looked shocked. The answer was so simple.

"You may be right," he admitted.

He gave it some thought. "Yes, you are right."

"My name is Fredriksen, and I can sure use the extra ten points on my grade."

"Well," he smiled sheepishly, "I was kidding about that. The grades had to be in by 1200 today. I didn't think any of you would be able to figure it out.

"Besides, I just said it was worth ten points. I didn't say you were going to get it."

I felt betrayed. It took two beers at the slop chute and an evening of Kilgallen's philosophy to calm me, only to have my anger return when I saw my low shop grade that week.

Much as I loved those planes, I doubted that I would ever get near enough to an F4U Corsair to turn my Zeus key in its slide fasteners. The men were in charge of this world of military aviation. They didn't seem to believe women were capable of becoming a useful part of it.

I hoped we could prove them wrong.

*　　*　　*

CHAPTER 12.
SINCERELY MELVIN

As soon as I unpacked my stationery, I mailed letters to each of the servicemen I wrote to in the Pacific Theater giving them my new address. None of those letters were answered either.

They couldn't all be dead.

I decided to write once more to Melvin, an Army corporal who had been to our home several times. His father was from the same town in Norway where my mother's parents were born, and he had seemed like one of the family. There was an answer to that letter at mail call a few weeks later. I took it to my bunk and read it:

> "Private Inga,
>
> "Yes, I got all three of your letters. However, now that you are a servicewoman, I no longer want to write to you because you have changed.
>
> "Please give my best regards to your mother.
>
> Sincerely, Melvin"

Feelings of rejection overwhelmed me. It's true I had changed, but was that any reason for him to stop writing? And how about all the others who had not returned my letters?

Had they felt the same way? Why?

Alone in the bay and needing someone to talk to, I marched down to the head and found Roth and Chici, (she pronounced it Chicky), sitting on a bench by the showers, having a smoke.

"Look at this!" I waved the letter in front of them. "I can't believe it. I thought he was my friend."

Roth greeted me with her usual smile, her round face reflecting the pleasure she seemed to find in everything around her. But after she read the letter, she became serious. Passing it on to Chici, she looked up at me and asked, "How much did Melvin mean to you?"

"He meant more to my mother than he did to me," I said. "But he asked me to write to him. I wrote to a lot of servicemen, but they all stopped writing when they learned I had joined the Marines. This is the only response I got, and it took three letters to get it. Is there something wrong with us?"

Chici shook her head. "Hey, remember all those tests we had to pass to get into this Marine Corps? There's nothing wrong with us."

She had once been married, and had been on her own for a while before enlisting. Her background was quite different from most of the girls in our class who, at twenty, had needed their parent's permission to sign up. I had a lot of respect for her opinion.

"Well then," I asked, "how would you explain this rejection?"

"I have a theory," she said. "I believe all men are bastards."

That came as a complete surprise. It would have been easier for me to believe that I had been at fault. Roth and I exchanged glances.

"It's true," she went on. "Every man wants to marry a virgin, right?"

"Of course," I agreed.

"But nobody expects a man to be a virgin."

Chici stopped to light another cigarette. "They know what they do when they leave home and put on a uniform. They just figure when we get away from the influence of our parents, we're going to do the same thing.

"What Melvin is trying to tell you is that he believes you are now a fallen woman."

"That's not fair," Roth protested.

"I didn't say men were fair. I only said they were bastards."

Roth had finished her cigarette. I followed her back to her bunk, where we could talk.

"I don't think Chici is right," she said. "My brother isn't a bastard."

She began to talk about their childhood, when they were growing up together on a farm in Colfax, Washington. "And we had this grove of trees down by the road. My brother and I used to play down there.

"One day he tied a rope around my chest and hung me from a tree. Then he walked away and left me hanging there."

She smiled, as if it were a pleasant memory.

"Didn't cars go by and see you?"

"One did. There was a bunch of guys in it."

"Did they stop and help you down?"

"No, they just looked at me and laughed. One of them said, 'Oh look, there's a girl hanging in that tree!'"

I thought about that as I went back to my bunk. Maybe Chici was right.

Maybe all men are bastards.

*   *   *

CHAPTER 13.
CONFIRMATION OF WHALEN

Grim determination had kept Kilgallen on her feet all day, and I could hear her groaning in the bunk above as she struggled through the painful nights. But with time, she healed. In a few weeks she was able to mount her bunk without the ladder, and her naturally ruddy complexion returned.

She stood straighter now, though she never threw her shoulders back to make an entrance like she owned the room and everyone in it, as we had been taught in boot camp. This may have been one more way of rebelling against the Marine Corps. I was more inclined to believe it a habit of humility that had been forged into her skeletal structure years ago, in reverence to the Divine Authority.

It wasn't long before everyone in class 52 knew of Kilgallen's background. We accepted her, though we never fully understood her, and she seldom spoke of her life in the convent. But one evening I got a glimpse of what it may have been like for her then.

Whalen had asked, with her usual blunt honesty, "Hey Kil, is it true that nuns shave their heads?"

I felt embarrassed for my bunkmate, until I heard an amused laugh from the bunk above me. "That story about nuns shaving their heads is nonsense."

Kilgallen threw her legs over the side and came down to talk. They sat together on Whalen's bunk, facing me. I continued to file my nails and listen as she went on.

"Most of us wore our hair short, because it had to be tucked under our coif. That's a tight fitting cap to keep our hair from showing under our headdress.

"My head was covered tightly for so many years that now my hair won't grow long. It was thick, and came down to my waist when I was a girl. Now I can't even get it to touch my collar. It makes me mad because I can't break that regulation."

"Maybe you should get a wig."

Whalen's suggestion went unnoticed as Kilgallen talked on about her past. "I was always getting in trouble at the convent. I'm a poet, a dreamer, and a lover. I didn't belong there."

"Yeah? Then, why did you go in?"

"I had to. When I was a baby, I got so sick the doctor said I wouldn't live through the night. They sent for the priest to administer last rites. Both my parents and my grandfather were there in the room with me. They were all waiting for me to die.

"Then my grandfather began to pray out loud. He promised God that if He would spare my life, he would give me to the church. That's when I opened my eyes and called for my mother."

Whalen whistled. "Boy, that was bad timing."

"Well, whatever it was, Grandfather was a very domineering man. No one in the family ever dared oppose him. We all just took it for granted that as soon as I was old enough, I would enter the convent. I began to study for it when I was fourteen, and I stayed in the convent until my grandfather died."

"I used to wonder what it would be like to be a nun."

"Are you Catholic?"

"Well, sort of."

Kilgallen laughed nervously. "You can't be sort of Catholic, Whalen. Either you are, or you aren't."

"See, my mother's family was Catholic. My parents never went to church or anything, but before they were married my father had to sign something promising us kids would be raised Catholic. They sent my brother and me to some school at this church."

"Catechism?"

"Yeah, I guess that's what they called it."

"Were you confirmed?"

"Maybe. I don't remember."

"Did you go before the priest, in a white dress?"

"Oh yeah, I remember that dress. I hated it. It was all lace and ruffles. Sure couldn't play ball in it. I never wore it again."

"Whalen, you are a Catholic. You need to start going to church. How long has it been since you went to confession?"

"I don't remember ever going to confession."

"Whalen, we need to talk. Let's go upstairs to the lounge."

"Yeah, well, I'm writing to my uncle right now. Some other time, okay?"

Kilgallen shook her head. Grabbing a towel, she left for the showers.

A bit later Bongiorni came by and said, "Hey, Whale, let's go see what's happening at the slop chute."

"Sure, Bon, I'll be right there."

She signed the letter quickly and sealed it. When Kilgallen returned from her shower, she learned that Whalen had gone out for a beer.

She sighed. Her work for God was not finished.

*   *   *

CHAPTER 14.
OUT OF BOUNDS

Kilgallen looked up from a letter she was reading. "Freddy," she said, "where can we go to talk?"

"How about the head?"

She took the letter with her and we sat on a bench by the showers. "This came today from my brother's friend, Chris. He's stationed at a cavalry base near here."

"Cavalry base? Do they still have those?"

She ignored my question. "He and some friends have invited me to bring three women Marines to be their guests at Ft. Reno for the weekend. They want to share their swimming pool and stable of horses with us. Will you go?"

"That depends. What would we be getting into?"

"Don't worry. These men are officers. They have been declared gentlemen by act of Congress."

"Oh, no! Remember what Captain Butler said about fraternizing? That could get us in a lot of trouble."

"Don't worry, it's different there. It's a quiet little Army base far away from any shore patrol." She took a deep breath. "Freddy, I really need to talk to him."

"Maybe you could go alone."

Kilgallen laughed helplessly. "How can I explain this? Chris says he will reserve rooms for four of us at the hotel in town. You won't get in any trouble. Wait here."

She went to the squad room and returned quickly with a snapshot. "Remember when I told you I used to be a nun? I showed you a picture of me in my habit."

I nodded.

"Here's another photo taken the same day. That's my brother James, on the left."

I was surprised. "He's a priest."

"Yes, and so is Chris. They met when they were both studying in Chicago. Chris spent a lot of time at our house then. He's the base chaplain now at Ft. Reno, and I want to explain to him my reasons for leaving the convent."

"Well, okay I'll go. Have you asked Lawson?"

"No. She looks too sexy. I know she can't help it, but she gives the wrong impression. I'm going to ask Peters. She's Catholic, and her behavior is always exemplary. You know, when I'm in trouble I always ask her to pray for me. She's so good, I can't imagine what she says when she goes to confession."

"Who else?"

"Maybe Graves. She looks wholesome, and she's had a lot of experience with horses. Besides, she's engaged to a major, so she's used to being around officers."

Kilgallen was planning her guest list carefully. I wondered what logic had led her to invite me, but I was afraid to ask. Both Peters and Graves agreed to go.

Chris's next letter mentioned that his friend Paul was from Boston. "Young is from Boston," she said. "She should go. I'll see if I can get her instead of Peters."

Young reminded me of a porcelain doll. She had big round eyes, a small button nose, rosebud mouth, and a pleasant expression that never seemed to change. She said she would go, and Peters was told she had been replaced.

Two weeks later Kilgallen packed our bathing suits and dungarees into her suitcase, and we were first in line for liberty cards.

We caught a train out of Oklahoma City and found double seats facing each other. After we had gone some distance Young became nervous. "Kil," she said, "it seems like we're going quite a distance. Are you sure we won't be going out of bounds?"

"We're probably beyond the 50 mile limit now," she answered, "but it shouldn't be much further. Anyway, I just love breaking these asinine regulations."

Graves smiled. "So we'll not only be fraternizing, we're going out of bounds as well. That ought to be good for a deck court, with Captain Butler."

Young did not see the humor in it. "You didn't tell me that. I shouldn't have come. I'll just die if I get in trouble." She shook her head. "A deck court with Captain Butler? I think I'm going to be sick."

"Hey," said Graves, "we're all in this together. Let's just relax and enjoy the weekend."

She was twirling short black curls around her index finger and pulling them out nervously, but she showed no other indication of concern. I wished I could be that calm about it. The whole idea was not setting well with me.

"Don't worry. The Army isn't going to bother us," Kilgallen insisted.

When our train pulled into the El Reno station, Young said she wasn't feeling well, but her comment went unnoticed. It was a small, quiet town. We were the only ones getting off, and the station was almost empty.

As Kilgallen stepped out she spotted a rather slight, kindly looking Army captain approaching the train. Orange red hair was showing beneath his overseas cap, and the cross on his collar reflected the bright sun.

She handed me the suitcase and walked up to him reverently, arms extended. They clasped hands in greeting.

"Mary Gertrude Kilgallen," he said. "It is wonderful to see you again." Turning to us he added, "And you ladies must be our guests. I'm Father Riley. I'm delighted you could come."

Behind him stood three officers, all with graying hair. He gestured toward the tallest. "This is Major Sherman Barnes. He takes care of the horses."

Sherman smiled. "I have four beauties for you to ride."

I had never been anywhere near a horse in my life.

Father Riley went on to the next officer. "Lt. Ralph Jensen is in charge of the kitchen. He's going to fix a breakfast for you tomorrow morning that you'll never forget."

Ralph was on the last notch of his belt, a tribute to his culinary art. "I'd like to do that, Father, but I'll first have to get permission from Karl."

All the men laughed. Evidently the reference to Karl was an inside joke.

"And Captain Paul Martin, here, oversees the grounds. He just had the pool cleaned again especially for you ladies."

"I hope you brought your bathing suits," said Paul.

Kilgallen took the suitcase back from me as she introduced us. "And this is Mary Young. She's from BOSTON!"

She watched Paul, expecting his face to light up. It didn't. She asked, "Paul, aren't you from Boston?"

"Well, I once lived there. It was many years ago."

Young was turning green. "Where's the head?"

"She means the ladies room," Kilgallen explained.

Graves and I rushed her into the station. It was so small we didn't need to ask directions. We got her there just in time. Her noon chow came up, along with the coke she drank on the train.

She splashed her face with cold water. There were no towels, so she went back outside dripping wet.

Father Riley was concerned. "Are you all right, Mary?"

Kilgallen answered for her. "She'll be fine."

We rode across the tracks to the hotel in an Army jeep while Sherman, Ralph, and Paul followed on foot. It was a two-story frame building in need of paint. Father Riley came inside with us and the other officers climbed into the jeep to wait.

The lobby resembled something out of a western movie. A large oval hand braided rug dominated the center floor. A few old men sat around it in faded chairs, chewing tobacco and spitting into tarnished brass spittoons.

The priest approached the desk. "I'm Captain Riley, and these are the four ladies I reserved rooms for."

"Oh yes, the four . . . Marines."

The desk clerk was a woman in her middle years, with harsh black hair tied tightly back, held fast with a large comb. She set her jaw disapprovingly and reached for the keys.

Father Riley waved as he left. "I'll be back for you in an hour."

Kilgallen answered, "Good-bye, Father."

The clerk, glancing out the window, watched him join the other officers in the jeep. Shoving the keys at Kilgallen she said, "He's awfully young to be your father."

"He's not my father. He's a priest."

"Oh?" She raised an eyebrow. "He looks like a soldier to me." She shook her head as we left. I suspected the whole town would soon know we were there.

We had two rooms on the second floor, across from each other. They were sparsely furnished except for a profusion of small hand braided rugs.

Kilgallen walked into one room and put her suitcase on a bed. Young followed her in, so Graves and I shared the other room, leaving both doors open.

I soon heard Young ask, "Where's the head?"

Kilgallen answered, "It's probably down the hall."

"You mean we don't have a private bathroom?"

"El Reno is not Oklahoma City, and this is not the Skirvin Hotel."

"What will I do if I get sick again?"

Graves called out, "You'd better be ready to run fast."

Kilgallen ordered, "You're not going to get sick again."

"Well, my stomach still feels awfully funny."

"You can't get sick now."

Father Riley was back with the jeep in an hour. As we left with him through the lobby, the woman at the desk avoided eye contact, pretending to examine some keys.

Young came along under protest. "You'll feel better," Kilgallen insisted, "after you've had something to eat."

Young was obviously aware of every bump in the road. Graves

changed places with her in the back seat so she'd be on the out-side, "Just in case." She made it to the base, only a bit worse for the ride.

Sherman, Ralph, and Paul were waiting for us at the Officer's Club, standing at the bar near the door. There was a grand piano at the far end of the room, with a dance floor in the center. The tables scattered around it seemed to be waiting expectantly for the Saturday night crowd.

A large autographed photo of Jack Holt, the movie star, domi-nated one wall near the bar. I was a fan, having seen him in "The Great Train Robbery."

"He's stationed here," said Sherman. "Been making training films. That man sure knows how to handle a horse." Our hopes of seeing him were crushed when he added, "But he's gone for the weekend."

I chose a seat by Graves, where we had a good view of his picture, and we ordered. The extensive collection of cocktail glasses behind the bar was quite a contrast to the supply in our slop chute, where the only choice was between a large coke or a small glass of 3.2 beer.

Softly, Young asked for "Just ice water, please."

Later, in the dining room, she said she wasn't hungry. Ralph recommended the prime rib dinner, so Kilgallen ordered that for her, insisting she eat some of it.

Over dessert, Father Riley turned to Kilgallen. "Mary, have you heard from your sisters lately?"

"The two youngest are still at home, going to school. Betty and Margaret are in California. Betty is a WAVE pharmacist mate stationed in Long Beach. She married a Marine Captain. Margaret is still too young to enlist. She's working at the Navy base."

She sighed. "I pray to be sent out there to be near them."

After dinner we went back to the lounge. A large, amiable woman was at the piano now, playing and singing requests while the officers dropped tips in her jar.

Young groaned as we sat down. "Where's the head?"

"Do you need it now?" Graves asked.

"No, but I want to know where it is."

She ordered more ice water.

The evening passed quickly. Graves and I danced with some of the younger officers there, and Father Riley had us back at the hotel before 2300.

During the night, Graves and I awoke to a commotion across the hall. I opened the door in time to see Young make a run for the head, but it was occupied.

"Kil," she moaned, "what am I going to do?"

Kilgallen pulled a swim cap from the suitcase and handed it to her. "Here," she said, "use this."

I told Graves what was happening. "It better not be my cap," she said.

The next morning Graves learned that it was her cap. "Kilgallen," she scolded, "why didn't you give her yours?"

"Mine leaks. Don't worry, I washed it."

Graves put the cap to her nose. "It still stinks."

Kilgallen scrubbed on that cap, trying to get rid of the smell, until Ralph came to pick her up for church. "Father told me to be sure and get Mary back in time for Mass," he said.

Young insisted on staying in bed until check out time. Graves and I left with them to attend the earlier Mass service. As Kilgallen climbed into the jeep she muttered, "I wish I'd stuck with Peters."

Before performing the later Protestant services, Father Riley joined us for breakfast. The officer's mess hall was empty when we arrived. It was smaller than I had expected and homey in a rustic way, with yellow flowered curtains. We took a large table close to the kitchen and Ralph approached the cook cautiously. He said, "Good morning Karl!"

Karl recognized his name. He came out, smiling. In a heavy German accent he asked, "How do you want your eggs?"

Father Riley looked at Paul and Sherman. They shook their heads and laughed. "I'm betting on Karl," said Paul.

Ralph took a step forward. "Karl," he said slowly, "I'll cook breakfast this morning."

Karl nodded, grinning. "How do you want your eggs?"

Ralph glanced back at our table. "Any of you ladies understand German?"

None of us did. He shrugged. "Neither does anyone else on this base. Karl's a prisoner of war. He's a good cook, but the only English we've been able to teach him is 'How do you want your eggs?' and he has no idea what that means. I guess we'll have our eggs any way Karl wants to fix them."

Ralph joined us at the table and we watched Karl put bacon on the grill. Our eggs came to us soft boiled in little cups, with the top half of the shell removed.

"This is how Karl wants our eggs," said Ralph.

After breakfast we changed into dungarees and Sherman took us to the stables. Graves was soon stroking the horses, talking to them. Kilgallen and I approached the animals with less enthusiasm. It had been a long time since she rode, but it soon came back to her. I wasn't so lucky. My horse seemed to know I was new at this. He gave me a lot of trouble.

Then, as we neared the river, he began to cooperate. I thought I was getting the hang of it. He waded in obediently and led me straight to the deepest part in the center. Then he sat. Caught off guard, I lost my hold and slid off into the chilling water.

Graves heard me yell. She came back and grabbed the reins of my reluctant steed, leading him firmly out the other side. "Take my horse," she said.

My boondockers felt like sunken ships. I struggled to my feet and waded out, soaked gaberdine dungarees clinging to my body.

Sherman helped me up on the other horse. "I'm sorry," he said. "That critter never behaved this way before."

Only with me, I thought.

We had to check out of the hotel before noon. Graves helped Sherman care for the horses while Father Riley took Kilgallen and me into town to pick up Young.

As we entered the lobby, an Army corporal came out of the dining room. "Father Riley," he nodded in recognition.

The priest smiled. "We missed you at Mass this morning, Nolan."

The woman at the desk looked surprised. "He really is a priest," she muttered.

We got Young on her feet, checked out of the hotel, and took her back to the base for lunch. She looked a little better than when we left her that morning, but again she ordered, "Just ice water, please."

While Graves and I enjoyed a swim, Kilgallen had a serious talk with Father Riley. Young sat quietly by the pool, sipping ice water and watching the clock. When it was time, she smiled. "It's getting late," she said. "We have to start back."

As the jeep bounced down the dusty road, taking us away from the old fort, I turned for one last look. The main purpose of the base now was to supply trained horses and mules to the Army for travel through difficult terrain. Except for the swimming pool and a few jeeps, it probably hadn't changed much since the turn of the century. It was a piece of American History, still intact.

I watched the buildings grow smaller until they disappeared behind a bend. It was like the ending of a great movie of the old west, starring Jack Holt.

I was sorry the star hadn't made an appearance.

*   *   *

CHAPTER 15.
THE PRICE OF LIBERTY

During our first month on the late shift, Cpl. DiPalma marched us out to the weed fields every morning for drill. A small dachshund often trotted along beside us, to the right of our platoon. When the corporal announced, "The smoking lamp is lit," (that's Marine talk for take a smoking break) Whalen always went over to pet him. "He's a valuable dog," she once said. "He must belong to someone on the base."

Cpl. DiPalma explained, "His name is Salty. He belongs to Captain Butler's little boy Dickey. He comes to visit us whenever he can get out."

Whalen had some peanuts in her pocket. She offered them to Salty, and he wolfed them down. The next morning he met us coming back from chow and followed Whalen into the squad room. She shook her head. "I'm sorry Salt, I don't have peanuts for you today."

I gave Whalen some of my Baby Ruth bar for him. He gulped it down and wagged his tail. She turned to me. "Hey, he wants more."

I handed her the rest of it.

Whalen started taking something back from morning chow after that, in case Salty came by. He wouldn't stay home. The moment he saw a gate or door ajar, he squeezed his little body through to freedom and headed straight for our barracks. If he couldn't find Whalen, he'd come to any of us. And if we were gone he would go looking for us. He knew we were either across the street in the gymnasium or out in the weed fields.

Salty's frequent visits were making Jeter nervous. Whalen was feeding him some sausage one morning when she protested. "Y'all better quit feedin' the captain's hound, ya hear? It c'd git us in a heap a trouble."

Whalen laughed. "Har har har, how could a little dog do that? Do you think he's going to go home and tell Captain Butler we've been feeding him?"

Jeter's eyes flashed. "Well, he keeps sendin' that lieutenant around here lookin' for 'im. He doesn't like it when Salty won't stay home. We'd best start ignorin' him, or we're all gonna git in trouble."

"Okay Salt, here's the last of it." Whalen opened both hands to show there was nothing left. Salty looked up at her mournfully and licked her fingers.

"I'm tellin' ya, ya better quit that."

I thought Jeter was coming down pretty hard on Whalen. All of us had made friends with Salty, and there seemed to be no harm in it.

Cpl. DiPalma stuck her head in the door. "Class fifty-two, fall out!"

Salty knew what that meant. He fell out too, taking his usual marching position directly behind Whalen, so he could trot along at her side. Unable to master the thirty-inch regulation step, he marched to his own cadence, keeping a safe distance from our unpredictable footwork.

The Corporal, always aware of her image, pretended not to notice Salty so she wouldn't have to deal with him. That morning she took us out to a spot where the weeds were so high his short body was completely hidden. But the grass by Whalen rippled as he moved along at her side.

We had been drilling about thirty minutes when the captain's car drove up. The corporal halted the platoon. Facing the car, she snapped to attention and waited.

Capt. Butler's executive officer, a second lieutenant, got out and opened the back door for the captain's son. Dickey stepped out and pointed to our platoon. He ran toward us with the lieutenant following indignantly. The boy looked like he'd be ready for kindergarten in September.

The Corporal gave a snappy salute as they approached. The officer returned it routinely, impatient to get on with the matter at hand. "I've come for Dickey's dog."

"Dog, Sir?"

"Yes. You know, the little brown dog. Dickey said he always follows you. Where is he?"

Cpl. DiPalma looked around. "I don't see a dog, Sir."

Out of the corner of my eye, looking just past Whalen, I noticed a spot off to the right where the grass trembled ever so slightly.

The lieutenant gave the area a quick search. He couldn't see a dog either. Reluctantly, he turned and started to leave, but Dickey wouldn't give up. He began running around the platoon demanding, "I want Salty! I want Salty! I won't leave 'till I get Salty!"

I heard a loud yelp. Dickey's foot had come down on Salty's tail. The dog flew up in the air, jumping high enough to clear the weeds. The officer grabbed him up and pressed him firmly beneath his left arm.

One of Salty's hind legs was hanging out. Dickey started pulling on it. "Salty, you bad dog," he scolded. "When I get you home, I'm going to have to whip you!"

Salty looked back at us in a plea for help.

The lieutenant turned to Cpl. DiPalma. "So you didn't see a dog?"

"No Sir. I didn't see a dog, Sir."

He started back to the car with Salty still trapped under his arm. Dickey ran close behind, yelling.

The corporal acted as if the matter was closed. She did an about face and yelled, "Ten HUT! Right face. Forward, MARCH."

But I sensed a bit of sadness in her voice.

When we got back from chow that evening we learned that Jeter had been right. Salty got us all in trouble. Kilgallen was at the bulletin board shaking her head when I came in.

"I don't believe it," she said. "How could anybody be so asinine? Someone ought to write a book about this place."

From behind me, Whalen asked, "What's wrong, Kil?"

"Read it. You won't believe it."

"Attention all enlisted Women Reserves," the notice began. "I am tired of being teased about my son's dog fraternizing with enlisted Women Marines. If the dog is caught again in their area, or following beside one of their platoons, every enlisted Woman Marine on the base, without exception, will have base restriction the following weekend." It was signed by Capt. Butler.

Whalen laughed. "Sal must have put that up as a joke."

Sgt. Salisbury came out of her office. "It's no joke. The lieutenant brought it this afternoon. He told me to be sure to have it posted before you come in."

Whalen shook her head and went into the squad room to get her stationery. "Wait 'till Uncle Harry hears about this."

Jeter was reading it now, and she was furious. "If ah don' git liberty this weekend, somebody's gonna pay."

Walking briskly to our bay, she confronted Whalen. "Y'all gotta quit feedin' that hound, ya hear? Ah don' wanna git any base restriction."

"Hey, Jete, ya got something interesting coming up?"

"Ah don' have nuthin' comin' up. It's the principle. Besides, Ah'd git stir crazy bein' locked up in this place. Ah gotta git out!"

"But Salty's already in here when I feed him."

Jeter's eyes flashed. "He only comes in 'causa you feedin' 'im."

Erickson looked up from her manual. "Jeter, knock it off. I've noticed you petting Salty a few times."

Jeter grinned sheepishly. "Well, that was before this. You won't catch me pettin' 'im again, and none a' you better, either. We all gotta cooperate on this."

Whalen wasn't too impressed with the sermon. She was concentrating on her letter. "Har har har, just wait till my uncle hears about this one!"

Friday morning we were falling out for early drill when I spotted Salty in the distance, heading straight for our barracks. Cpl. DiPalma was about to call us to attention when she saw him. She decided to wait.

We watched as his little legs moved swiftly, bringing him closer and closer. Then it happened. Salty stepped off the curb and over the line, into the women's area. Soon he was prancing around our platoon excitedly.

Jeter shouted, "Git that hound outta here!"

Nobody moved.

She fell out of rank and disappeared into the barracks. Returning with about ten feet of line she called, "Come on, Salty. Come here boy."

He trotted over. Quickly, she secured the rope to his collar. Leading him back across the street, she tied the other end of it to a young tree in front of the gymnasium and hurried back to take her place in the platoon.

The corporal called, "Ten hutt! Right face! Forward, march!"

We moved away, leaving a bewildered little friend alone to ponder the wisdom of fraternizing with enlisted Women Marines.

*   *   *

CHAPTER 16.
WAIT AND HURRY UP

The Marine Corps moves on a schedule we called "Hurry up and wait." They woke us at 0445 when 0500 would have given us plenty time. Wherever we went, we had to get there early.

Why?

To wait.

Whalen didn't take it seriously. She developed an attitude all her own, It was more like "Wait and hurry up."

When Sgt. Salisbury stuck her head in the door and yelled "MAIL CALL!" we all rushed upstairs to the lounge and waited as the name on each envelope or package was called in random order. All but Whalen. She remained relaxed on her bunk, asking one of us to "Pick up my mail, okay? Okay."

Whalen didn't stand around waiting for the march to morning chow either. We couldn't wake her up. She would only respond to "Class fifty-two, fall out!"

That woke her up fast. Shouting, "Hey, let's look alive!" she slithered out of the sack, being careful not to disturb the sheets. Once on her feet, she slapped on her overseas cap, grabbed dungarees and boondockers, and took off out the door.

She fell in directly behind me. As we stood at attention, waiting, it was my job to hide her from the sergeant's view while she got dressed. Fortunately, it was still dark.

Whalen did not return the men's dungarees that were issued in Camp Lejeune's Battalion Area. She explained, "When I went down to turn 'em in, everybody was gone."

She had the only set in our class. The heavier twill made a
rustling sound as she pulled the pants up over her pajama bot-
toms. When I heard the clink of her belt buckle I knew the pants
had been secured.

She stepped into her boondockers next, often not bothering
with laces. She could tie them later, while waiting in line at the
chow hall. Whalen wore a skivvy shirt for pajama tops so now she
appeared to be dressed. However, she had to leave her jacket on
because she hadn't yet put on her bra.

During the week we studied safety equipment we almost left
without her. Passing a room full of inflated life rafts on our way to
class, she took a second look at them. "Hey," she said, "what a
great place to sack out!"

Whalen usually spent the smoking break asleep on the floor in
the classroom. Someone would wake her up when the break was
over. But the day she wasn't there, nobody missed her. There were
enough empty chairs around that an extra one after the break wasn't
noticed.

When the instructor finished his lecture on the pilot's ejection
seat, class was dismissed for lunch. Mustering outside for the march
back to the chow hall, Cpl. DiPalma eyed us suspiciously. "Who's
missing?"

Someone said, "Whalen."

Remembering the remark she had made earlier, I said, "Corporal, I think I know where she is."

"Take someone with you and go get her."

Bongiorni and I headed back into the building. "She's probably down here," I said, nodding toward the hallway on our left.
"That's where she saw a display of life rafts that looked good to
her."

"That character," Bongiorni laughed. "I think she's getting
too much saltpeter."

Whalen had chosen a two-man life raft. We found her lying
comfortably on her back, head hanging over the inflated bow. Her

arms and legs spilled out in four directions. Totally relaxed, the position of her head caused a faint snore.

Bongiorni nudged me and pressed her index finger to her lips. Then, kneeling beside Whalen, she bent over close and shouted, "CLASS FIFTY TWO, FALL OUT!"

Whalen sprang to her feet. "Hey, let's look alive!" She glanced at Bonjiorni. "Aw it's You, Bon. You're kidding. How'd I get here? What time is it?"

She looked at her watch and scrambled outside. By the time Bongiorni and I got back to the platoon, Whalen was already in place, standing at attention. The corporal frowned, making us look like we were the ones who caused the delay.

But her attitude got her in trouble one morning when our class was scheduled to take part in the flag raising ceremony. Whalen's hair was still in pin curls when the order came to fall out.

That would have been a nightmare for anyone else, but it didn't bother Whalen. "Hey it's raining out there," she said. "My head will be covered. So, who'd know?" She threw on her trench coat, flipped the havelock over her hat, and headed out the door.

It was some distance from our barracks. By the time we arrived at the flagpole it had stopped raining.

The lieutenant ordered, "Remove havelocks."

Whalen was caught. The officer ordered that she report to her the following afternoon in full uniform. She didn't look too happy when she came back. "Lt. Sterner gave me a week of barracks restriction," she said. "I hate that. 'Going My Way' is playing at the theater tonight."

Then she grinned. "You know, she still didn't trust me. She made me take off my hat and set it right by her own on the desk, to make sure my hair wasn't up in pin curls again."

Sgt. Salisbury entered the squad room. "Whalen," she said, "Lt. Sterner just called. She wants you to bring back her hat."

Of all the lines we waited in, pay call was longest. Everyone in the barracks lined up alphabetically for that ritual. The line wrapped around the entire lounge, ran the full length of the hall, and down the stairs.

Abramovitz never complained, and I didn't have it too badly, but to Whalen, near the end of the line, it was unacceptable. When Sgt. Salisbury shouted, "Pay call," she settled down to start a letter to her uncle. She had made a deal with Pellier.

After we were paid, we had free time while the line worked its way through the alphabet. Whalen treasured every moment she could snatch as "free time." While others waited their turn in the pay line, she relaxed on her bunk. Often she laughed out loud at what she had just written. "Har har har, listen to this," she once said. "A penny here, a penny there, and the first thing you know, two cents are gone."

As soon as Pellier was paid she would come to our bay and say, "Whalen, they're down to the P's."

That was her tip that it was getting close to her turn. She started paying attention. Every few minutes, she called out, "Teaford, Telfer, Tierney." If there was no answer, she assumed they were not yet down to the T's.

Her system worked for a while, but I knew something was wrong the day I saw Zufall walk past fingering her money, while Whalen was still resting comfortably on her bunk.

Teaford, Telfer, and Tierney had gone to Ship's Service.

I turned to warn her, but it was too late. Sgt. Salisbury followed right behind Zufall. As she approached, Whalen called again, "Teaford, Telfer, Tierney."

The Sergeant let her finish before she asked, "Whalen, don't you want to get paid today?"

Dropping everything, she bolted out of the bay and took the stairs three at a time. Stopping suddenly in front of the payroll table, she clicked her heels, saluted the officer, and announced, "Private Whalen reporting for pay call, Sir!"

The lieutenant waited for the sergeant to return before she paid out the remaining cash. Later, Sgt. Salisbury came into our bay with a warning for her. "Whalen," she said, "you were lucky this time. Don't let it happen again."

From that day on, Whalen always went upstairs as soon she got the message from Pellier.

* * *

CHAPTER 17.
THE POUNDING
OF THE WAVES

Sgt. Salisbury announced that the WAVEs aboard the base invited us to join their softball team. Whalen thought she had a better idea. "Why don't we start a team of our own? We could beat those WAVEs."

The sergeant hesitated. "Do you think we could?"

"Hey, we're Marines, aren't we? Sure we can beat 'em."

She made no promises, but a few days later a notice for tryouts was posted on the bulletin board, and that afternoon she brought in a sign-up sheet.

I could run bases as fast as any of them, but I could never hit the ball. I stayed out of it for the good of the team. Whalen and Jeter signed in our bay, Graves and Peters in the next. Moving on through the barracks, the sergeant soon had more than enough for a team.

When they returned from tryouts, Whalen was surrounded by fans, wanting to know where she learned to pitch like that. "My uncle taught me," she said. "He's really good. He got me a job on a women's softball team back in New York."

Bongiorni looked surprised. "Whale, you never told me you played professional baseball."

Sgt. Salisbury heard that. "Whalen, did you play pro? Because if you did, maybe it wouldn't be fair for you to play on our team."

"Aw no, Sal. It was nothing like that. See, I worked for this aircraft company. They put me on salary and I came in to inspect hydraulic fittings a couple times a week. Then I practiced with the company team and played in all their games against the other defense plants. Naw, I didn't play pro."

"Then what would you call it?"

"Well, they called it hydraulic assembly inspector."

"I'll think about it," she said, as she left for her office. When the team list was posted, Whalen's name was there. After a couple weeks of practice they challenged the Navy to a game. The WAVEs jumped at the chance, looking forward to an easy victory. They didn't know about Whalen.

A date for the game was set, and our team felt confident. We didn't expect Whalen to pull what she did on the last Wednesday night before the game. Bunking next to her I saw it all, and there was nothing I could do about it.

It was a warm, still summer night. The barracks would not cool down. Whalen and Bongiorni had gone off on Wednesday liberty. It was getting close to lights out, and they weren't back yet.

Whalen often had close calls. When the lights were turned off, someone always yelled a "lights out" warning into the head, and she would bolt out of there like she was stealing second base. By the time Sgt. Salisbury reached our bay for bed check, Whalen appeared to be fast asleep. If the sergeant noticed a toothbrush still clenched in her fist, she never mentioned it.

But that night she couldn't ignore what happened. She had come to the door and flipped the switch, calling "Lights out," and Whalen and Bongiorni weren't even in the barracks. This time they could both be in trouble.

Someone stuck a boondocker in the emergency exit at the other end of the squad room, leaving it ajar. If they came back soon they might be able to slip in that way, undetected.

In the darkness, staring at the empty bunk next to mine, I heard the side door close, then soft whispering. It had to be them. Could they make it?

Whalen dashed the length of the squad room and ducked into

our bay just before the sergeant reappeared at the door. Jeter whispered, "Git in bed and cover up!"

Whalen threw herself down on her bunk and pulled up the wool blanket that had been folded neatly at her feet. Turning her back to me so the sergeant couldn't see her face, she threw her cap on the deck and wrapped the blanket up around her neck to conceal her uniform.

It looked suspicious enough that she snuggled under a wool blanket while everyone else was on top of the sheets half naked, trying to cool off. But the sergeant couldn't overlook the purse that was hanging out over the top of it, still strapped to the buttoned down shoulder tab beneath.

It was too late to warn her. The sergeant's flashlight was shining directly on the bag. She came in and lifted the blanket, exposing Whalen in full uniform. "I'm sorry Whalen," she said. "I'll have to ask you to wait for me in my office."

"Oh sure Sal. I didn't mean to cause you any trouble," she apologized as she left.

They had become good friends at the practices. It was a difficult situation for both of them, but Sgt. Salisbury was a Marine first. She did what she had to do.

The rest of the bed check went without incident. Bongiorni, bunking further down in the squad room, was able to crawl in bed unnoticed. She was amused the next morning when she found out what happened. "Ha ha, Whalen got caught. Isn't that a kick?"

Kilgallen wanted answers. She asked, "What did Sgt. Salisbury say to you in the office last night?"

"Aw, she just gave me a week of barracks restriction."

That sobered Bongiorni. "Does that mean we have to cancel our plans for liberty in Okie City this weekend?"

"Yeah, and that's not the worst of it. I can't play ball, either. Sal is really upset over it."

Bongiorni shrugged. "What's so bad about that? I haven't played ball since I was a kid."

"But Saturday we play the WAVEs."

Now, that was bad. Without Whalen, we wouldn't stand a chance against them.

I had duty Saturday afternoon so I missed the game. I was coming in off patrol when the team returned with news that the WAVEs had clobbered us.

Whalen shook her head. "I'm sorry Sal, it's my fault."

"No, Whalen. I'm the one who put you on restriction. If it's anyone's fault, it's mine."

A little of that goes a long way. I went down to see what was happening in the head.

Monday our friendly rivalry with the WAVEs became less friendly when notice was posted that the medical records for class 52-44 had been lost. If they were not found before we finished the course, we would have to take the entire series of boot camp shots again, so they would have a record of them.

"How asinine," said Kilgallen. "They know we've had our shots. This is not to protect us from disease. It's to cover for their incompetence."

Lumpkin took it the hardest. "How could those WAVEs, over in the dispensary, lose thirty-six medical folders? I just hate those shots."

It was hard to forgive them this one, especially after they creamed us at baseball.

Whalen's restriction ended Thursday. She and Bongiorni made reservations at the Skirvin Hotel for the weekend. They were going to "do" Oklahoma City.

When we came back from Review, Sgt. Salisbury had the tray of liberty cards on her desk, waiting for us. She handed Bongiorni her card, but she was having trouble finding Whalen's. The line lengthened while she went through all of the W's, searching.

"Whalen," she shook her head, "these cards are stored at base headquarters. It looks like they forgot to put yours back."

She called headquarters, but there was no answer. The WAVEs had gone off duty and the office was closed until Monday. The sergeant was very upset.

"Aw, that's okay Sal," Whalen tried to comfort her. But Sgt. Salisbury looked close to tears. She was too decent for that job.

Whalen smiled. "I got an idea, Sal. Why don't we challenge them to a rematch?"

Sgt. Salisbury liked the idea. She tried to arrange another game with them, but most of their team had graduated.

They quit while they were ahead.

*   *   *

CHAPTER 18:
HE IS MY BROTHER

Catlin's top bunk was across the aisle from me. Lumpkin, below her, would not allow anyone else to sit on her bed, so at times Catlin would join me on mine. One day after mail call she came over to talk.

"I just got a letter from my brother," she said. "He'll be in Oklahoma City a week from Saturday on his way home on furlough. He wants me to meet him there."

Hunnicutt, well known to the sailors aboard the base as "Hunni," was walking by and overheard. "Does he look like you? If he does, I want to meet him."

"Actually, everyone says we look a lot alike," she replied, "only his hair is a lighter brown, and he's tall. We've always been very close. I can hardly wait to see him again."

Kilgallen, above us on her bunk, was reading a letter. She leaned out over the side. "Lawson and Freddy and I are reserving a room at the Skirvin that night. Why don't you join us?"

"Thanks," she said. "I'll get a room there for Herb too."

"Maybe we can find some sailors who would be willing to share their room with him," she suggested. "That would save him some money."

Catlin shook her head. "It wouldn't work. Not with the strict regulations here against fraternizing."

"Your brother's an officer?"

"He's a an Army pilot."

Lumpkin, across the aisle, shook her head. "Then you can't fraternize with him either."

"But he's my brother."

"If Captain Butler won't let his enlisted son use the front door, or sit at the table to eat with him, I'm sure he's not going to let you socialize with your brother."

"What can I do?"

Roth broke out in one of class 51's favorite songs. To the tune of "The Billboard March," she sang:

"Oh there's a chaplain, in twenty-two,

That you can tell your troubles to-o-o-."

Peters picked up on it. "That's a good idea. Why don't you go to building 22 and talk to the chaplain?"

Catlin seemed interested, but Kilgallen thought she had a better idea. "He would probably arrange a short visit in the chapel while he hangs around to make sure the MPs don't arrest you. Why not meet him in the room we reserved at the Skirvin? We'll take off and you can talk in private, maybe even have dinner sent up."

"Sounds great," said Catlin. She called her brother and told him to go directly to the Skirvin Hotel and ask for Kilgallen's room number. She would wait for him there.

Saturday she left the base with us. When we got to Oklahoma City we went directly to our room at the hotel. Later we left Catlin there to wait for her brother and we took off for dinner and a movie. We saw "Gaslight," starring Ingrid Bergman, Charles Boyer, and Joseph Cotten. When we returned she was gone.

Kilgallen wasn't concerned. "She probably went back to the base after their visit." She sat and took off her shoes. "Wasn't Joseph Cotten wonderful?"

We gave no further thought to Catlin until we returned to the base late the next day and learned what happened. She had gone to the lobby to pick up a paper, and saw her brother there. She signaled him not to speak, nodding for him to follow her.

He stayed some distance behind as she went to the room, entered alone, and closed the door. A bit later he knocked and she let him in.

As they hugged, she glanced over his shoulder through the open door and thought she saw a shore patrolman watching them. Soon she heard a knock. Answering it, she was greeted by two shore patrolmen.

"You're coming with us," said the taller one.

"He's my brother. I just want to have a visit with him before he goes overseas."

"We have our orders."

As she followed him out, the shorter one looked first at her, then at the young officer. "Geez, he looks just like you. He must be your brother! If I'da known that, I'da left you alone."

At her deck court Capt. Butler reprimanded Catlin and gave her barracks restriction. "If you had any stripes I'd have those too," he added. "Even if it happens to be true that he is your brother, you must understand that fraternizing will not be tolerated in the Marine Corps."

Kilgallen was devastated when she heard the news. "I gave her some bad advice. Peters was right. She should have talked to the chaplain."

She stood by her locker a moment. "There must be something I can do about the way they're treating us."

Then, smiling, she added, "Maybe there is something." She reached for her stationery and climbed up on her bunk.

"I'm going to write a book about this place."

*   *   *

CHAPTER 19: PAYDAYS AND LETTERS FROM HOME

They say that in the Navy the pay is so divine,
They give you fifty dollars and take back forty-nine.
Author unknown

After allowances were taken out for my dependent, War Bonds, insurance, and a collection of other charges, pay call for me was usually more trouble than it was worth. We were paid in increments of five dollars. If, after deductions, less than that amount remained in my account, I wouldn't get anything.

More often than not that was the case. I waited in line, behind Honora Ferris, until my name was called. Then, as I stood at attention before the officer she would say, "Private Fredriksen, nothing." I would respond, "Thank you Sir," do an about face, and leave no richer than before. Were it not for the loans Kilgallen repaid, paydays would have little meaning for me.

I could put up with that for a while. I was earning money again. With the sewing machine upstairs, I had more tailoring jobs than I could handle. Lately some WRs were bringing me winter uniforms to be altered, a sign that autumn was on its way.

One evening, while I was working on one of Hunnicutt's winter blouses, Lawson came upstairs to talk to me. "Aren't you afraid you'll get caught?" she asked. "You know, we're not supposed to have a job on the side. I'd hate to see you get in trouble over this."

I hadn't thought of that. Sgt. Salisbury had noticed me at the sewing machine many times and said nothing beyond a simple greeting. "Surely they wouldn't consider this a job."

"Captain Butler would. You really ought to get a work permit. You wouldn't have any trouble proving a hardship."

"Well, it's true I didn't get anything at the last two pay calls, but I have a place to sleep and plenty to eat, so there is no hardship. Besides, as soon as my mother is married, I'll start getting full pay and everyone will have to alter their own uniforms."

I checked Hunnicutt's other winter blouse to see if there was enough hemming tape to shorten them both.

"Why don't you ask Sgt. Salisbury what you need to do to get a permit? I'm sure she'd help you."

She was making me feel uneasy. The sergeant would be no problem, but going through the chain of command, Captain Butler would want to stick his nose in it.

"I'm afraid to," I explained. "Sgt. Salisbury must know, and she hasn't said anything. If Capt. Butler refused the permit, she would have to stop me."

Lawson shrugged. She went back downstairs, leaving me alone with a lot to think about. News from my mother had been unsettling. In her last letter she had written:

"Tom is no better. He seems to be getting weaker with each passing day. I located a little stewing beef and made him a nice pot of stew. I added carrots and onions and string beans from my victory garden. I had a taste, and it was good, but he hardly touched it.

"I try to get him to have the doctor come. He refuses, says he won't have anything to do with doctors. He is a stubborn man.

"Gust comes to see him too." I didn't know any Gust. "He raises rabbits so he cooked one for Tom. It was baked in a tasty tomato sauce, but Tom said he couldn't eat it.

"Gust lives just down the hill. Sometimes he walks me home. He said he's going to bring me a rabbit tomorrow. Now what will I do with a whole rabbit, without you here to help me eat it?"

She was lonely. I should not have left her alone. It had never occurred to me that Tom would be sick for so long.

There wasn't enough tape to hem the second blouse. I decided to call it a night.

There was a chill in the air the day I got the next letter from my mother. The envelope was penciled black around the edges, her way of warning me that inside there would be news of a death. I opened it slowly, fearing what it might say. It was only a brief note.

> "My Dear Daughter Inga,
>
> "Tom died last night. I found him this morning when I went over to try to get him to eat something.
>
> "I called Gust and he came right over. We're trying to locate his daughter in Idaho.
>
> " I will miss him.
>
> "Your loving mother"

I had refused to consider the possibility of Tom's death. My mother had always needed someone around to take care of her. When Tom told me of his desire to marry her, I felt my presence there was no longer needed, that I would be in the way. Well, Tom was gone and she needed me now.

I got out the box of Marine Corps stationery from the PX in Camp Lejeune. It had an eagle, globe, and anchor embossed in gold at the top of the sheet, with "Semper Fidelis" beneath. I couldn't find more like it at the Navy's Ship Service here, so I had been saving it for special occasions. I'd better use it up now, while it's still appropriate.

"Dear Mom," I began. "I wish I could be with you now in your time of grief. I will apply for a family hardship discharge tomorrow, and come home as soon as I can.

"I don't know how long it will take . . ."

It became impossible to hold back the tears. Was I crying for my mother or for myself? Maybe both. I hadn't realized how deeply the Marine Corps had become a part of me until now, knowing I must give it up.

A hand touched my shoulder gently. "That letter," it was Pellier's voice, "I noticed it was edged in black."

"Pelly, I have to go home."

"Let's go to the head where we can talk."

We sat on the bench opposite the showers and she listened to my story. "Think about completing your training first, Freddy," she advised. "We're almost finished, and it could help you to qualify for a better job when you go home."

She was right, of course. I started the letter again. This time I wrote that I would apply for a discharge soon.

My mother's next letter described the funeral. "There was a great spread of food at Tom's house after the service," she wrote. "Gust cooked most of it, including a large platter of baked rabbit. I made potato salad. Potatoes and green onions came from my garden, and eggs from our hens.

"After everyone left, Gust helped me with the dishes and then he walked me home. He came in for a cup of tea because I was out of coffee.

"Gust is a nice man."

She mentioned my dog Sam, the chickens, and her victory garden before ending the letter. Maybe she would be all right for a few weeks by herself. It looked like she had a good friend close by.

About the time we went into our winter uniforms and I was getting ready to apply for my discharge, there was another mysterious letter for me at mail call. Again, it was in my mother's handwriting, but there was a strange name in the upper left hand corner. It read: "Mr and Mrs Gust Kahrostopolis."

I was shocked. "Oh, no! She didn't!"

Kilgallen heard. "What's the matter, Freddy?"

"I don't believe it. My mother just married a man I haven't even met. How could she do such a thing?"

Bongiorni was passing by. She laughed. "Your mother is old enough to get married without your permission."

I couldn't open the envelope. I didn't know what to think, or even how to feel. I stuffed the letter, still sealed, into the top shelf of my locker.

Kilgallen asked, "Aren't you going to read it?"

"Why? I already know what's in it." I rested my head in my hands. I needed time to think.

"Let's go to the slop chute for a beer," she suggested.

It turned into one of those two beer nights. Kilgallen had a way of helping me to see things from another perspective.

"She must have been lonely when your father died."

"Yes, she must have been."

"And when Tom died too, she was left alone again."

"Uh huh."

"Now she's not alone. Why can't you be happy for her?"

A couple sailors came by, beers in hand. One asked, "Mind if we join you?"

Kilgallen urged them to sit down. "You're just in time to help us celebrate." Motioning to me she said, "Freddy's mother just got married."

"Oh, yeah? Hey, that's great!"

The other sailor added, "Let's drink to that!"

We drank to their happiness until it was getting close to lights out. By the time we got back to the barracks I was feeling better about it.

After bed check I slipped out of the sack. Taking my mother's letter from the top shelf of my locker, I tiptoed into the head where it was light enough to read.

"We were married in the courthouse yesterday," it began. "I'm moving down to his house. There is no need now for you to come home until the war is over."

*   *   *

CHAPTER 20:
INDIAN "JOE"

"Chici's been hurt!"

Tierney's voice broke the Sunday morning stillness in the squad room. I hurried down to their bay. "What happened?"

"I don't know, but look at her shoulder."

There were two wide bands of adhesive tape on her left upper arm, running horizontally just above her vaccination.

Bongiorni strolled in behind me. "She must have had quite a night. Let's wake her up so we can find out what happened."

I looked at my watch. "They close the chow line in twenty minutes. If I know Chici, she'll need a cup of coffee."

Bongiorni laughed. "You know Chici all right."

Tierney removed the last bobby pin from her hair. A short, black ringlet fell to her forehead as she bent and gently tapped Chici's shoulder. Always quiet and reserved in her ways, she whispered, "Last call for coffee."

There was no response.

"What's the matter, is she dead?" Bongiorni bent down and gave her a firm pat on the cheek. Louder, she said, "Come on Chici baby, you need a cup of coffee."

Chici opened one large brown eye. "Is that what everybody's drinking?"

"Yeah, that's it. That's what everybody's drinking. But they're closing the bar. You don't have much time."

Chici became aware of the three of us standing over her bunk. "What the heck's up?"

Tierney pointed to the bandage. "We're wondering how you hurt your arm."

Chici glanced at it like she was seeing it for the first time. "God, I don't know."

Bongiorni tried to refresh her memory. "After review you said you were going to Norman with some sailor you met at the slop chute."

"What the heck was his name?"

"That's what I want to know." Bongiorni grinned. "You weren't introducing him around. Not that I blame you. He was kinda cute."

"Was he?" Chici began to show some interest. "Geez, I hope he calls. I hope I gave him our number."

She began pulling on the adhesive. Tierney warned, "You better not do that. It looks professional. You should leave it alone 'till you can get to sick call."

"I don't care if it's the only thing holding my arm together. I have to find out what's underneath." She got a grip on one corner of the top tape and gave it a hard yank.

I gasped. She had the profile of the head of an Indian tattooed on her arm. Mostly blue with a red feather sticking up in back, his eye just cleared the lower tape.

She was devastated. "Tell me it's just a bad dream. Tell me I'm still asleep."

Bongiorni gave it to her straight. "It's no dream, Chici. You got yourself a tattoo."

"Well." She answered with surprising courage. "We might as well see the rest of it."

She loosened another corner and ripped off the bottom tape. The entire head was about the size of a quarter, with the feather standing up almost an inch. Beneath it, in capital letters with quotation marks, was the name "JOE."

Tierney asked, "Who is Joe?"

"I don't know any Joe."

Bongiorni was intrigued with the mystery. "He didn't look Indian."

"Who didn't look Indian?"

"The sailor you were with. I saw you both going out the gate. He had light brown hair."

Now Chici was really confused. "God, I wish I could remember him."

"I think," said Bongiorni, "you need a cup of coffee to clear your head."

Chici dressed quickly. She was pleased that the sleeve of her skivvy was long enough to cover "JOE." "I guess I'll have to break the habit of rolling up my sleeves," she said.

There was no line at the chow hall. Chici filled two cups and Bongiorni, Tierney and I each poured one for ourselves, just before they dumped the coffee. It always tasted better on Sunday, after the urns had been cleaned for Saturday inspection.

As soon as we sat down, Bongiorni started pumping Chici for more information. "Tell me, what does an Indian mean to you?"

"I'm half Indian," she said. "My father was Cherokee."

"Was his name Joe?"

"No, it was Smokey . . . Smokey Kitchen."

"Who is Joe?"

"Damned if I know."

Pellier and Jeter walked by on their way to empty their trays. "Hey Chici," Jeter teased. "How was that date with Joe last night?"

"Joe?"

"Yeah, I saw ya leavin' together. He's sure cute."

"You know Joe? What do you know about him?"

"Too bad he's shippin' out. Didn't he just finish Metalsmith?"

"Oh yeah, sure. Metalsmith." I could see that Chici was beginning to remember something. After Pellier and Jeter left, Chici talked more freely. "It's coming back to me. Yeah, now I remember Joe. He's a nice kid, but he can't hold his liquor."

Chici remained sober during the weeks that followed. She kept her skivvy shirt on in the squad room with the sleeves rolled down, but occasionally someone would notice "JOE" as she was stepping out of the shower. Word got around and we became accustomed to seeing him.

Before our time in Norman was over, it got her in trouble. The Navy had not found our medical records, so we had reported to the dispensary for the first in our series of shots. A doctor was giving the injections this time, and the line moved fast. They were soon down to the C's. I was close enough behind Chici that when she rolled up her sleeve I saw the doctor stare in disbelief.

"What is that?"

Chici blushed. She had forgotten about "JOE." Softly, she replied, "A tattoo, Sir."

He picked up a note pad. "You're Chici?"

"Yes Sir."

"When did you get that . . . thing?"

"About a month ago, Sir."

"Who did it?"

"I don't remember, Sir."

"You don't remember?"

"No Sir. I don't remember, Sir."

He had finished writing and started to wave her on when he remembered the reason for her visit. He put an extra thrust behind the needle as he jabbed it into her arm. She stiffened, took a quick breath, and went on her way.

That evening Sgt. Salisbury came in to talk to her. "Chici," she began, "you have barracks restriction until next Tuesday at 0900 when you will appear before Capt. Butler for a deck court. In the meantime, you will only be allowed out to attend classes and chow with your group. You have been charged with having a tattoo."

Lowering her voice she added, "I'm sorry."

After the sergeant left, Chici shook her head. "What will I do, stuck in here for a week? I'll go crazy!"

Whalen, who had been through it, offered some advice. "I

wrote a lot of letters to my uncle." She paused. "I wonder if he read all that stuff."

"I don't have anybody to write to."

In the days that followed, we tried to help Chici pass the time. Kilgallen found a shop in town that sold a shorter bottle of beer that fit in our purse. We each smuggled one in to her. After the ride back from Norman the beer wasn't very cold, but Chici didn't complain. Later I put the empty bottles in a sack and disposed of them in a trash can at the slop chute.

Bongiorni gave her a deck of cards and we learned that Chici was a whiz at blackjack. Keeping her entertained that way was costing me money. By Tuesday I was almost broke.

The morning of her trial Chici was dressed in full uniform, ready to face Captain Butler, before I could get the shoulder straps buttoned on my dungarees. Kilgallen studied her. "Chici, you look like you didn't sleep last night."

"I didn't."

"How are you going to defend yourself?"

"I won't. I'll just take my punishment and get it over with. I figure a few more weeks of playing blackjack on restriction and I'll have enough money to take the whole class out for a bash."

"Good!" said Bongiorni. "We can have a big fat pahdy!"

I couldn't get too excited about the way they were planning to spend my losses.

At breakfast Kilgallen gave Chici some advice. "You should defend yourself," she said. "This is asinine. Men don't get deck courts for having a tattoo."

"That's right," Tierney agreed. "They told us we were to re-ceive no preferential treatment."

Bongiorni laughed. "I'd hardly call this preferential treatment."

"This is preferential for the men," Kilgallen stated. "I think you have a legal argument here."

Chici shook her head. She wouldn't fight it. "Don't forget, I'm up against Captain Butler. Defending myself will only get me into deeper trouble."

Sgt. Salisbury called, "Class 52, fall out."

Chici leaned against her bedpost. She got a few pats on the shoulder and words of support as we filed out for the march to class, and she was left alone.

We were all on edge that morning. I lost my pencil so I couldn't take notes. Nobody could go to the head because someone lost the head chit. And Kilgallen dropped her Dzus key inside the engine cowling.

"Stars And Stripes Forever" blasted out over the loud speakers as we marched back to the chow hall. I was hoping Chici would be there waiting for us, but she wasn't.

Kilgallen, Bongiorni and I were starting on our ice cream sandwiches when I heard Chici's voice behind me.

"Got room for one more?"

She had changed into dungarees, and she was smiling.

Bongiorni grinned. "Hey, it's the tattooed lady! Sit down and tell us what happened."

I moved over to make room on the bench. She set her tray down and announced, "I'm off the hook!"

Kilgallen looked surprised. "He let you go?"

"Yeah, he had to. But first he admonished me for unladylike behavior."

She stopped to laugh, not wanting to be rushed.

Kilgallen was curious. "What happened?"

"Captain Butler had the whole office going through the Marine Regs, looking for something to charge me with. But get this. The only thing they could find on tattoo was that it's a bugle call played at the end of the day to summon the men to their quarters.

"I think the captain was close to tears."

Chici paused dramatically and rolled up her sleeve to display "Joe."

"This will be a great story to tell my grandchildren, when they ask me what I did when I was in the Marine Corps."

*   *   *

CHAPTER 21.
WHEN WINTERS CAME

Oklahoma was hit with a sudden, bitter cold in the autumn of 1944. The order making winter service the uniform of the day was on the bulletin board Friday night, to be effective Saturday. Our winters were stored in our sea bags. We had to work fast. Sgt. Salisbury unlocked the door to the storage room upstairs and we stripped the shelves.

Lines formed fast as we waited our turn at the irons to press a blouse, skirt, shirt and field scarf (that's Marine talk for tie) for Saturday morning review. We had to finish before lights out.

Unfortunately, one detail had been overlooked. Having gone through boot camp in the summer, we were never taught how to tie a field scarf. Kilgallen had spent a winter in uniform at Washington D.C. She was the only one in the squad room who would know how to dress herself.

The next morning I watched her make the knot hoping to learn how it was done, but she moved too fast. I asked, "Kil, would you show me how you tied that?"

Jeter and Pellier came over to watch. Graves, in the next bay called, "Anybody know how to tie this thing?"

Kilgallen asked, "Am I the only one?"

Several WRs crowded around our bay and Kilgallen faced her students. "You tuck the tie beneath the shirt collar with the narrow end coming down on the left side."

I muttered, "Now, which is my left side?"

Kilgallen laughed nervously. "Come on now, we don't have time to kid around."

I wasn't kidding around.

She draped it around my neck. "Bring the narrow side down about this far."

Someone from class 51 yelled, "But you're doing it backwards to me."

"All right, we'll start over." She moved into the center aisle and climbed on a chair. "Let's all face the front of the building and you can watch me from the side."

That worked better for me. I managed to get the idea. When we had finished, though, only a few ended up with both ends the same length.

She continued the lesson until Cpl. DiPalma called us to fall out. Most were still in their slips, working on the field scarf. I was no better off. Even though my tie had turned out all right, and I had my skirt on, I couldn't find the emblem for my hat. It wasn't with the rest of my winter emblems.

Sgt. Salisbury came in to see what was causing the delay. "Just tie the field scarf and button the blouse over it," she said. "You can even up the ends later."

That may have solved their problem, but it was no help for mine. I searched for my emblem until I saw Whalen leave. Then I knew I had to do something fast. I decided to march in Review without the emblem, and hope nobody noticed. But when I took my winter hat from its box, there was my eagle flying high, just as I had attached it back in boot camp.

Soon after we went into winters Jeter asked, "Anybody wanna go inta Norman with me ta git pictures taken? My mama wants one of me in my uniform."

"I hate that," said Whalen, "but my folks asked me for one a while back. So did my uncle. Maybe I could have a bunch made, call 'em Christmas presents. That way, I don't have to shop."

Several of us agreed to make appointments with the photographer in Norman before we left, so we could exchange pictures, but Kilgallen would have no part of it.

She was writing one of her long letters to her mother. Looking down from her bunk she said, "I never allow my picture to be taken, but I'll go along with you Saturday if we take chow cuts and have lunch in that Copper Kettle over on White Street. It's such a nice little tea room!"

"Your parents will want a picture of you in uniform," said Pellier, who had no parents.

"They already have an ugly one of me in my habit. It's there on the mantel, between pictures of my two gorgeous sisters in their pearls and low cut necklines. Every time I go home, I have to look at it. I promised myself I would never have my picture taken again.

'... my face—I don't mind it
For I am behind it;
It's the people in front get the jar.'
... Anthony Anderson Euwer."

Whalen disagreed. "Aw, there's nothing wrong with your face, Kil. You have a good face."

"You haven't seen my gorgeous sisters." She sighed. "But I do have nice legs. They're just like Marlene Dietrich's."

She lifted a pants leg and posed for us. Whalen seemed impressed. "Hey, you could send your folks a picture of your legs to put on the mantel."

Kilgallen did not take part in the exchange of photos.

While we could now wear winter uniforms on liberty, we were stuck with our skimpy women's dungarees out on the line. They wouldn't issue warm work clothes to our class because we would soon be leaving. For us, there was little protection from the bitterly cold winds sweeping across the apron.

We put the wool lining in our trench coats and wore them when we worked outside on the planes. We had to be very careful not to get grease on them, because we also wore them on liberty.

Those ugly red and green machine operator's caps came in handy to protect our heads from the cold. They were just thin rayon snoods, but by wrapping the wool scarf beneath them, it kept our ears warm, while still appearing to be in uniform.

Almost everyone in our class developed varying degrees of what the Navy called "cat fever," with a cold and sore throat. The dispensary was crowded the morning I went in with a runny nose. It got me out of the freezing temperature for a while.

Lumpkin, the class goldbrick, was first in line. She had no fever or other symptoms, but she whined about a multitude of miseries including cramps from her period.

The doctor was sympathetic. "Why don't you go back to the barracks and rest today?"

Ward was just ahead of me in line. I could hear her chest rattle as she breathed, and she looked terrible.

When her turn came, the doctor took her temperature. "I'd like to send you home," he said, "but I already have one girl in the barracks. That's my quota for the day. Your fever isn't too high. You'll be all right."

He gave her a couple APCs (the Navy cure-all, a combination of aspirin, phenacetin, and caffeine,) and sent her back out on the line.

After lunch I asked Sgt. Salisbury for one of the warm sleeveless jackets we wore when we walked guard duty, for Ward. It was too little too late. She was taken to sick bay that evening with pneumonia.

I visited her the next day at lunch break. "You know Freddy," she said, "the doctor insisted I didn't have much fever yesterday. I told him my normal temperature is 97.4, but I don't think he believed me."

I couldn't decide if I was most angry at Lumpkin or the doctor. But at least, for Lumpkin there was some retribution. She had forgotten a lesson she should have learned the day she "fainted" at review.

There was no liberty card for her that weekend.

*   *   *

CHAPTER 22.
FROM Z TO A

Lumpkin was getting nervous. "We're starting our last week of classes, and we haven't had our third shot yet," she whined. "Why don't they give it to us now and get it over with? This waiting is driving me crazy."

Whalen looked up from a letter she was writing. "Gee, Lump, one more little shot isn't going to hurt you."

"Little shot? Not hurt me? Why, they're going to stick a big old needle in my arm. I don't mind telling you, I dread it."

Grabbing her toothbrush, she stomped off to the head.

"The whole thing is asinine," Kilgallen declared. "Those medical records are probably sitting in the bottom drawer of some little ensign's desk."

Lawson smiled. "What do you want to bet they find them right after Zufall gets her shot?"

It was hard to understand Lumpkin's attitude. Shots were no problem for me. I just rolled up my sleeve, placed my left hand on my hip, and looked the other way while I repeated to myself, over and over again, "I'm going to get a shot but I don't care."

It worked so well they usually had to tell me to move on. Whalen was right. One more shot wasn't going to hurt any of us. Yet, while I couldn't work up much sympathy for Lumpkin, I had to agree with Kilgallen. She had pretty well described the situation with her favorite word. Asinine.

We reported to the dispensary for our last shot on Friday, already lined up alphabetically when the doctor came in. Abramowitz rolled up her sleeve. "Why do I always have to be first?" she asked.

A WAVE pharmacist mate picked up the top card and read, "Zufall?"

The doctor looked up. "That can't be right."

"These are all backwards," she said. "Wood is next, then Whalen, Ward, Tierney, Telfer, Teaford. . . ."

The doctor shrugged. "Let's take them from Z to A this time. You can straighten those out as we go along."

Abramowitz rolled down her sleeve and walked to the back of the room and Zufall led the other end of the line around to meet the doctor.

Whalen grinned. "Hey Zu, Wood, for once we're at the head of a line. Wanna go to Ship Service after?"

Shot lines move quickly and efficiently. They were up to the L's when a WAVE hurried in from the office. "There's a call for you, Sir. They said it's urgent."

The doctor relaxed his hold on Lumpkin's arm. He was putting away the needle when she yelled, "Don't just go off and leave me standing here like this! Give me the shot first!"

He looked surprised, but she got the shot before he left to answer the phone. He returned quickly. "They just found your medical records. The rest of you are dismissed."

Lumpkin was still there, exercising her arm. I thought I saw a tear roll down her cheek. By the next morning that arm was so swollen she couldn't get it through the sleeve of her blouse. She reported to the dispensary, and was promptly admitted to sickbay.

Lawson and I paid her a visit before we went on liberty. Her arm was almost twice its normal size. Wrapped loosely in gauze, there was something yellow oozing out from beneath the bandages.

"You know where I made my mistake," she said, fingering the gauze. "I should have let that doctor leave to answer the phone."

*   *   *

CHAPTER 23.
TOP MAN

We often joked about which of us might be awarded the certificate suitable for framing and the ring from the people of Oklahoma City. We knew it was impossible. "Top Man" would always be just that. No woman could ever attain it, with our lower shop grades, no matter how hard we crammed for the written tests.

But without a doubt, if there was a "Top Woman" award, it would go to Erickson. She seemed determined to learn all there was to know about everything, whether or not it would be on the test.

Her quest for knowledge once proved embarrassing. It happened the day she and I were paired off to examine one of the small planes parked on the apron. We were to locate and check off all the parts that were listed in our manual.

I was standing on the catwalk with a clipboard, looking over her shoulder as she sat in the cockpit searching for the instruments. We were almost through when she spotted something she didn't understand. Picking up the loose end of a long tube attached to the floor of the plane, she puzzled over it. "Freddy, do you know what this is?"

"No idea," I said. "It's not on the list, so it won't be on the test. Did you find the altimeter?"

"Wait," she said. "I'm curious."

"Eric, there's not much time . . ."

It was too late. She had called the instructor over. Showing him the tube she said, "This is not on our list, but I want to know what it is."

He grinned sheepishly. "You know what it is."

"No, I don't. What is it?"

"Sure you do." He turned to me. "You know what it is don't you?"

I shook my head.

"You two are kidding me."

He looked first at Erickson, then at me. We stared back, innocently. "You're not kidding. You really don't know. Well . . ." He thought a moment. "I guess you'd call it the pilot's relief valve." He left hurriedly.

"I should have known," she said, "by the funnel on this end."

About the second week of engines we began to notice that Erickson was no longer spending her evenings studying at her bunk. Graves, her bunkmate, asked if anyone knew where she was.

Peters, in the next bunk, was her buddy. She knew. "Eric went to the library."

"I don't blame her," said Graves, "it's hard to study around this place."

"Oh, it's not that. Eric can study anywhere. She meets a sailor there. He's Aviation Machinist on our shift, the same week as we are. He thinks he has a good chance at the Top Man award, so Erickson offered to help him study for it."

Kilgallen asked, "How did she meet him?"

"She was at the library doing some research on the Pratt Whitney engine for last week's assignment. They both reached for this book at the same time."

Kilgallen was impressed. "Why didn't I think of that? What's he like?"

Peters said, "I haven't met him, but I guess he's okay. his name is Steve. He's taller than Erickson, even in heels, and comes from her home state of Michigan."

Kilgallen smiled. "It sounds like it might get serious."

As we went into the final weeks, Steve started checking the grade lists posted in the barracks of the other two men's Aviation Machinist classes he was competing with. His grades topped them all, and it was no wonder. Erickson was studying with him almost every night, helping him to increase his lead.

But she continued to spend all of her weekends with Peters. Sunday morning they attended early Mass together on the base before going into Norman for Erickson's Christian Science services. Then they were off to explore the local culture.

One evening, observing that Erickson was again missing from her bunk, Kilgallen could no longer stand the suspense. "Freddy," she said, "let's go to the library."

"Why?"

"I want to get a look at this Steve."

"We can't go there just to spy on Eric."

"Then we'll bring our books and study. C'mon."

"No. It wouldn't be right."

"Not right? To go to the library and study? We've as much right to be there as they have."

"What would we say? 'Hi, Eric. How about introducing us to your friend?' No."

"Wouldn't you like to know what he looks like?"

"Well . . ."

"If you don't come with me, I'll go alone."

Kilgallen reached into her locker. She brought out her manual and a notebook filled mostly with artistic doodling.

Reluctantly, I reached for my cap. "Why do I let you talk me into these things?"

We had a little trouble finding the library. Neither of us had been there before. When we reached the door, Kilgallen opened it slowly, peeked in, and stared for a moment. Then, closing it, she turned to me and whispered, "Let's go."

As soon as we were back on the street she said, "I saw him and he looks just like Joseph Cotten."

I had to take her word for it.

The last class began with a review of all the subjects covered during our five months at Norman. The instructor crammed our brains with answers to the test questions that would follow. When he finished, we picked up our pencils and went to work.

Time went fast. The test papers were collected before I finished, and the instructor faced us solemnly. "I'm sorry to have to tell you this," he said, "but women aren't meant to do this kind of work. The only way we'll ever make aviation machinist mates out of you ladies is to marry you off to aviation machinists."

When our final grades were posted, there were no surprises. Erickson was first by a wide margin. True was second, Jeter a close third. All of them chose El Toro for their next assignment. They would report there, following a 15 day leave.

The rest of the class pulled a month of mess duty.

Erickson took a chow cut the day of the awards assembly, to meet Steve at Ship Service for hot dogs before the ceremony. Later I saw him walking her back. They stopped just outside the women's area to talk. Kilgallen was right. He did resemble Joseph Cotten.

When Erickson came in she said, "Steve checked the last grade list in the barracks of all the sailors graduating with us. He's sure, now, that he made Top Man. He's taking me out for dinner tonight, to celebrate."

Kilgallen smiled. "Looks like it's getting serious."

Erickson ignored the comment.

There wasn't much time to get showered and dressed. I was still tying my field scarf when I heard Cpl. DiPalma call, "Class 52, fall out!"

On our last march to the auditorium I noticed Kilgallen's head still bobbed an instant after everyone else's. By the time we arrived the hall was already filled with graduating sailors.

As the speeches began, Captain Butler's Dobermans sat attentively at his side, seeming to understand everything that was taking place.

Kilgallen, at my side, dozed intermittently until it was time for the awards. After Aviation Metalsmith and Aviation Gunner top men received theirs, it was Steve's turn. Aviation Machinist was the longest class, with twice the number of students. The award was considered the greatest honor. I saw Steve glance across the aisle and wink at Erickson.

"This award," the Naval officer glanced at the paper in his hand. He didn't finish the sentence. "I think there's been a mistake here," he said.

Handing the report down to his secretary, a WAVE seated in the front row, he asked, "Are you sure this is correct?"

She read it and nodded. By now Capt. Butler's dogs were getting nervous. They sensed something was wrong.

"Well," he began, "it's the first time this has ever happened. The Aviation Machinist Mate award for Top Man this week goes to a woman, Pvt. Leslie Kay Erickson."

Erickson didn't move. Jeter gave her a nudge.

"No. No, Steve was supposed to win!" she responded.

Kilgallen leaned forward and poked her. "Go up there and accept it!"

She rose slowly and began the long walk to the front of the auditorium. She didn't glance across the aisle, but kept her eyes fixed straight ahead.

It had never occurred to Steve to ask Erickson what her grades had been. He buried his face in his hands. By now, his classmates had burst into loud, unrestrained laughter.

Watching her climb to the stage, I felt tremendous pride that one of us had achieved this award. Graciously, she accepted the certificate suitable for framing and the man-sized ring from the people of Oklahoma City. She said "Thank you Sir," did a sharp about face, and left quickly.

The ceremony over, we were dismissed and allowed to proceed back independently. As we left, Steve reached out to Erickson and grabbed her arm. "Kay, we have to talk."

She returned to the barracks a bit later, looking stunned. "I can't believe this. I just can't believe it." She sat on her bunk and fingered the ring. When she placed it on her thumb, it came to rest at the base of it.

Peters sat down beside her. "What happened?"

Erickson took a deep breath. "Steve was furious. He never wants to see me again. He said I embarrassed him in front of his entire class, because he had told everyone he won. When he was beat out by a woman, they laughed at him."

"There's a lesson here gals," said Bongiorni. "Don't ever be smarter than your man. Unless, of course, you don't mind losing him."

Erickson chuckled. She didn't mind.

Besides, it really was very funny.

*   *   *

CHAPTER 24.
THE PARTY

One evening shortly before graduation, I went to the slop chute with Kilgallen and Lawson. After we picked up our beers, we discovered there were no empty tables. Kilgallen paused beside three sailors who were seated in a booth for six, and called back to us, "There's no place to sit."

The remark was not meant for us, but for the sailors. The big one in the corner looked up. "Hey, c'mon join us."

Kilgallen gave him a surprised smile and sat down beside him. I took the aisle seat next to her and Lawson, on the other side, settled in between the other two sailors.

The more mature one by Kilgallen said, "I'm George." George must have been twenty-five or twenty-six. Probably married, I thought. "And this is Wes and Jimmy."

"That's Jim," the younger sailor corrected him. He ran his fingers through loose brown curls and glanced across the table at me. "I'm from Seattle."

I said, "Hey, I was born there." My family moved to Chicago when I was ten, but Jim was elated to find someone who knew where Queen Anne Hill was.

Wes looked a little older, with close-set eyes and a serious expression. He placed one arm behind Lawson to tap Jim on the shoulder. "Hey," he said, "wasn't George the hottest pilot in our class?" He did not remove his arm.

"Yeah." Jim sighed. "He was in the top ten percent at Corpus Christi. He would have qualified for the Marines. Boy, he could be flying those Corsairs now."

It sounded like they had flunked pilot training. Kilgallen asked, "How did you wash out?"

Wes glanced admiringly into Lawson's big blue eyes. "Let George tell it," he said.

"Biggest disappointment of my life," George began. His voice trailed off, and the three sailors shook their heads.

Kilgallen turned to George. "So what happened?"

"It was our last training flight out of Corpus. We were going to get our wings that Saturday. Five of us were flying in formation on our way home, flying over the gulf."

"There were five of you?" Lawson asked.

"Yeah." George sighed. "The other two got sent here too."

Kilgallen was getting impatient. "Tell us what happened. You must have done something really stupid."

"Well, there's a high bridge spanning the Laguna Madre. We used to talk about how it must feel to fly under it."

"All of you flew under the bridge?" I asked.

"No, just one of us."

Kilgallen frowned. "If only one of you flew under it, how come all of you got washed out?"

George answered. "They didn't get the identification of the plane."

Lawson said, "Well, you must know who did it."

Jim clenched his fist. "Yeah, we know who did it."

I sensed it was not one of the three.

"They didn't ask us," George explained. "We wouldn't have told them anyway. Besides, they had trained too many pilots so anyone who came up for discipline got washed out. We all got sent here for Aviation Gunners Mate."

I was reminded of a song McGinnis sang, to the tune of "Stars and Stripes Forever":

Be kind to your washed out cadet
For he may be an aerial gunner.
He sits in the rear of the plane,
And he never, ever, complains.

Now you may think that he is afraid.

Well, he is. . . .

Theirs was the saddest story Kilgallen had heard in a long time. She wanted to cheer them up. "Hey, how about coming to our graduation party?"

Lawson and I exchanged glances. This was the first either of us had heard of it. Wes looked crestfallen. He glanced down at Lawson. "You're graduating? But we just got here."

"This is our last week," Lawson explained.

Kilgallen asked again, "Well are you coming or not?"

"Sure we are," said George, and it was settled.

When Kilgallen suggested they bring the other two washed out cadets, it was time for us to talk. I reminded her it was getting late. As we left, the sailors promised to save us a table the following evening.

Once outside I said, "Kil, I'm not throwing any party."

"I just now thought of it. Those sailors look so unhappy, and we have to celebrate somehow."

All week she made plans for the party over beer muster at the slop chute. She started taking Jeter and Pellier along after Al and Jack, the other two cadets, joined us, and the sailors started saving two adjoining tables.

Jim always singled me out. I heard all about his high school graduation, prom night, and Dad's plans for his college. He even said I reminded him of his girl friend back home.

The week passed quickly while Kilgallen tried to get the party organized. The sailors offered to bring the liquor. Kilgallen volunteered us for the rest. We would reserve two rooms for us at the Skirvin Hotel and have the party there. She suggested the sailors get their rooms in the same hotel so they would not risk being on the street after curfew.

"I'll call the hotel tomorrow after lunch and make our reservations," said Kilgallen. "You guys had better do the same."

"Why make two phone calls?" George asked. "One call can do for all of us all, and that will take care of it."

Kilgallen protested, but George ignored her. "We have a phone booth just outside our barracks," he said. "It's no problem. How many of you will there be?"

She turned to Lawson. "Graves thought maybe she'd come," she said. "And Hunnicutt will come if she didn't have a date."

Hunnicutt, well known among the sailors as "Hunni," was a quiet little gal in thick glasses. She usually carried a novel tucked under one arm, but she had more dates than any of us.

Kilgallen counted. "That makes seven. Anybody else?"

"Never mind. I'll take care of it," said George, and the subject was dropped.

Graves decided not to join us, but Hunnicutt wanted to know where we would be, in case she didn't have a date. We took off for Oklahoma City after graduation, going directly to the hotel. The five sailors were already there, waiting in the lobby.

George approached us, grinning. "It's all taken care of," he said. "Come on, I'll take you to your rooms."

"We haven't paid for them yet." I started for the desk.

George stopped me. "That's all taken care of."

Kilgallen was getting suspicious. "You're not paying for my room."

"Okay, okay, you can pay me later. Let's not argue about it here in the lobby. It doesn't look good."

We wanted to look good, so we followed George quietly to our rooms. Before leaving, he handed a key to Kilgallen and she told him the party was set for eight. She closed the door and sighed. "Whew! I was worried there for a while."

I looked around. We had two large rooms with a wide sliding door open between them. Each room had its own bath. There were two double beds in one room, and three more in the other. Several folded cots leaned against the walls in both rooms. It was probably more than we needed.

Kilgallen and Lawson tried out the beds and promptly fell asleep, so Pellier, Jeter and I slipped out to pick up things for the party. We saw the sailors in the lobby, but they were busy talking and didn't notice us.

Jeter frowned. "Why don't they go to their rooms?"

We picked up what we needed at a little store a couple blocks away. When we got back the sailors were still in the lobby. They saw us and waved.

George smiled. "See you around eight."

I couldn't figure out how I got into this mess. I'd be glad when it was over.

Lawson was awake now, but Kilgallen was still sleeping. Pellier put the cokes on ice and we laid things out for the party. Then we woke Kilgallen and went to dinner.

When we returned to our rooms we found the five sailors already inside, dipping into the chips and drinking rum and Coca Cola. Jeter eyed them suspiciously.

"It's not 2000 yet. How'd y'all git in?"

George said, "Hey, it's 1930. That's close enough."

"But how'd y'all git in?"

Smiling sheepishly, George came up with another key. "We were holding out on you."

Kilgallen grabbed it.

George appointed himself bartender. He added a little soda to a glass of Scotch and handed it to Kilgallen.

She made a face. "You put too much Scotch in this."

"You'll be glad I did when the ice melts."

But she was thirsty. The ice didn't have time to melt. George quickly filled it again with more of the same.

It wasn't much of a party. We didn't have a lot in common with these sailors. They had recently arrived, we were about to leave, and there's just so much to be said about Queen Anne Hill. It got late, and the sailors seemed reluctant to leave. Kilgallen asked George what floor their rooms were on. That's when the truth came out. "These are our rooms too." He winked. "We only needed one reservation, because we're all going to end up together anyway."

It took a while for his remark to work its way through the Scotch. When it did, Kilgallen rose in righteous indignation to her full five feet eight inches. "How dare you!"

She straightened her field scarf and searched through our hats until she found the one with her name on it. Grabbing her bag and trench coat, she headed for the door.

I tried to stop her. "Kil, where are you going?"

"Back to the base. Are you coming with me?"

"We can't leave now. It's too close to curfew."

"Watch me."

And she was gone. Lawson turned to me. "What can we do? I don't want to stay here, and I'm afraid to go out."

"We have to stay, but it will be on our terms."

I glanced over at Jeter. She had set up a cot in the corner, and was already asleep. I put up another alongside her and dropped my purse on top of it.

"That one's mine," I said. "Now, you guys take the other room, and we'll see you at breakfast."

"Hey, it's still early," Jim argued.

Wes grinned at Lawson. "You need another drink."

"I'm getting married next month on my furlough," said Pellier. "What am I doing here?"

Al glanced at Jack. "I'd say the party's over." After they disappeared into the other room, there was a knock at the door. It was Hunnicutt.

"I don't have a date," she said, "and it's past curfew. I need to sleep here tonight." She noticed the three sailors. "Wow! What have we got here?"

Lawson explained, "They were just leaving."

"Aw have a heart," George pleaded, eyeing Hunnicutt.

She picked up on it. "Yeah, let's let 'em stay."

Pellier watched with mild amusement as Lawson pointed toward the door to the next room. Looking straight at Wes she ordered, "Out!"

I gave Jim a shove in the same direction. The three backed off slowly, watching for a sign from Hunnicutt.

The GIs back home never behaved like this. Disgusted, I closed the doors between us, turned off the light, and hit the sack.

Hunnicutt was already spread out on the bed by the sliding doors so Pellier and Lawson shared the one next to my cot. I don't know how long I had been asleep when I was awakened by a soft knock at the hall door. I got up and opened it quietly.

It was Kilgallen, and she was covered with a white powder. She had left a trail of it on the carpet in the hall behind her. I motioned her in and followed her to the bathroom. She looked in the mirror. "I don't believe this!" Taking off her hat, she scooped the powder from the crown into the toilet.

"If that asinine shore patrolman hadn't been standing there in front of the train station, I could have made it inside," she said. "I ducked into an alley and waited for him to leave. But he stayed, and another one joined him. When the last train left, I figured I was stuck in the alley for the night."

She paused, shaking her head. "Then one of them started across the street, toward the alley. When I turned to run, I knocked over this barrel of flour behind the bakery. The lid came off and I tripped and fell into it."

"Where's your other shoe?"

"I had to leave it. There wasn't time to look for it."

"Come on in," I said. "I'll fix a bed for you."

"Are the sailors gone?"

"Yes. They're all in the other room."

"Is that door locked between us?"

"No, we couldn't lock it, but it's closed."

"No lock on the door? Then I'm not going into that den of iniquity. I'll sleep here, in the bathroom."

Her mind was made up. "I'll find you a blanket."

Jeter's pillow had fallen. I took it. I put on my wool blouse and gave her my blanket. "Where do you want me to spread this out?"

"On the floor."

"You could get stepped on."

"I'm not sleeping in there."

She folded the blanket into the bathtub. Then she put the pillow on the sloping end and climbed in, covering up with her trench coat. I turned off the light and went back to my cot.

When I awoke the next morning Kilgallen was gone, and so were my shoes. The doors between the two rooms were still closed, and there was no sign of the sailors. I was hoping last night had been just a bad dream, but no. The flour was still there.

Jeter was already awake. "Let's go to breakfast," she whispered. "Ah'm starved."

"I can't, Jeter. My shoes are gone."

"Where'd they go?" She laughed.

"Kil must have taken them."

"You can't go out in your stocking feet."

"I know. Just bring me back coffee with cream, and a roll."

Lawson, Pellier, and Hunnicutt woke up and went to breakfast with Jeter. I found some hotel stationery and started a letter to my mother.

Kilgallen had pulled some stunts in the past, but this one topped them all. Without shoes, I had no idea how I was going to get back to the base.

I was wondering just how much to tell my mother about the party when the door burst open and Kilgallen rushed in, holding up her other shoe. It was covered with flour.

She kicked mine off. "Gee these are tight. How can you stand them?"

I followed her into the bathroom. Her uniform seemed to be in pretty good shape, but her red hair looked like it was turning white.

"I can't go to church like this." She moistened a washcloth to wipe the flour from her shoe. "I just have time to make the next Mass. I won't be back."

As she was leaving she paused at the door. "I'd better make sure I've got everything."

She hurried to the chest of drawers. As she was checking them, Jeter, Pellier, Lawson, and Hunnicutt returned from breakfast with my roll and coffee.

When Kilgallen opened the bottom drawer, she stood up and put both hands on her hips. "For the love of Mike," she exclaimed, "what, in heaven's name, is that?"

I looked. How do you explain condoms to a nun? "We used to see those in the alleys back in Chicago when I was a kid." I cleared my throat. "We called them rubbers. They're . . ."

"I know what they are. I want to know what they're doing in here."

By now we were all standing around, looking down into the drawer at the remnants of last night's party.

Kilgallen counted them. "There's three!" She gasped. "That means three of you . . ."

Hunnicutt smiled. "Or one of us three times."

It didn't take many like her, wearing our uniform, to ruin the reputation of us all.

*   *   *

CHAPTER 25.
THANKSGIVING MESS

Erickson, True, and Jeter, top three in class 52, enjoyed Thanksgiving at home. The rest of us spent the holiday in the mess hall, walloping pots and sweating over a hot steam table.

Lumpkin had joined us, fully recovered from her reaction to that last shot. She acted as though she was in charge, seeming to enjoy working with the food. "Those WAVEs don't know anything about carving turkey," she complained. "Just see how they've butchered these."

They looked all right to me, but I shook my head in disgust. No use exposing my ignorance. After all, she was the one with the degree in domestic science.

Women's classes were on the early shift, so the cooks had been busy most of the night preparing the feast. We had spent the morning helping them, and I was starved. Unfortunately, I had chow line duty. We would be the last to eat. The galley and mess hall were filled with tempting aromas. I didn't think I could last much longer.

We served the dishwashers first. I decided that's the job I would volunteer for the next time I pulled mess duty, no matter what it did to my nails. I just couldn't work on an empty stomach. I was starting to cut more pumpkin pies when a cook rushed in and yelled, "Ensign Gerber needs one of you in her office right now."

She was looking at me, so I followed her back. It was not a pretty sight. The officer had found a bloodied mouse, long dead, flattened behind a drawer in her desk. The cook was very upset, but the officer remained calm.

"I was wondering what I kept smelling," she said.

They left me to handle it alone. After disposing of the mouse and scouring the drawer, I felt like my hands would never be clean again. I scrubbed them for a long, long time. When I returned, most of the classes had already been served.

The noon whistle blew. The civilians on the base were working a half-day, so they were free now to go home for their holiday dinner. I thought, how nice.

But they didn't go home. Instead, they lined up outside their chow hall, next to ours, complaining that the door was locked. Lumpkin reported it to Ensign Gerber, and asked if we should open their line.

The officer followed her into the dining room. "They weren't supposed to eat here today," she said. She thought a moment. "There probably won't be many, just a few who don't have a home to go to for Thanksgiving dinner."

She turned to me. "You . . . Private. Get some help to set up their line and open their door."

Having been volunteered again, I took Kilgallen, Lawson, and Graves with me, leaving Lumpkin with a skeleton crew. Kilgallen complained as we brought out the food. "Serving civilians is not our job. Why don't they go home?"

Lawson was filling the coffee urn. "Ensign Gerber said maybe some of them didn't have a home to go to."

"They can't all be homeless," Kilgallen answered. "Have you seen that line?"

I glanced out the window. It looked like every employee on the base was out there waiting to be fed. I hadn't seen that many civilians in one place in months. They reached clear out to the street and half way down to Ship's Service.

The cooks finished carving the turkey and left. The officer was gone now too. There were only a couple sailors still in the galley. They played poker while they waited for us to finish up so they could carry out the heavy garbage cans.

I opened their door and began serving turkey and dressing to the civilians while Kilgallen spooned out gravy with potatoes, both sweet and mashed. She was so disgusted she was spilling gravy everywhere. It burned into the steam table. We would have to scrub that off before we could eat, and I would have to put up with my hunger pains a while longer.

When I gave them turkey, they just stood there, holding out their tray, expecting more. Kilgallen had to ask, "What kind of potatoes?" to lure them on.

I had never served civilians before. They didn't know how to keep the line moving.

The third time I called for more turkey there wasn't any. "And we're out of gravy too."

A civilian passing my station heard that. "I can't eat my biscuits without gravy."

Kilgallen suggested, in that case, he not take biscuits.

"What's the matter, didn't you cook enough food?"

"We paid our money. Now they have to feed us."

The civilians were revolting.

I locked their entrance and we fed what we had to those who had already paid. What food was left Lawson took to the women's mess hall, and we drained the steam table to clean it.

When we finished, I picked up some celery sticks that had been left behind and took them with me to our dining room. I was surprised to find that the line had been emptied and cleaned out, except for a little celery.

Lawson asked, "Where's the food?"

Whalen leaned on her mop. "That's all that's left."

"I don't believe this," said Kilgallen. "They didn't even leave us a piece of pumpkin pie."

Graves went back to the kitchen to see what was there. I heard a sailor say, "Everything's gone. You gals cleaned us out."

"Those civilians you mean," Graves answered. "There's nothing left out there but celery sticks."

A sailor handed her a large jar from the table. "Here," he said, "stuff 'em with peanut butter."

She brought the jar back to the dining room. At least there was plenty of coffee. I hoped they hadn't planned on serving leftovers for dinner. There seemed little reason to sit down, but I was tired and the coffee was hot.

Graves picked up a celery stick and loaded it with peanut butter. "When I get out of this Mickey Mouse Marine Corp . . ."

But Kilgallen seemed pleased. She sipped her coffee and smiled. "What a great chapter this will be for my book!"

*   *   *

CHAPTER 26.
CHICAGO

All of us believed we were bound for Cherry Point, but Kilgallen never stopped praying for California. Campbell was the only one looking forward to east coast duty, closer to her home.

Soon after we returned from our last day of mess duty, Sgt. Salisbury entered the squad room with our orders. "Class 52, you're all going to El Toro, California."

Kilgallen smiled. "I'm glad I made that last Novena."

Campbell's disappointment was lost in the excitement everyone else was feeling at that moment. She shook her head. "I should have studied harder."

We had some time to pack and make travel plans. Day coach train fare was half price for military. Kilgallen and I made reservations to Chicago, leaving Oklahoma City together on the morning of December 9th.

I planned to spend a couple days with my sister and brother there, and visit with school chums before going on to Portland, Oregon to see my mother and meet my new stepfather. Pellier was getting married there, and she had asked me to be her maid of honor. We would report to the Marine Corps Air Station at El Toro fifteen days later, before midnight of December 24th.

It was raining when we boarded the train. By mid morning there was talk of flood conditions to the north. When we slowed down Kilgallen pressed her nose to the glass, straining to see the rear of the train as it came around the bend.

"The water is almost half way up to the window."

"We're hardly moving now," I answered. "How do they know the tracks aren't washed out up ahead? I hope we can get through."

Kilgallen faced me solemnly. "I hadn't thought of that. I don't want any long delays getting into Chicago."

She reached into her purse. Bringing out the small silver bag containing her rosary, she leaned back, closed her eyes, and relaxed. Her lips barely moved as the beads slipped through her fingers.

Just like Kilgallen, I thought, to retreat into her prayers at a time like this, leaving me alone to worry the train through the flood.

When she had finished she opened her eyes and put her rosary back in its case. After a moment's pause she said, "Let's go to the diner and get some lunch. I'm starved."

We ordered the usual hamburgers and French fries with coffee. Kilgallen seemed in good spirits, despite the high waters. "My father said he would meet me at the station," she said. "I can hardly wait to see him again."

I couldn't dismiss our situation that lightly. It seemed to me we were in danger of having a lengthy delay on our arrival time if, indeed, we would arrive at all. It didn't look good.

But when we started back to our seats I noticed the train had picked up speed, tossing us from side to side as we moved through the cars. Glancing out a window, I saw that the water had receded. Were we past the flooded area? Or was this God's response to something Kilgallen had asked of Him?

Before we reached our coach, she spotted an Army chaplain traveling alone. She stopped to talk to him and I continued on alone. I had some time now to myself, some time to think. It had been over three years since I left Chicago. I had changed. Those I left behind probably had not. I'd forgotten how to talk to civilians. Would we still have anything in common? It had been more than eight months since I had even been inside a house. By the time she returned, I was suffering a full-blown case of furlough anxiety.

"Kil, when you go home, what do you talk about?"

"Well, I let them talk first. After a while they wind down. Then they ask me how my life is going. I tell them the truth, but they don't believe me. I finally give up and we settle into a discussion of the weather, how the children have grown, and the problems my Grandmother is having with her dentures."

She wasn't much help.

We arrived at Chicago Union Station the next day just after lunch, only a bit behind schedule. Kilgallen spotted her father and disappeared into the crowd.

I saw my sister, Dawn Gaines, hurrying toward me. I was struck by her delicate features, so like our mother's. She looked so small, so thin, and so tired. She had written she was working a sixty-hour week at the defense plant.

This war was tough on civilians.

"I got the afternoon off." She smiled. "Everyone wants to see you. We'll go to Mrs. Miller's first." She took my hand, as she had so many times in the past, and led me out to the street.

We caught a Madison Street car, and were soon there. Mrs. Miller's large frame filled the door as she invited us in with her usual Southern hospitality. I started for the living room, but she steered me into the kitchen.

I wasn't hungry.

"I remember how you used to like my scrambled brains and cornbread," she said. "I'm cookin' you up a good mess of it."

Despite having lunch on the train, I managed to clean my plate and even enjoy a second piece of her hot cornbread.

Next stop was Mrs. Grimson's for fried chicken and biscuits. I started to explain that I had just eaten, but Dawn kicked me in the shin. I ate.

Then off to see Dawn's Mother-in-law, Mrs. Hanson, who remembered how I had always enjoyed her spaghetti and meatballs. I was the only one eating. These people didn't want to visit with me. They just wanted to stuff me.

About the time I decided I couldn't hold another bite, Dawn's husband, Bill, came in, wearing his policeman's uniform. "Come on Inga," he said, "finish up. I'm taking you and Dawn out to Lloyd's place for dinner."

I felt like I had already eaten dinner . . . three times.

Bill, a jovial Irishman, apologized for being in uniform. "They want us to wear it whenever we go out," he said. "The department is having trouble getting enough able bodied men. This way it looks like there's more of us, and we always appear to be on duty."

Lloyd, my brother, lived in Lombard. I hoped his wife Lill had planned something light. I loosened the hook on my waistband and left with them.

When we got to Lloyd's house, he opened the door wide. Recognizing a familiar aroma coming from the kitchen, I knew I was in trouble. "Do I smell turkey?"

My brother nodded, grinning boyishly. He looked even taller and leaner than I had remembered him. There was still the same dark mustache that he had grown years earlier, hoping to look older.

Lill came out from the kitchen wiping her hands on a towel. She was about my height, with a cute button nose and a friendly smile. A baby cried in a back bedroom and we followed her there to meet my three month old niece, Susie. Lill let me hold her while we talked. "You told us in your letter," she said, "that you didn't get a Thanksgiving dinner, so I cooked another one just for you."

"It smells wonderful!"

I hoped it would be some time before it was ready, but soon Lloyd ushered me into the dining room and lifted hefty two year Lee into his highchair.

Lill said, "Everything's ready. We've been waiting for you."

It pleased me that Mary Jo, my six year old niece, asked to sit beside me. Lloyd spoke of a machine he was designing for the military that was so secret he couldn't even tell me about it.

Meanwhile, Lill was heaping my plate. I tried to remember how hungry I had been on Thanksgiving Day.

For much of the meal, Bill entertained us with a collection of lively jokes he had heard on the beat, being careful to clean them up for the mixed company. There seemed no end to his repertoire.

That night Mary Jo happily shared her room with me, and I spent much of the next day getting reacquainted with her. Late in the afternoon, after she had stared at me for some time, I asked her what she was thinking.

"Well," she said, "I was just wondering. Don't you have any clothes, Aunt Inga?"

I had made plans to spend that evening with school chums. Lily and I were going to visit Elsie for a few laughs. We had a lot of happy memories to share. Elsie and Lily were both married, but their husbands had shipped out, and they had each moved back with their parents. It would be just like old times.

At least, I thought it would.

Dawn and Bill came for dinner again and later dropped me off at Lily's house on Jackson Blvd. I was back in my old neighborhood. Lily hadn't changed. She was my height, my weight, and we both had the same fair complexion. People sometimes asked if we were sisters.

We walked together the short distance to Elsie's, just as we had done many times on our way to school, years earlier. Lily rang the doorbell and we waited. She rang it again, and yet again. Had she forgotten we were coming? She rang once more. As we turned to leave, her mother came to the door.

A tall, quiet woman, she had been a nurse before her marriage. Solemnly, she said, "Please wait in the living room while I get Elsie ready for your visit."

There was mystery and sadness in her voice. Lily and I sat quietly for what seemed a long time before she came back downstairs. "You can go up now." She turned to me. "She's very tired and upset, but she wanted to see you."

I couldn't imagine what was going on. As I climbed the stairs, I looked back at Lily. She was shaking her head. Why hadn't anyone told me Elsie was ill?

I hardly recognized her. Her face was ashen, the freckles just a darker shade of gray. Her brown eyes were red and swollen from crying, and it looked like her mother had borrowed every pillow in the house to prop her up.

This was not the girl I remembered. The only thing familiar about her was the reddish brown naturally curly hair. Usually swept up, it fell now to her shoulders.

Lily asked, "Did you lose the baby?"

"Yes." She wiped her eyes.

"How far along were you?"

"A little over three months. It was a boy."

"I lost a baby too, after Ralph shipped out."

"You did?" She looked surprised.

"I wasn't as far along as you were. My mother took care of me. I didn't tell anybody, not even Ralph. He had enough to worry about, just trying to stay alive."

This reunion was not turning out as I had hoped. Instead of a pleasant visit with old friends, it felt like I was surveying the losses on the home front. Except for memories, I had little in common now with the two closest friends I had ever known, and I couldn't have picked a worse time to find that out.

Her mother appeared in the doorway holding a tray. Attempting a smile she said, "Tea and oatmeal cookies?"

We didn't stay long. I found my way back to Lombard and went to bed early.

In the morning I would have a train to catch.

*   *   *

Top left and right: Sisters
Bottom left: The Fredriksen kids
Bottom right: left to right-Bill and Dawn Gaines,
Freddy, and brother Lloyd

CHAPTER 27.
EN ROUTE

The whole family came to the Union Station to see me off. Sorry to leave so soon, I had to move on, if I was to make Portland in time for Pellier's wedding. Boarding the train, I selected a window seat where I could wave good-bye to them.

The engine fired up and I heard the familiar hiss of escaping steam, followed by the powerful sound of chug, chug, chug. The train began to move, slowly at first, then faster. I lost sight of the faces of my loved ones, and wondered when I'd see them again.

The chug chugs gradually became choo-choo choo-choos. The train took on a gentle sway, and I was on my way. A young mother sat beside me now, holding a baby in her arms. I gave her my seat by the window.

"I'm going to Portland to be near my husband until he ships out," she said. "We probably won't have much time together, but every moment counts. I know they tell us we should stay home and wait, not follow our husbands around, but I want to be with Joe as much as I can. Nobody knows how long this war will last, or what might happen before it's over."

It was a good-sized baby, already getting restless. She shifted him to her other arm. Her face was pale and thin, and she looked tired. The baby was lively. She had trouble restraining him.

She folded a clean diaper and draped it over her left shoulder. "I'm pregnant again. Our second baby is due early in May. Joe will probably ship out before then. When he does, I'll go back home and wait at my mother's, in Kankakee."

The woman looked about my age. I thought of Elsie and Lily,

living with their grief. For the moment, I was glad I was single. But such thoughts never lasted long. At least they had someone to wait for. I had no one. And next month I would be twenty-three.

"Joey!" His mother pulled him back. "You can't go out there." I put my suitcase across to block the aisle. She took a graham cracker from her sack to hush the crying.

Joey got his fill of crackers early in the trip. Before the day was over he had managed to visit two soldiers across the aisle from us, a Coastguard officer and his wife behind them, and the four servicemen sitting in front and in back of us. His mother had been constantly aware of his wanderings, never relaxing her vigil.

"It's all right. Let him be," they would say. But she never took her eyes off of him for more than a moment.

She ate sandwiches from her bag, and the porter brought the baby's bottles as she needed them. When I went to the diner for lunch, Joey took a nap on my seat.

The day passed and night came. Joey finished a bottle and ate most of a banana his mother had mashed for him. He was getting sleepy.

"I'd like to let you have my place for him," I said, "but I've checked, and every seat in the car is taken."

"It's all right. I'll hold him on my lap," she answered. "He'll probably sleep through the night."

I was glad of that, for my sake as well as hers.

The next morning she looked exhausted. I asked, "How did you sleep?"

"Oh, I couldn't let myself go to sleep. I was afraid he might fall, or crawl away."

Her situation was even worse than I had imagined. "When I get back from breakfast, I can take him for a while if you'll let me, so you can have a nap."

A hopeful smile crossed her face. "Oh, would you? That would be so nice."

I went back to the diner at the first breakfast call, wondering how I was going to control that unpredictable ball of energy. I had never taken care of a baby before, and this one appeared to be quite a challenge.

After a good breakfast and a stop at the head, I was as ready as I would ever be. Joey had just emptied his bottle. The mother handed him to me. "It's time for his nap." She brought the back of her seat down as far as it would go and stretched for a moment before closing her eyes.

Joey was even heavier than he looked. He gave me a one-sided smile and put his head on my chest. Frowning, he moved away from the emblem and settled further out on my shoulder. I felt his rubber pants and thought my uniform would be safe. This might be easy.

But Joey was suffering some discomfort. He reared back and gave out a loud, wet, belch that brought up a good portion of the milk he had just finished drinking. It hit the eagle globe and anchor, and poured down from there.

Joey looked at the mess and frowned. Then he switched to the other shoulder and promptly fell asleep.

I glanced at his mother. She was already out, and that clean diaper was still folded neatly over her left shoulder.

By the next morning I smelled heavily of sour milk. Wiping my blouse with a damp cloth had removed the stain, but not the stench. I was in no condition to meet my new stepfather, or to be maid of honor at Pellier's wedding.

It was sprinkling when we pulled into Portland the next day. I had lived here less than three years, but quickly adopted it as home. It felt good to be back. I caught the Foster electric bus. Taking a back seat, I opened my window to blow away the stench.

I was curious about this Gust. His last name, Kahrostopolis, sounded Greek. Had he been born there or here in the states? I hoped he wouldn't mind having me around for a few days. I wasn't sure how I would fit in, or even if I could fit in at all.

My mother had moved to his house, about a half-mile further out of town. I rode the bus to the end of the line. Getting out, I noticed it had stopped raining. I flipped down my Havelock and started up the hill.

Almost half my furlough days were spent. I had survived a flood, barged in on a dear friend as she grieved the loss of her baby, and been spit upon with milk now turned sour. Surely my luck would change.

*　　*　　*

CHAPTER 28.
THE STEPFATHER

I found my stepfather's house to be smaller than the one my mother and I had shared, and quite run down. But I could see that she had already staked out her flower garden along the path to the door. Soon it would be bright with daffodils, hollyhocks and roses, bringing color and beauty to an otherwise drab looking house.

A blue star hung in the window, indicating a member of the household was away in the service. My mother's new husband must have a son, I thought.

I knocked softly. The door sprung wide open, giving me my first look at Gust. "Welcome to your new home!" he roared, beaming a wide smile.

About my height, with thinning gray hair, he was stocky and powerful looking despite advancing years. "Me and Mama, we waiting for you. I kill my fattest bunny for you. I just start skinning him."

That explained the blood on his shirt.

My mother stood at his side. Short and plump, her white hair rolled in what she had always called, "A little toot on the top of my head." She smiled expectantly, seeming to await my approval of her new husband.

"Gust really knows how to cook rabbit," she said. "He's fixing a good dinner for you today."

I grabbed her for a quick hug before Gust ushered me to a large kitchen in the back of the house. "You see?" he said, pointing to the lifeless creature. One pink eye stared up at me. Looking at the slain animal, I wondered if it was still warm.

I turned to my mother. "I see you've started your flower garden."

She nodded. "By late spring they'll be as tall as the ones at our house." Mom was at home wherever her flowers grew. "I'll start my victory garden next. I brought some carrots down from my house to have with our dinner."

"Mama, she like her vegetables. She raise them, I cook them for her. But I'm in charge of the meat!" He pounded his chest. It looked like he was in charge of everything, and my mother didn't seem to mind.

The phone rang and Gust answered it. "Freddy? No, we got no Freddy here."

"Oh, that's for me . . ." He had hung up.

"My buddies call me Freddy. That must have been Pellier. She's getting married here in Portland tomorrow."

The phone rang again. I started toward it, but Gust got there first. "Yes, now you ask for Inga. Now I know who you talkin' 'bout."

He gave me the phone and stood nearby, listening.

"Freddy, we were married two days ago by the chaplain on Jeff's base in Vancouver. Sorry you couldn't be there.

"We're leaving for three days at Timberline Lodge. We want to ski Mt. Hood. Then Jeff has to report back for duty, and you can reach me at the Broadway Hotel."

As I hung up my mother asked, "Did you see your star in the window?"

"Oh, is that star for me?"

"That your star," said Gust. "Mama bring it down from other house, she want to put it up here. I say put it up. We don't have no son fighting in war, but daughter go join Marines. Neighbors don't know difference."

"I put that star up right after you left," she said. "I told Gust it goes wherever I go until you're home again."

Gust added, "You will come live with us after war. I build nice room for you side of house. I know lot of single Greek men in town. I get you good Greek husband, make lots money, you don't have to worry."

I couldn't believe what I was hearing.

My mother frowned. "Gust, maybe she'd like to pick out her own husband."

"No, no. That's not Greek way. Greek father take care of daughter. I take care of Inga."

She shrugged. She would stay out of it.

Gust went back to his work and I followed my mother into the dining room. It was impossible for her to hear me over Gust's loud voice booming out from the kitchen.

"I tell Mama I sell her place, she live here with me now. If she be my woman, she live in my house."

My mother nodded agreement. "We're comfortable."

I couldn't talk to her here. We would have to get further away from him. I asked, "Mom, is there a place where I can put my suitcase?"

She led me to an alcove off from the living room where a rollaway bed had been set up. "You'll sleep here. Gust made a place in the corner where you can hang your clothes."

He was still talking, but we were far enough away that with my mother's hearing loss, she didn't pick it up. We sat on the bed and she asked me about Lloyd and Dawn, and the grandchildren. We talked until we heard "Come and get it!"

I followed my mother as she hurried in. Gust made a wide flourish toward the feast he had spread on the table. "I do cooking in this house," he boasted.

The rabbit had been baked in the oven of an old wood burning stove. There were carrots, potatoes, and onions tucked around it in a large iron skillet. It was topped with Gust's own tomato mixture, and he made a cream sauce spotted with slices of home cured olives for the baked potatoes. I could understand why Mom seemed to have put on a few pounds.

"Wine is from grapes I grow in side yard."

My mother added, "He piles them into my wash tub and stomps them down with his bare feet."

I thought this might be a good time to stop drinking.

He filled our plates and poured the drinks before he sat down. "Mama, she no drink wine. She like her coffee."

"I come United States, fight FIRST World War." He emphasized "first," as if to imply it was best. "I fight for this country. I now American citizen."

He filled my glass again. It wasn't empty.

"When I come to America, I cook Greek way. Army send me to school, learn to cook American way. I still cook Greek way. They don't know difference.

"And," he went on, "I get pension from government. I am disabled veteran."

He didn't describe his injury, and I didn't ask. He looked pretty healthy to me.

Gust would interrupt his story now and then, urging me to take more food "to fatten you up." I later heard him use the same expression in reference to his rabbits.

"People buy my bunnies, no need ration stamps. Pay more money instead." He motioned to the hides stretched on drying racks in the kitchen. "Then I sell furs, make more money. Mama don't need your help now."

"You don't have to worry about us," my mother said. "We're comfortable."

I could cut the meat with a fork. "This is the best rabbit I have ever tasted," I said. "Could I have the recipe for your sauce?"

I had no idea what I would do with it.

"No recipe. I just make. Next time you watch, then you make recipe. You like it? Have some more." He scooped another thigh into my plate and smothered it with sauce. This could be habit forming.

As the days passed and I noticed my skirt getting tighter, the day came to contact Pellier. I called the hotel and we made plans to meet at the USO the next morning.

Gust listened carefully to my end of the conversation. When I hung up he asked, "You go downtown tomorrow?"

"Yes. I'm meeting my buddy at the USO in the morning to make plans for our trip to California."

"Tomorrow morning, eh?" He grinned. "How about you run errand for me downtown?"

"I'd be glad to. What can I do for you?"

"Well, let me see . . . I think I want you bring me pound bacon from Sam's butcher shop. That's it, pound bacon."

My mother frowned. "But Gust, we have plenty bacon."

"Never mind," he said. "This for something else."

She nodded obediently and went back to her dusting.

The next morning Gust sat down at a small desk in the corner of the kitchen. "I write note, you give Sam."

When he finished he folded it twice and held it out to me. "Don't let anybody wait on you but Sam. You give him this."

"I will. Any particular kind of bacon?"

"The note explain everything. He know what kind of bacon I talkin' bout. He put it on my bill." He handed me a ration book, smiled, and patted me on the back. "You like Sam. He nice man."

At the USO I found Pellier seated at a table, talking to a young civilian. He pulled up a chair for me and I joined them. A volunteer brought coffee and donuts.

"Freddy, this is Cliff. He's driving to Los Angeles, leaving the evening of the twenty-second. He has offered to take us along,"

Cliff was wearing the eagle pin we had come to know as the "ruptured duck," indicating he was a WW II veteran. He had an honest, open face. His eyes were large and wide set, as clear blue as my father's had been. I felt we could trust him, and I could always use a free ride. "It sounds great."

"Before you decide," Cliff warned, "you should know I'll be driving a truck. I came in here to see if some GI going that direction wanted to come along. I hadn't planned on two women. It won't be as comfortable as a car, but it's a big rig with a bed behind the seat of the cab. You could both sleep back there."

I asked, "When are you going to sleep?"

"Well, I stop for a few hours in San Francisco. I'll climb up in the sack while we're there and you two can take off and have a look at the city."

Pellier looked at me expectantly. I said, "Let's go."

"I'll have my truck loaded by eight-thirty, and be at the northwest corner of Front and Glisan by nine tomorrow night. If you're not there, I'll wait for you."

We exchanged phone numbers but I warned him about the telephone surveillance at my house, asking that he not upset Gust with knowledge of our plans. He agreed, and left.

I finished my coffee and had another cup while Pellier told me about her wedding. "It was very simple, very nice. I wish you could have been there."

She didn't stay long. "Jeff is getting off this afternoon," she said. "I want to be at the hotel when he arrives. Could we have dinner together before we leave tomorrow night? He wants to meet you."

We decided to meet at Ireland's, at 1900.

I was about to board the bus for home when I remembered the bacon. I checked my bag for the note. It fell open as I took it out, revealing a full page of writing, all in Greek. I hoped Sam could understand it.

The shop was busy. I waited my turn, then asked for Sam. The butcher called to a man working at the other end of the counter. "Hey Boss, this little soldier lady wants to speak to you."

"I'll be right there," he said. As soon as he finished with his customer he came over. "What can I do for you, young lady?"

I handed him the note. He was taller and younger than the other butchers, with a slightly receding hairline and a slightly expanding waistline. I judged him to be in his forties, probably just past the draft age.

After reading the note, he looked up with an amused smile. "So you're Gust's girl, eh?"

"He married my mother a couple months ago. I just met him last week."

"That's right. I heard about it." He glanced around at the crowded shop. "Hey, we're awfully busy right now. Could you come back in a half hour or so? I'd like to take you to lunch."

I thought the only thing to be picked up here was a pound of bacon. "Thanks, but I've had lunch," I lied.

He weighed out a generous pound, wrapped it, and handed it to me. "Too bad. Maybe we can get together later."

I got out of there so fast I forgot to give him the ration book, and he didn't ask for it. I had heard about friendly butchers, but this Sam carried it too far.

When I reached the house Gust greeted me at the door with a big smile. "Well, what do you think of him?"

"Think of who?"

"Sam."

I looked at my mother, then at Gust. "What's going on?"

Mom explained. "Gust thought Sam would make a good husband for you, so he wrote him a note."

"That's Greek way," Gust boasted. "I take care of daughter, find good husband. Sam own business, work hard. He need wife. He take good care of you. You don't have to worry."

I didn't know whether to protest violently or run like hell. Gust grinned. He seemed to be waiting for me to express some appreciation. My mother sat at the table, watching me carefully.

One more day, I thought. One more day and I'll be out of here. I hoped Gust wouldn't try something like this again in the next twenty-four hours.

I hung my trench coat near the stove to dry and asked, "Is there any coffee?"

My mother answered, "Yes, there's plenty. The Bordens next door don't drink coffee, so they give us their rations. She doesn't believe in reading coffee grounds either."

She filled my cup and added a rounded spoonful of the grounds, as she always had when she was going to tell my fortune. "Remember, when you finish, to drink the last drop so there won't be any tears."

Gust laughed. "Maybe we find husband for Inga in the coffee cup."

My mother went right along with it. Taking my cup she said, "When I was your age I had already been married a year, and I was pregnant with Lloyd."

She searched my cup. "I see a disappointment very soon, but don't worry. It will work out all right." She gave it a turn. "Otherwise, everything looks clear."

"Do you see husband for her in there?"

She studied the cup again. "She hasn't met him yet."

"Well," he said, "we keep looking."

Later, when I mentioned that I would be leaving the following evening, Gust said, "I go with you to station, take care of you."

I had survived without a father for ten years, and had taken care of both my mother and myself. I didn't need this. "Pelly's husband wants to meet me, so I agreed to have dinner with them in town before we leave."

Knowing this man believed a woman incapable of boarding a train by herself I added, "He will see that we get off all right. You won't have to worry about me."

The next afternoon, when my mother sent me to the store for bread, I called Cliff. He was leaving soon to start loading his truck. Everything was going according to plan.

*   *   *

CHAPTER 29.
CLIFF HANGERS

It was hard to say good-bye to my mother. She seemed content in her new life, but I knew I could never be a part of it. She couldn't know why I hugged her for so long.

Gust insisted on accompanying me to town, but he left after he met Jeff, knowing I would be "taken care of."

Pellier and her husband had arrived at Ireland's ahead of me. Jeff was a likeable Army sergeant of average height, and slim. He seemed serious as he motioned me to the empty seat across from him.

"I told Sally I wanted to meet you," he began, watching me thoughtfully, "because I needed to ask you to promise me you'll take care of her for me. Would you do that?"

Here was another man who thought a woman couldn't take care of herself. What role was I to play? Nursemaid? Chaperone? But he was about to ship out, and he wanted some reassurance that he was leaving his bride in good company.

I glanced at Pellier. She shrugged.

"Well?" he asked.

"Sure, Jeff."

I looked at my menu. "The chicken here is excellent."

The three of us were on the northwest corner of Front and Glisan well before 2100, waiting for Cliff. We were still there, waiting, at 2200. Jeff called Cliff's number. There was no answer. By 2230 it was beginning to rain. We gave up and headed for the depot.

There were no more trains to Los Angeles that evening. The

next one, leaving in the morning, was scheduled to arrive in Los Angeles just two hours before midnight on Christmas Eve.

"I still have our room," said Jeff. "You two take it, and I'll catch a bus to the base."

He didn't have to go back to the base that night. There was a last minute cancellation at the hotel and I grabbed it. The clerk said, "It's a double bed. You'll have to register as two."

Using my first and second names I registered and paid for both Inga and Violet Fredriksen.

Some champagne was left from the wedding. I went with them to their room and helped finish it off. After Jeff filled our glasses, Pellier loosened her tie, rolled up her sleeves, kicked off her shoes, and climbed up to stand on the bed. Lifting her glass, she toasted, "To Cliff. Toujours gai! Toujours gai! Toujours gai!"

Jeff frowned. Her French side was showing. He got out his camera to take our picture. Pellier borrowed one of Jeff's cigarettes for effect, and again, repeated the toast.

We drank to Cliff until the champagne ran out. Then I left a wake-up call at the desk and went to my room. Alone in my bed, I thought of what my mother had seen for me in the coffee grounds. "A disappointment very soon, but don't worry. It will work out all right."

She was certainly right about the disappointment. I never knew her to be wrong, but the rest of her prophecy seemed unlikely. Trains never ran on schedule anymore.

Jeff had to leave early for his base the next morning so Pellier and I found our way to the station on our own. No doubt that would have worried Gust, had he known.

The trip to Los Angeles was uneventful. The sun came out about the time we hit California and Pellier approached the state with her usual intellectual curiosity.

We made friends with the servicemen seated around us. Pellier got into a bridge game with a group of soldiers across the aisle and I played pinochle with some sailors seated further back.

It was difficult to relax on the train, knowing that when we hit

Los Angeles, finding our way to the base would be chaotic. A soldier who was stationed near El Toro was of some help. He said, "What you need is a Santa Ana red car."

We pulled into the Los Angeles station a little after 2230. I took off to inquire about the red car while Pellier searched for a nickel to call and report we would be late.

When I spotted a military bus with EL TORO MARINE CORPS AIR STATION engraved across the side, I didn't know whether to approach the driver or make a run for Pellier. I headed for the bus. As I drew near the door opened, and a deep voice called from inside, "Going to El Toro?"

"YES!"

"Hop in."

It seemed too good to be true. "Could you wait while I get my buddy? She's over there in that phone booth."

"Hop in."

He drove the bus up close to her. When he opened the door I yelled, "Pelly, get aboard!"

She hung up, grabbed her suitcase, and joined me.

We passed through the gate at 2350. Five minutes later we were in our barracks reporting to Sgt. Fredrickson, (no relation,) the NCO on duty.

"I was concerned for you two," she said, "but you made it with five minutes to spare. Now you have a twenty-four hour liberty. "Merry Christmas."

*   *   *

Sadie and Gust

"Toujours gai!"
22 December 1944

Freddy and Gust

CHAPTER 30.
CHRISTMAS DAY 1944

Pellier woke me up with "Merry Christmas, Freddy!"

We had made our beds quickly in darkness the night before. Now we could get a better look at our new home. We were on top deck by the window, and I had the upper bunk.

It was quiet. We seemed to be alone in the squad room. Evidently everyone else had arrived early enough the day before to check in, make their beds, and take off on liberty. None of the bunks had been slept in.

We had more room here than at Norman. The bunks were still separated into bays by lockers, as in Norman, but now there were only two double bunks to each bay instead of three, with more space between the bunks and the lockers. A dresser stood in the center between the two double lockers. It had a mirror and four large drawers, one for each of us. With so much luxury I could learn to love this place.

I jumped down and went to the window. There wasn't much out there but sand and a few young trees. The buildings were beige stucco, of recent construction. "What a beautiful, clear day!" said Pellier. "That must be Mt. Baldy to the north."

I had never heard of Mt. Baldy, and had no idea which way was north, but I did know a clear blue sky when I saw one. "It's too nice to waste," I said. "Let's grab a quick breakfast and take off."

The chow hall was nearby, and it had a juke box. I dropped a nickel and the Andrews Sisters sang "Rum and Coca Cola."

This place had class.

As we took our trays a mess girl called, "Bacon, ham or sausage, and how do you want your eggs?"

"We have a choice?" I asked. "No beans?"

"Beans for breakfast? You must have just come in from Oklahoma. You're in the Marine Corps now, not the Navy. How do you want your eggs?" It was a nice change.

Over sausage and two eggs sunnyside, I asked Pellier, "What can we do today that's within our budget?"

"We could visit the UCLA campus. I hear it's lovely."

The price was right, and I had always wanted to explore higher learning.

We asked a corporal at the desk for directions. "Go out past the gate and look for the signs. Stand behind the one that says LA. Drivers going to Los Angeles will pick you up."

I asked, "Isn't that hitch-hiking?"

"Everybody does it here. If the line is too long, there's a military bus that leaves the gate about every 15 minutes for Santa Ana. You can catch a red car into LA from there."

As we were leaving, a florist arrived with a huge bouquet of roses. The NCO looked at the tag. "They're for a Callahan," she said. "It's from some lieutenant. The note says, Thank you for packing my parachute. It opened."

"Callahan? She was in my platoon in boot camp!"

I was elated. Not only had she freed one Marine to fight, but she had also saved the life of another.

We stood behind the LA sign for a while. It was a warm, still day. Nothing stirred, not even the leaves in the bean fields across the road. We soon realized that everyone with a car had already left. When the military bus came, we climbed aboard.

Later, on the red car, Pellier approached an old timer and asked directions to the University. "Now, there's a USO in Pershing Square," he said. "I can show you exactly where it is, because I transfer there to go to my daughter's. They have all kinds of information on what to see in Los Angeles. They can tell you how to get there.

"And say, if you get hungry, there's an interesting place to eat just a block down on Olive. It's called Clifton's Cafeteria. It has grass huts, waterfalls, and a ceiling of flowers made of neon lights. Makes you feel like you're in the South Pacific."

"Thank you," Pellier answered. "It sounds like a memorable place to have our Christmas dinner."

When we entered the USO, two mature women were talking to a lady at the desk. We went to the other end of the counter and began looking over the display of possibilities. We could take a bus out to Hollywood and actually stand on the corner of Hollywood and Vine. I wished I had brought my Brownie box camera.

The lady at the desk came over to talk to us. "Looking for something to do today?"

Her expression supported a determined smile and there was something in the tone of her voice that made me suspect she already had plans for us.

Pellier answered, "We just came in last night. We don't have much money, so we thought we might . . ."

"Of course. I have just the thing." She motioned toward the two women at the other end of the counter. "These ladies want to invite you to their home, to have Christmas dinner with them."

"Well, that would be very nice," I said, "but we planned to eat at Clifton's Cafeteria later. Right now we want to see some of the city."

"Yes," Pellier added. "We just came in for directions to the University. I hear their campus is charming."

"Nonsense! You can't eat in a cafeteria on Christmas Day. You must have a nice home cooked meal. Now, these ladies will be delighted to have you. They'll bring you to their home for a holiday feast. Later when you're ready to leave they'll take you wherever you want to go."

She motioned for them to come and join us. "They don't want to impose on you," she said, "but I told them you'd be happy to . . ."

"Oh my yes," said the taller one with the purple feather in her hat. "We must have you for dinner."

She turned to the smaller woman at her side and they had a secret chuckle. The other explained, "Marvie made us promise we'd bring back a service woman this time. We had a service man for Thanksgiving, and he didn't take much interest in Marvie."

Both ladies appeared to be post-menopausal. This little Marvie, I thought, must be a grandson to one of them. Expensively dressed, they looked enough alike to be sisters. Each carried a few extra pounds and had concealed the natural color of both their skin and hair.

"Won't Marvie be surprised," said the taller one, "when we bring back TWO servicewomen?"

Pellier shook her head in a last futile attempt. "That's very nice of you, but we've already made other plans. We just came in for directions to the UCLA campus."

The volunteer looked disappointed. "These ladies have been here for almost an hour," she said. "They promised Marvie they'd have a servicewoman to Christmas dinner, and they can't go back now without one."

She looked around and sighed. "The streets are almost empty. It doesn't look like anyone else is going to show up. Would you go with them, for Marvie?"

Pellier whispered to me, "I'm a sucker for little kids, especially at Christmas time."

So was I. We agreed to go.

Their car was one of the last Packards made before the war. We climbed into the back seat. It was roomy and comfortable.

"I'm Maude Norvelle," said the larger woman behind the wheel. "And this is my sister, Agatha Chester."

"Please call us Maude and Agatha," said the other.

I introduced myself and then my buddy. "This is Sally Pellier."

She corrected me. "It's Benson now. Thursday we will have been married two weeks."

Maude shook her head and looked at Agatha. "We've got two of 'em all right, but one of 'em's married."

I wondered why that was important.

The house was in a neighborhood that looked like a Hollywood movie set. It was Spanish style white stucco with a red tile roof. Three live palm trees stood tall in front, and against the house a row of bright red poinsettias were growing right out of the ground instead of from pots. I noticed there were two blue stars in the window.

Maude turned off the ignition. "Well here we are. I wonder how Gert's doing. We've left her alone with those two for quite a while."

"But most of the work was done," Agatha assured her. "She could manage." Turning to us she added, "Gert is our sister. This is her place, and she's having our Aunt Bessie down from the home in Santa Barbara. Aunt Bessie can be . . ." She paused and giggled, "quite a problem. But we love her. She's really a dear."

Maude opened the door and entered without knocking. "Yoo hoo, we're back."

Agatha stepped aside, insisting I go in next.

A woman came out of the kitchen to greet us. She was as tall as Maude, but thinner, and her face had a freshly scrubbed look. Her graying hair had probably been carefully combed earlier, but now it looked disheveled. She wiped a hand on her apron before extending it to me.

"I'm Gert," she said, "Gert Van Tassle. And this," she motioned to a tall, quiet young man standing beside her, "is my nephew, Maude's son Marvin."

So this was Marvie, the child we couldn't disappoint at Christmas. The kid must have seen at least twenty holiday seasons, and appeared to have weathered them well. He stood beside his Aunt Gert and nodded a half smile.

"Marvie, this is Inga Fredriksen," his mother said. He nodded again. "And this," she paused. "What is your married name again, dear?"

"Sally Benson, but I think I'll continue to use my maiden name, Pellier, as long as I'm in the service."

"Yes. Anyway, she's married."

It seemed to make little difference to Marvie.

A bedroom door opened and a plump white haired lady a couple inches shorter than Agatha appeared in a red velvet dress that trailed to the floor. "Haloo, haloo," she called. "Merry Christmas, everybody!"

"Aunt Bessie," Maude started toward her, "I wondered where you were." She bent down and hugged her.

Aunt Bessie adjusted her glasses. "I've just had my hair marcelled. Don't mess it up."

Gert shook her head and whispered to Agatha. "She hasn't been out of the house."

Agatha smiled at Bessie. "Your hair looks real nice."

Bessie boasted, "Landon and I are going to the Governor's ball this evening."

Taking us aside, Agatha explained, "Landon was her husband. He's been dead twenty years, but we can't tell her that. He was a gardener at the capital up in Sacramento."

Marvie went to a back room to throw darts. I suspect he had requested they invite a servicewoman instead of a man in the hope that she would be less intimidating.

Maude removed her hat, stroked the long purple feather, and placed it on top of the piano, near the dining room. Then she left to help Gert and Agatha in the kitchen. They would have to set another place at the table.

Aunt Bessie entertained us, talking incessantly of Landon, while Maude and Agatha brought out the food. Then Maude left to call Marvie.

Maude took her place at one end of the table to carve and motioned Marvie and me to either side of her. My attempts to draw him into conversation were futile. He was a quiet boy.

"Of course, Marvie was called to serve," Maude began, as she sliced the ham, "but they didn't take him." She put back a lock of hair that had fallen to his forehead. "I got a note from our family doctor for him to take along to the draft board. He has so much trouble with his sinus."

Marvie whipped out a clean handkerchief and attempted to blow his nose. It was dry. Evidently he was having a good day.

"He's continuing his education now." She turned to him. "Aren't you, dear?"

He nodded. "Third year at USC."

Agatha said, "Gert has two boys in the war. One's a sergeant, with the Army in Europe, and the other's in the Navy. He's out in the Pacific somewhere."

That explained the two stars in the window.

Before we finished filling our plates, Aunt Bessie burst out in song. "Love me and the world is mine," she began, stopping any further conversation. Her next number was "My Mother's Eyes." She had started on "Paddlin' Madelin' Home" when Gert reminded her that her dinner was getting cold. By then Marvie had finished eating, excused himself, and left to throw more darts.

Bessie looked at her food for the first time. Gert and Agatha kept her eating until she emptied her plate.

"There," she said, "I ate it all, and I didn't spill a bit on my new dress." She turned to confide in Pellier, "Landon loves this dress.

"Now I'll play the piano and we can all sing."

"Yes," said Agatha. "You girls go on out and sing with Bessie. The three of us can clean this up."

I would rather wash the dishes.

Bessie did fairly well on the piano, considering her advanced years, but the only song we all knew was "Jingle Bells." We sang that until all the dishes were put away.

Gert emerged from the kitchen first, wiping her hands on a towel. "We haven't opened all of the presents yet. There's still a few left under the tree."

Maude went back to get Marvie while Gert and Agatha sorted through the remaining gifts. There was a package for Pellier and me to share, addressed to "Guest Serviceman." It was a carton of Chesterfields. Cigarettes were difficult for civilians to find. We thanked them for their thoughtfulness. They didn't seem to notice that neither of us smoked.

The largest gift was from Gert to Aunt Bessie. She took the red ribbon off and tied it in her hair some way. When she opened the box she gasped, "Oh, my! Oh my!" She held up a handmade white bed jacket, quilted with red hearts embroidered around the bottom and up the front. She acted like the Queen of England had sent her the crown.

"Oh my," She repeated, slipping it on over the red velvet dress. She took Maude's hat from the piano top and set it on her head so that the purple feather went off at a rakish angle. Then, after posing a moment, she burst out in song. "I'll take you home again, Kathleen . . ." As she sang, she did a fancy little two-step right out the front door.

She was heading for the street. Gert called, "We can't let her go out there alone!"

She took off after her, with Maude and Agatha close behind. Marvie went back to his darts.

I looked at Pellier. We grabbed our hats and followed them out. Bessie was making good time up the street, with the red bow dangling to about the middle of the bed jacket. She turned right at the corner, on to a main boulevard, still singing and enjoying herself thoroughly.

We tried to stay close enough to help if we were needed, while keeping sufficient distance to attempt some semblance of military manner.

It turned out Aunt Bessie didn't need any help. They let her dance completely around the block, trailed by her unique group of followers, as she sang one old favorite after another. She was starting on "When You and I Were Young, Maggie," as we arrived back at the house.

Gert was determined to cut her off before she started around the block again. She got in front of her and stopped, bringing the whole platoon to a halt.

"Aunt Bessie, I baked you a pumpkin pie."

"Oh, that's my very favorite."

Forgetting to finish the song, Aunt Bessie turned and followed her into the house. As soon as we were inside, Gert locked all the doors. "They warned me at the home she might do this."

While they were cutting the pie, Aunt Bessie disappeared. "She has to be in the house somewhere," said Gert. She left to search the back rooms and found her asleep on one of the beds.

She called to us, "Come look at this."

The hat was set off center now, causing the feather to tremble each time she exhaled. "She's tuckered out, said Gert. We'd best let her sleep."

Pellier and I left soon after we finished the pie. We were back at the base before dark. The same corporal was still at the desk. She asked, "Are either of you Benson or Fredriksen?"

"Right on both counts," said Pellier.

"Well, there's been several long distance calls for you from a man up in Portland, Oregon. He said his name is Cliff."

"Cliff!" we exclaimed in unison.

"Yes, that was his name. He said to tell you he broke his arm while he was loading the truck. Does that message mean anything to you?"

"Yes, thank you," I said. "It means a lot to us."

* * *

CHAPTER 31.
PAPIER-MACHE IN THE ATTIC

As WRs drifted in off liberty, our squad room took on the look of a class 52 reunion. Pellier and I shared the first bay on the left with Ward and Tierney. Kilgallen and Lawson were in the next bay with Roth and her buddy Sattler. Our class filled the entire squad room.

We were all together again except for Erickson, True, and Jeter. Having arrived a month earlier, they had been billeted in another barracks. Erickson, now a corporal, was secretary to the base commander. Jeter made PFC. She was driving a motor scooter as messenger out of the same office. I heard True was working in the control tower.

Our arrival was premature. The hangars we would work in were still under construction. Sgt. Fredrickson gathered us all in the upstairs lounge to discuss work details. I sat on the floor between Lawson and Kilgallen to listen.

"We need some volunteers to be cooks," she began. "They will be trained in our galley for permanent job placement, and housed separately, due to shift work."

Lumpkin was first to volunteer. I thought I would rather pick up cigarette butts.

She moved on down the list, asking for typists and general office workers. Finally she said, "They can use three people in the art department, and the rest of you can police the area, or take a month of mess duty."

Kilgallen, Lawson and I threw our arms up in unison.

"Okay, you three report to the theater attic at 0800 tomorrow."

I asked, "Can we wear dungarees?"

"You'll need dungarees in the attic."

She made a face. It couldn't be that bad.

Kilgallen was ecstatic. "I am a poet, a dreamer, and an artist," she said. "They should have put me in the art department in the first place. I've wasted a lot of time scrubbing grease from under my fingernails." She held up her hands, as a surgeon would after scrubbing. "These are the hands of an artist!"

The theater was easy to find, but the door to the stairway was closed and unmarked. It creaked ominously when Lawson opened it. The stairs were narrow and dark. I found a switch and turned on the light.

Reaching the top, I saw that the attic only went across the front end of the building. There was a projection booth in the center, with the art department to one side of it.

The walls were lined with drawers, and two long work tables ran the length of the room. A file cabinet stood in the corner, and a utility tub on one side held brushes soaking in cans of water. But where was the paper?

The room looked like it hadn't stood inspection since it was built. I wondered if anyone even knew it was here.

An NCO came up the stairs behind us. "I'm Sgt. Baker," she said. "I'm in charge of the art department."

She looked a bit older than Kilgallen and shorter, stockier. Her brown hair, beginning to gray at the temples, was swept back in a bun.

"I taught art to eighth graders for five years," she went on. "I have a bachelor's degree in art."

Kilgallen topped that. "I taught art in high school for six years, and I have a master's degree in art."

Sgt. Baker changed the subject quickly. "Well, let's get started. We have a lot of posters to do. Kay Kyser will be here next week, and then Bing Crosby."

While she was removing poster board from a drawer, two more WRs came in. I learned that Paula, the tall, slim, blonde corporal, had worked in New York as a commercial artist. Punchy, a shorter, pleasant looking brunette PFC, had drawn cartoons for a greeting card company. I was out of my league.

While conditions there were crude, the quality of work was not. Paula was good, and she was fast. I would learn a lot from her. Punchy had a habit of doodling when she was thinking. She filled scraps of paper with cartoons of Women Marines in humorous situations, leaving them scattered about on the tables. I admired them, and wished I could do as well.

Kilgallen always took time to add a bit of flair to her work, giving it a touch of class. Her posters would often show ornate detail around the edges, causing Sgt. Baker to urge her to "finish up," reminding her of the volume of work still to be done.

Kilgallen tolerated these interruptions, but she would not be rushed. Sgt. Baker may have the stripes, but she had the master's degree. "She's just a harmless character," Kilgallen once said of her. "One of those people who never do any harm, but they never do any good, either."

Shortly after we started work in the attic, Sgt. Baker had a request from an officer for a large eagle, globe, and anchor.

"This will be a dirty job, but somebody has to do it. Any of you had any experience with papier-mache?"

I loved working with it. "Yes, I have."

Kilgallen remembered my scarecrow she had seen in the bakery window in Oak Park. "Freddy's good at it."

I got the job. I collected all the old newspapers and flour I needed from the mess hall. In the squad room I begged for wire coat hangers and the recreation department donated an old basketball for the globe.

By 0800 the next morning I had it all there, ready to start. First I crafted a solid wire base, twisting it up around the ball and shaping it.

Then the fun began. Tearing newspaper into narrow strips, I

mixed it with a flour and water paste until it could be easily shaped. I covered the ball and wire with it, and smoothed it out. With more wire, using my dress hat emblem as a model, I shaped an eagle and an anchor, encasing them in the mixture as well.

We were beginning to clean up for the day when Sgt. Baker reminded us, "Make sure you put all of your work, and all of the paper, away in a drawer before you leave."

"This won't fit in a drawer," I said.

She pursed her lips. "All paper must be put away at the end of every day." The sergeant, handling both pieces carefully, put them away in empty file drawers. I saw no reason for that. It would dry better on the table.

The surface was still damp the next morning, but Sgt. Baker was in a hurry. I would have to paint them. Using show card colors I mixed a good blue for the oceans and various shades of brown and green for the land, with an icy blue-white at the poles. Lawson suggested I put a spot of dusty pink about where Oklahoma's red dirt would be, and we had our little inside joke.

My eagle was handsome. I painted him, and the anchor, the next day, and left them overnight in a file drawer. The next morning I affixed the eagle to fly high on the globe, and wired the anchor, now battleship gray, across the back. It stood solidly on the table. By Monday it would be dry, ready to varnish.

Sgt. Baker had left early for a dental appointment. Paula and Punchy cleaned up and were gone too, but Kilgallen and Lawson stayed with me while I looked for a place to store my work. With the eagle and anchor attached to the globe, it wouldn't fit in the filing cabinet. "Why can't I just leave it out on the table? It should dry better there."

"Sgt. Baker can't object to that," said Kilgallen. "There isn't any other place for it. Anyway, I think it's asinine to put it all away every night. It just has to be taken out again the next morning."

We left it on the table.

By Monday morning I was anxious to finish the job. Kilgallen and Lawson dawdled, so I went on without them.

I was second to arrive at the attic. Sgt. Baker was first, and she was furious. She stood at the top of the stairs, wringing her hands and shouting down at me, "You disobeyed my order!"

There was a good reason. I tried to explain.

"It's ruined! Eagle, globe, and anchor, all ruined!"

How could that be? I looked. She was right. There was nothing left but bare wire, a deflated basketball, and bits of mache dangling here and there.

"What happened?"

"Rats! That's what happened. RATS!"

"You mean there's rats up here?"

"They're all over this building. Why do you think I insisted that you put your work away every night?"

By now the rest of the crew had arrived. They gathered around the table, staring quietly at the remains. Sgt. Baker firmed her jaw and glanced around the room at us.

"Any of you had any experience with clay?"

*   *   *

CHAPTER 32.
FRATERNIZING

Pellier and I were starting back to the base after a weekend in Los Angeles. While we waited for a red car, she noticed some stuffed animals being sold on the sidewalk. A life-size cat with long white hair caught her eye.

"Freddy," she said, "last week they told us we could have stuffed animals on our bunks. Isn't that cat adorable? He looks like he's curled up on someone's lap."

A little later he was curled up on her lap for the ride to Santa Ana. A Marine pilot passing by noticed the cat. "That's some mascot you have there," he said.

Pellier turned and gave him her enchanting smile. "I just picked him up. He needs a name. Do you have any suggestions?"

He took the aisle seat behind me and bent forward. I sensed that it wasn't the cat he was interested in. Remembering my promise to Pellier's husband that I would take care of her for him, I checked to make sure she was wearing her wedding ring. It was there, a plain gold regulation band. Surely he had noticed.

Not wanting to get caught talking to an officer, I decided to stay out of it. I ignored them both. Reaching for my bus schedule, I gave it my full attention and hoped he would soon lose interest.

I heard my name. "And this is Freddy."

Then louder, "Freddy?"

I looked up.

"This is Lt. Mike Casey." She turned to him. "And this is my buddy, Inga Fredriksen."

The officer had a friendly smile and he appeared to be a gentleman. Probably a cat lover. I relaxed. They talked during the entire trip, while I memorized the time table.

When we reached Santa Ana a military bus was waiting. It was more than half full and all the window seats were taken, so Pellier and I took separate aisle seats. Lt. Casey didn't sit down, though there was still seating further back. Instead, he came to stand by me. "Pelly tells me you're from Portland," he said.

I was afraid to answer. "I am? I mean, she does?"

"I have an aunt who lives on Sandy Blvd. Do you know where that is?"

"Oh. Yes. The Sandy bus goes out there."

I couldn't talk to this man. I glanced up. He had reddish brown hair and a good face, spotted with freckles. In civilian clothes he would have been easy to talk to. But he was in uniform, and those gold bars on his shoulder were intimidating.

"I'm a farm boy from Nebraska. Ever hear of Red Cloud?"

I shook my head.

"That's all right. Hardly anybody has."

On the first turn, an inebriated Marine rolled over on me. When I pushed him back he woke up enough to realize he needed a cigarette. He managed to get one in his mouth and light a match, but he couldn't bring the two together. When the match burned down dangerously close to his fingers, I blew it out.

He gave me the matches. "Light thish fer me?"

My vigilance wouldn't end there. After I lit his cigarette, I had to protect him from burning a hole in his uniform or, worse yet, in mine. Keeping watch on him for the short trip back to the base relieved me of any further conversation with the lieutenant.

When we arrived at the base, the officer stepped to one side, allowing me to leave first. "You know," he said as I passed, "you'll make a good wife some day . . . for some old drunk!"

As Pellier and I walked toward our barracks, I noticed he was following us. When there was no one else within hearing, he spoke. "Freddy, may I call you?"

He called me two nights later, inviting me to dinner.

"How can we manage that?" I asked. "We can't even walk down the street together."

"I've been talking to the big boys," he said. "They told me how it's done. Meet me outside the gate at the Santa Ana bus stop Friday at 1800. Just act like you don't know me, and take a window seat."

When I told Kilgallen about it she was thrilled. "Freddy, you're going to fraternize? That's great!"

She was a lot more excited about the idea than I was. With visions of a deck court, I didn't have much hope of enjoying the evening. Nevertheless, Friday at 1800 I was standing at the bus stop in my last pair of nylons, wondering what I was getting myself into.

Lt. Mike Casey had arrived earlier. He fell in line behind me. When the bus came, he followed me in and took the seat beside me without comment.

I felt uneasy. This officer could get me in a lot of trouble. He wrote something around the edge of his bus schedule and handed it to me.

It read, "When we get out, follow me."

I followed him to the Greyhound bus station. He boarded a bus ahead of me, and paid for two to Balboa without looking back. He lingered in the aisle until I sat down, then slid in beside me. Before we left the station, a shore patrolman stuck his head in the door. By now the bus was full, mostly with military. He glanced around, and motioned the driver on.

After we were well on our way to Balboa I heard, "We can talk now. We just had to get out of Santa Ana. The Navy in Balboa will leave us alone. Relax."

I couldn't relax. I knew that he believed I'd be safe with him there. I just wasn't sure that I believed it. Breaking regulations was against my nature, and this time I couldn't blame it on Kilgallen.

"Do you like seafood?"

I remembered I was hungry. "I love it."

"Well, it's Friday, and one of the other pilots in my outfit told me about a place in Balboa that serves excellent abalone dinners. We'll go there."

I had never heard of abalone. It turned out to be a real treat. I was thoroughly enjoying the meal when a Navy shore patrolman entered the restaurant. There was no place to hide. He glanced around the room, looked straight at me, and smiled. Then, giving a nod, he left quietly.

Whew!

After dinner we went to a nice cocktail lounge where we danced and talked until late. I was able to relax and enjoy the evening. But when we boarded the bus to go back to Santa Ana, that uneasy feeling came back.

A week later we dared to attend a movie together. "The Keys of the Kingdom," with Gregory Peck, was playing at the Broadway in Santa Ana. We couldn't talk on the bus, and Mike walked several feet behind me to the theater.

Sitting beside him in the dark, I felt safer. We shared a box of popcorn and Mike put his arm around me. But after the movie there was no place where we could go to talk without being seen. He followed me back to the bus stop and later watched me walk alone to my barracks. We had spent an entire evening together without speaking to each other.

The next time Mike called, he invited me to go with him to visit his Aunt Rosie in Santa Monica. He assured me that the Los Angeles area was safe territory for fraternizing. "And bring your bathing suit," he added. "Aunt Rosie lives on the beach."

Saturday evening we enjoyed an elegant dinner at the Cocoa-nut Grove. Xavier Cugat's band was playing there. When we joined a conga line weaving among the tables, I suddenly came face to face with a WR officer sitting with a group of civilians. Lucky for me, she appeared not to notice that the officer behind me had his hands on my hips.

That evening I stayed at the Library Park Guest House. It was a temporary housing unit set up for servicewomen, in the park next to the downtown library.

Mike spent the night at his Aunt Rosie's.

The next morning he took me to Mass. I had never been inside a Catholic Church before. I didn't know how to act. "You don't have to do anything," he said. "Just sit there."

I sat, feeling rather conspicuous and odd. It didn't help when the priest began to speak in English. His message that morning was a warning to the young people against marrying outside the Church.

He must have seen us come in together.

The sun felt good as we left after the service, and we agreed that it was warm enough for a swim. I loved the ocean. We took a bus to his Aunt Rosie's. She was still at church when we arrived.

I went in the bathroom to change into my bathing suit. When I came out Mike was waiting in the hallway, trim in his red and white swim trunks. He had a couple of towels over his shoulder and a large bottle of sun tan oil in his hand. "Think we'll pass for a couple civilians?" he asked.

It was the first time I had ever felt completely comfortable with Mike. It was as if, by some magic, all of the military taboos had melted away. Is this how it feels to be a civilian? I couldn't remember.

We went to the back porch and sat on the steps overlooking the beach. Mike opened a bottle of sun tan oil and we shared it.

Somehow, the bottle caught on a towel. It fell to the cement deck and broke, spilling oil everywhere. He found some rags and tried to soak it up, but when we started off for the beach, we left some evidence behind.

We swam and built a sand castle, while Mike kept an eye on the house for a sign of his aunt's return. When he spotted her on the porch he said, "Aunt Rosie's home from church. We'd better get back."

She was waiting for us. A handsome, outspoken woman seeming to be in her early sixties, she eyed me critically. "Michael, what's the idea of robbing the cradle?"

"You mean that old bag? Aunt Rosie, she just turned twenty-three. She's six months older than I am."

Even after she saw my uniform folded on the bathroom hamper, she was still not convinced. "Well, she's awful skinny for twenty-three."

"Freddy's just a late bloomer," he said in my defense.

Later, as I tied my field scarf, I heard the teakettle whistle. Rosie called out, "Lunch is ready."

She had made tuna sandwiches using lettuce and sliced tomatoes from her victory garden. Rosie and Mike reminisced over lunch, sharing stories of the old days, back on the farm. But when we had finished eating she straightened up. Her face took on a stern expression.

"Now, Michael, I want to know something. Who butchered a hog on my back porch?"

Mike took all the blame. "I spilled that. I'm sorry. I tried to wipe it up."

"Reminds me of one time back home," she began. "You weren't mor'n eight or nine. Coming in from gathering eggs, you tripped on the top step." She turned to me. "You never saw such a mess of scrambled eggs in your life."

Then to Mike, "Be careful, Son, in those airplanes."

We stayed until quite late, knowing it might be their last visit together for a long time. The pilots at El Toro were shipping out fast. His orders could come any day.

Our next date was to be our last. It was Friday, and again we went to the seafood restaurant in Balboa. As we entered I recognized True sitting at a table with a Marine pilot. Mike called to him. "Field!" Then, to me, "He's the one who told me about this place."

"Casey! Why don't you join us?"

"Shall we?" Mike asked me.

"I'd like that," I said. "I didn't know True was dating an officer."

Mike seemed surprised at my remark. He took my hand and

led me to their table. I hadn't talked to True since she left Oklahoma right after graduation. I noticed she had made corporal.

As we joined them, the pilot beamed. "You're just in time to
help us celebrate. Martha and I have been married one week today."

I knew what that could mean. If they found out an enlisted
WR had married a Marine officer, he was sent overseas immediately. I asked, "Aren't you afraid you'll get caught?"

"If they ship me out," he said, "at least I know Martha will be
waiting for me when I get back."

Mike explained, "We're not avoiding combat duty. We want
to get out there and do what we've been trained to do so we can
get this war over with."

True nodded. "But Glenn hopes he can go over with his own
outfit, the men he's trained with. They're used to flying together.
They're like brothers."

I looked at these men with their gold wings, who were like
brothers, and wondered what the future held for them.

After dinner True and I made a trip to the head. I asked her,
"How could you keep this a secret? Nobody in our class has any
idea . . ."

"I couldn't take that chance."

"But Mike knew."

"Mike knows how important it is that the group stays together. Glenn knows he can trust him."

"You can trust me too," I said, knowing that if Kilgallen ever
learned of this she couldn't keep it to herself.

Soon after we rejoined the men, the honeymooners excused
themselves. Mike and I went again to the familiar cocktail lounge
to dance and talk until it was time to leave.

On the bus back to Santa Ana, Mike seemed at a loss for words.
That was unusual for him. Carefully, he began. "Our departure
could come at any time, of course. If I don't call you Wednesday
evening, you can know I'm gone."

I thought of Kilgallen and her prayers that her orders would be for El Toro. "Don't forget your rosary."

Mike did call Wednesday night. He called from a pay phone, and it was very brief. "I theenk I am not long for thees plaez," he began. Then, dropping the phony accent, he added, "Field hasn't been able to get through to Martha. He asked if you would tell her he tried. There's a line waiting for the phone. See you after the war."

"I'll tell her. Yes, see you after the war."

He hung up. The threat of a deck court that had been haunting me was over. In its place was a genuine, personal concern for the safety of a good friend who had gone off to fight in a terrible war.

I would miss him.

*   *   *

CHAPTER 33.
A REAL SKIRT WATCHER

Shortly before Mike shipped out, notice was posted of an impending review to take place early in February. We had a week to get ready. Having grown used to the more relaxed lifestyle here at El Toro, I couldn't get excited about another review.

A sergeant in the recreation department was assigned the job of whipping us into shape. She knew how to umpire a game, but her knowledge of drilling a platoon was limited. She didn't seem any more thrilled about it than we were.

Every afternoon she marched us to the parade ground, some distance from our barracks, to put us through the routine. It was on the job training for her. While she lacked Cpl. DiPalma's style and sense of authority, she was a good Marine and we tried to cooperate.

On the morning of the review, Pellier was first up. She raised the Venetian blind and looked out. "Freddy, did you hear the wind howling last night?"

I opened one eye. "No, but I sure hear it now."

"Come take a look."

A layer of sand several feet high was whipping across the base. It bent young trees almost to the ground and picked up everything loose in its path. I watched a mess girl lean into the wind, fighting her way to the chow hall, and a WR's hat flew by traveling faster than she could run to catch it.

"So this is what a Santa Ana is like," said Pellier.

"What's a Santa Ana?"

"It's a powerful wind that occasionally rushes in from the

Mohave Desert through the pass. It can become very destructive by the time it reaches this area." She smiled. "Well, that cancels the review."

It looked to me like it would cancel everything. It was going to take a lot of courage just to head for the chow hall. I kept a firm grip on my hat all the way to breakfast.

By the time I got back to the barracks, my hair was standing straight out, looking as if the wind was still blowing it. I would have to wash it, put it up, and hope to get the hair dryer before my date with Mike that evening.

Sgt. Fredrickson stuck her head in the squad room. "We're expecting a call any moment from headquarters canceling the review. Until it comes, just stand by."

I stood by on one foot, and then the other. I started a letter to my mother. The sergeant came in and reminded us again to "just stand by."

Roth went to the head for a smoke and Peters left to keep her company. I found the corked sprinkler top and fit it into my coke bottle. On my way to the laundry room to sprinkle a shirt to wear that evening, I heard the sergeant announce, "They haven't called yet. You'll have to start getting dressed."

"WHAT?"

"Until we receive a call that the review has been cancelled, you'll have to carry on as if you are going. Sorry."

I stuffed the shirt back into my ironing bag and reached for a pair of cotton lisle hose.

"Drat it!" said Tierney. "When are they going to get around to telling us it's cancelled? Back in Iowa we'd call this a real skirt watcher. We can't march in that."

"Oh, no?" said Roth. "We're Marines. We'll do what we're ordered to do."

"But surely they want it called off too," I reasoned, "because if it isn't, they'll have to go out there to watch us pass in review."

Sgt. Fredrickson interrupted. "No word yet. Keep dressing."

I was in full uniform, checking to make sure my eagles were flying high, when I heard her say "Fall out!"

"Fall out?" Tierney looked shocked. "Did I hear her right?"

Roth shrugged. "See? I told you."

Once outside, the wind hurried me along to the area where we would muster. We groped our way into some kind of platoon formation. I was third in line in the back row. I would march in the right squad.

Our drill sergeant went inside, hopeful of a last minute reprieve. When she came back out she said, "We have to go now."

The wind carried her voice away from us. I could hardly hear her order, "Platoon, attention . . . left face . . . forward, march." Then she added a command of her own. "Hang on to your hat!"

I got a firm grip on mine before we turned the corner and leaned into the wind. Abandoning the regulation step, I fought for every inch, blinded by sand blasting in my face.

I soon learned it wasn't just my hat I had to hang on to. My skirt kept blowing up around my hips, making me wish I were in the center squad. I clenched my hat with my left hand so I could hold my skirt down on the outside. It wasn't working. I could have used another hand.

By now several other women's platoons had joined us. Our group was somewhere in the middle. With the wind tossing us about unmercifully, it was impossible to maintain our lines.

The sergeant marched abreast of our squad leader. She appeared to be shouting, but I could hardly hear what she was saying. Not that it mattered. We couldn't keep cadence anyway.

We moved out of the women's area and managed to get past the theater. When we reached the Bachelor Officer's Quarters, on my right, I imagined Mike, relaxing inside with his pipe and a good book. How nice for him.

As we left the buildings behind and headed for the open parade ground, the winds became even stronger. After what seemed an endless struggle, I heard "Platoon halt." We had arrived.

But where was everybody? Except for the other platoons of

WRs, the grounds were deserted. So was the reviewing stand, and the band hadn't even shown up.

Our sergeant seemed at a loss to know what to do next. She talked to the other platoon leaders and we waited.. and waited.. and waited. Still, there was not a man in sight.

The leaders deliberated for some time before deciding to return to the barracks. Then it was hard to keep from running. The wind, now coming from behind, hurried us along.

As soon as I reached the squad room I flopped on Pellier's bed, exhausted. Taking the mirror from my purse, I folded a clean handkerchief into a sharp point and began picking sand out of my eyes.

Kilgallen passed by on her way to the office. She was mumbling, "I have to find out what's going on."

She soon returned shaking her head. "How asinine! How totally asinine! The reason we were not told the review had been cancelled was because the order that came down from headquarters said only to notify all MEN!"

Somehow, she managed a smile. "Well, anyway, I have another great chapter for my book. I'm going to call it 'From The Boudoirs Of Montezuma!'"

That evening, after Mike and I reached Balboa where we could talk, I found out what he had been doing while I was struggling past the BOQ. "You ladies really put on a show for us today."

"You were watching us?"

"You paraded right past my window. You didn't think I was going to look the other way, did you?"

"Well, at least you couldn't recognize me."

"Right squad, third from front. Oh, and Field wants to know where you got that pink slip."

*   *   *

Freddy, Ward, and Roth at home in the upstairs lounge

Roth and Tierney wait for El Toro bus at Mary's-home of the best hamburgers in the world

Sattler and the red car

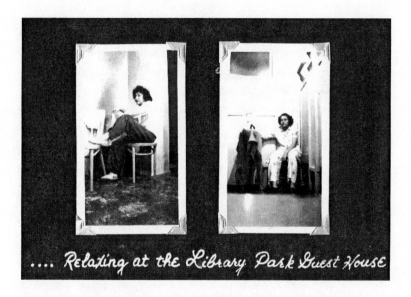

.... Relaxing at the Library Park Guest House

Left: Peters dries her things over the heater
Right: Loeffler waits while the iron heats up

CHAPTER 34.
JETER AND THE GOVERNOR

When Erickson came to our barracks to visit with Peters, I often enjoyed listening to her tales of what was happening in the office of the base commander. My favorite was the story of Jeter's adventures with the governor.

It seems that Jeter enjoyed the freedom of her job as messenger out of the office, but she soon became impatient with a governor that had been installed to limit the speed of her motor scooter. Even when she pressed her foot to the floorboard, it would not go faster than the speed limit which, on a military base, was fifteen miles an hour.

Jeter had remarked, "I c'd run faster 'n that!"

She located the device and adjusted it up to twenty.

"Folks'll never notice," she said.

And they didn't.

But that was still too slow for her. "Golly, I c'd run it up to twenty-five, and nobody'd say anything, not with the base commander's insignia on it."

Erickson laughed. "Now she's going ten miles over the speed limit. I wonder how long she'll get away with it."

Still, she was not satisfied. She raised it once more, pushing it up to thirty, "Just in case I'm ever in a hurry."

And Jeter was always in a hurry.

Lawson and I saw her whiz by one morning on our way to the theater. We waved, but she was going so fast she didn't see us.

"She'd better be careful," said Lawson.

Getting around the base at such speed left Jeter time to pursue other interests. She was curious to know what was going on at the Officer's Club. Upon investigating, she learned that doughnuts were delivered there every morning, and placed on a counter near the back door.

She figured if she stayed low, out of sight, she could crawl to them, reach up, and grab a couple without being seen. It soon became a part of her daily routine. She would bring her hand up quickly to snatch one, wrap it in one of the sheets of waxed paper stored under the counter, and slip it in her pocket before grabbing another for Erickson.

With both doughnuts tucked safely out of sight, she left quietly the same way she came in, on her hands and knees.

Very early in her game an officer had reached for a doughnut, only to see a hand come up from behind the counter and snatch it away. Curious, he stalked the interloper, and Jeter had been discovered.

Instead of reporting the theft, he shared the story with fellow officers and they gathered every morning to watch. Word got back to the secretary of the base commander. "No wonder Jeter won't let me pay for the doughnut," said Erickson. "She's been stealing it!"

Early one day in March, a surprise encounter brought an abrupt end to the officers' entertainment. It had rained heavily throughout the night, but the sky was clear as Jeter started off on her rounds that morning. She quickly delivered all but one large manila envelope. It was to be taken to hangar A, at the ABG-2 construction site. She decided to stop by the Officers Club to pick up her doughnuts before making that trip.

The officers were already gathered inside, exchanging small talk while they awaited her arrival. The door opened slowly and they heard the familiar swish of dungarees, brushing against the cement deck. Reaching up, her nimble fingers snatched the first doughnut. She wrapped it quickly and slipped it in her pocket. But when she reached for another, a frightened mouse scampered out from the shelf below.

Jeter screamed and jumped up, in full view of the officers. They burst out in loud, unmerciful laughter.

She hadn't planned on getting caught. Bolting out the door, she mounted her scooter and pushed the gas pedal to the floor.

Speeding down an incline, she made a sharp turn to the right, barely making the bridge. Then, veering to the left, she overshot, diving off the other side into a deep drainage ditch. The water was high enough that morning that it buried the scooter.

Jeter struggled to her feet and searched frantically in the murky water until she found the envelope. She tossed it on high ground. Then, turning her attention to the scooter, she tried repeatedly to dislodge it, but it wouldn't budge.

The officers, having followed her outside, were now lined up on the bank, obviously enjoying her misfortune. Ignoring them, she pulled the soggy doughnut from her pocket, removed the wax paper, and cast it to the birds nearby.

A group of enlisted men were gathered along the other side of the ditch now, amused. To Jeter they seemed less threatening than the officers. They hadn't caught her stealing doughnuts, and she wouldn't have to salute them.

She turned to them and tried to appear helpless. "Hey, you guys," she called, "how about y'all givin' me a hand?"

*   *   *

CHAPTER 35.
DANCING AT THE
HOLLYWOOD CANTEEN

Los Angeles went all out to entertain the GIs stationed in the area during World War II. We could pick up free tickets at the USO in Pershing Square for many of the top shows in town.

Some even put on matinee performances on Sunday afternoon just for us. Pellier and I often attended these. We saw "Ken Murray's Blackouts" at the El Capitan, "The Drunkard" playing at The Theater Mart, and an indecent play that was embarrassing to me called "Maid in the Ozarks" at the Belasco Theater.

We found a two-story house in an older part of Hollywood that was available to servicewomen every Saturday night. All the rooms upstairs had been converted into dormitories and filled with cots. Fifty cents got us two clean sheets, a pillowcase, and all the coffee we could drink Sunday morning.

Two gentlemen managed it. Andy, the older, was white haired, round and jolly. Rex was young, a college student who had not been drafted because of an earlier crippling attack of polio. They both made us feel welcome, and they never came upstairs when women were present.

A kitchen just a block away served a complete breakfast to military every Sunday. There was a kitty for donations, but it was largely supported by the community. I suspect housing was available nearby for the servicemen also, as many had breakfast there.

The second time we stayed in Hollywood, Pellier decided to

skip breakfast and just have coffee downstairs. I was hungry so I started off down the street alone.

Nearing the kitchen I noticed a Marine approaching from the opposite direction, with a young civilian girl clinging to his arm. When I moved over to make room for them, the Marine pointed his index fingers in front of him, like a kid pretending they were guns. As I passed he shouted, "BAM! BAM! BAM!"

The girl giggled. Evidently she was familiar with the term. Outwardly, I ignored them, but the feelings of hurt and anger churning inside me would not be denied. By the time I reached the kitchen, I was too upset to eat.

I took a cup of coffee, dropped a dime in the kitty, and sat down at an empty table to lick my wounds. A couple Marines came by and asked if they could join me.

"Sure."

Sipping coffee as we talked, I was beginning to feel better when one asked, "Hey, are you in town by yourself?"

"No. My buddy wasn't hungry so I left her at the house."

"I thought so," said the other. "You BAMs always travel in pairs."

There was that word again. Now I was furious. Raising my cup, I poured what was left of the coffee over his bacon, hash browns, and two eggs sunny side. He would have had it in his lap if I didn't have so much respect for the uniform.

I thought that might be a good time to leave.

Finding Pellier seated alone at the kitchen table, I let my anger fly. "Those bastards!" I shouted. "Those bastards!"

"Pretty strong language, coming from you," she replied with her usual serenity.

"Chici is right. All men are bastards, Pelly, and right now I wouldn't care if I never met another one."

She poured me a cup of coffee and added the cream, letting me ramble on. "I'm starting a club," I said finally. "We'll call it the All Men Are Bastards Club, and any WR who's disgusted with the way men treat us can join. Instead of going out with them so they can insult us, we'll just sit in the head at night and talk about 'em."

"All men are not bastards, Freddy. There are still plenty of decent men around who are not insulting."

"Sure, but they're all married. Pelly, I think you got the last one."

But I couldn't nurse my anger forever. It was time to get on with the day. Pellier searched her purse. "Here's our tickets for Ken Murray's Blackouts this afternoon. After that, how about taking a look at the Hollywood Canteen before we go home? They serve dinner and put on a good show every night."

It sounded great to me. "I hear they also have dancing to a live band afterwards. I haven't danced in ages."

"I won't dance, but I'll watch, and hold your hat."

That night Pellier did watch them dance at the Hollywood Canteen, but she didn't have to hold my hat, because I was watching too.

The place seemed friendly enough at first. We got in the chow line and there was Frances Farmer at the steam table, spooning out scalloped potatoes. She was one of my favorite stars. I was thrilled when she smiled at me.

After we filled our trays I noticed a delay in the line up ahead. Bette Davis was speaking to the volunteer who would be seating us. She turned to the two WACs just ahead of me. "You'll have to eat upstairs on that balcony," she said, shaking her head. "I guess servicewomen are not allowed to eat on the main floor with the men. I'm sorry."

One of the WACs turned to me. "What do they think we're going to do to them?"

Carrying our trays, we climbed a narrow stairway against the left wall to a rough, rather makeshift mezzanine. By the time the show started, there were about a dozen of us up there. I thought it rather odd that they would seat us separately, but the food was good and the show was great. The men gave Dinah Shore several encores when she sang, "They're Either Too Old or Too Young."

Later the main floor was cleared of tables and the band began
to play dance music. Two WAVEs started down to the floor and
they were promptly sent back upstairs. "We're not allowed to dance
here," one said. "The men can only dance with the junior hostesses."

I looked down over the rail. Some of the men were dancing,
but there weren't enough civilian girls to go around. They were
urging us to come and join them.

I wished that I could.

A WAC glanced down. "Look at that gal with the low cut
neckline. I can see her bra." She adjusted her field scarf. "And
that's not all I can see."

A line had formed to one side, near the door. Pellier said,
"There's Bette Davis, signing autographs. She's president of the
canteen."

A WAVE made a face. "Does she make the rules?"

Pellier shrugged.

We watched the super star smile at each serviceman in turn,
and sign his program. I decided I wouldn't offer her mine. I didn't
want a souvenir to remind me of this place.

A SPAR stood up. "I'm not going to sit up here and watch
everybody else dance. I'm getting out of here!"

We all rose together and filed down the stairs. Servicemen were
still begging us to dance with them as we strode past.

A woman was singing "I'm getting corns for my country, at
the Hollywood Canteen."

I got my corns at boot camp.

*   *   *

CHAPTER 36.
LOVE AND WAR

A group of Marine aviation machinists were working aboard the Navy base at North Island, near San Diego. Their unit, ABG-2, (Air Base Group Two) would transfer to El Toro when our hangars were finished, and we would join them then. However, there were many delays in construction, due to shortages of both material and labor. Meanwhile, WRs were arriving weekly from Norman.

We were offered the chance to transfer down to North Island to work there until our hangars were ready. It sounded like a good idea to me. We discussed it in the Art Department.

Kilgallen said, "I'm staying here."

Lawson agreed. "If Kilgallen doesn't go, I won't either."

"I think it's time we start working on those planes," I said. "I think I'll go."

Kilgallen shook her head. "Don't count on it. They'll probably stick you at some desk, shuffling papers."

I thought about that. Later I asked Pellier what her plans were. "I think I'll stay here, Freddy," she replied. "There's so much more to do, so many things to see. We've just begun to explore the culture here in Los Angeles. Besides, we're Marines. North Island would be another Navy Base."

I was tired of half cooked beans for breakfast, and I could always use more culture. Besides, there was that promise I had made to Jeff, Pellier's husband, to "take care of her." And Kilgallen may be right. I could end up behind a desk. I stayed.

Several from our class transferred down, including Whalen,

Bongiorni, and Graves. I would miss them. I would also miss Graves' picture of Major John, her fiance.

Their engagement was not all that it appeared to be. Even John was not aware of her true feelings. Evidently I was the only one she had told.

Perhaps I had caught her at a weak moment. I recall that it was August, back in Norman. That was the month class 52 had swimming. Graves and I were on the same biological schedule, so we had been excused from swimming on the same days, due to what Kilgallen called "the curse."

We had to march to the pool with the platoon anyway, then request that we be excused from swimming, and proceed back independently.

Once, on the way home, Graves suggested we stop for a Coke. There was a machine on the porch in front of building 22. I dropped a nickel and took out the bottle, using the opener on the side. Then I sat down beside Graves on one of the benches that lined the wall.

She was unusually quiet. To break the silence I asked, "What do you hear from John?"

"Freddy, can you keep a secret?"

"Well . . ."

"I don't love John."

How could anybody not love John? I loved him, and I didn't even know him. "Why not?"

"Because I'm still in love with Bob."

"Who's Bob?"

Graves picked up her right foot and placed the boondocker squarely on her left knee. "Bob and I have known each other since we were kids," she began. "We grew up together, dated all through high school."

She paused. Twisting a curl around her finger, she pulled it out and let it spring back. "All those years, we just assumed we'd get married someday. But when Pearl Harbor was hit, Bob enlisted in the Marines and insisted we postpone our marriage until after the war."

She stared at the bottle in her hand. "They shipped him out to the Pacific."

My eyes focused on the porch railing as I listened.

"Well, Bob got hit. Hard. He was hurt pretty bad. He wrote me from some Naval hospital out in California, told me doctors said he would never recover completely. So he broke the engagement. Said he didn't want to be a burden to me.

"I wrote back, pleading with him, but he wouldn't listen. He insisted we were through, and that was that. He stopped answering my letters. I doubt he ever read them. He even called his folks, made them promise not to tell me where he was."

She put her Coke down on the deck to blow her nose. "Some months later I met John at a sorority dance. We had a few dates before he shipped out, and he asked me if I would marry him when he came back. All my friends said I'd be crazy if I didn't.

"Well, I went along with it. I took his ring, hoping it would help me to get over Bob, but it didn't work. I know that some day I will have to tell John I can't marry him. But you can't write that to a man flying bombers out of North Africa."

I never told anyone what Graves had confided to me that day, but I never forgot it, either.

Before she left for North Island, I went down to her bay to say good-bye. Pellier was sitting on a bunk nearby. They talked as she packed her sea bag.

Graves had just removed John's picture from her locker door. He had a handsome face with twinkling eyes and a mischievous smile. His hat was set at a rakish angle, giving the impression that he didn't take life too seriously. Yet the message written in the corner, just below the oak leaf on his collar, was serious enough. It read, "To Pat, with all my love," and it was signed, "Yours for always, John."

"Well John, we're moving again." She wrapped the photo in a skivvy shirt and stuffed it into the sea bag.

Pellier said, "You know, when the war is over and you and John are married, you can set that picture on your mantel, right beside the one of you that's hanging on his locker door."

Graves' smile faded. She finished packing in silence. We helped her press everything down so she could get the lock through the hasp. Later a bus came by to pick up the group, and she was on her way to North Island.

News traveled fast between the two bases. I was surprised to learn, a few weeks later, that Graves had married.

*   *   *

CHAPTER 37.
STORE WINDOW
REFLECTIONS

Truth is stranger than fiction, but it is because fiction is
obliged to stick to possibilities; truth isn't.
Mark Twain: Pudd'nhead Wilson's New Calendar

Pellier had tickets to the servicemen's performance of "The Drunkard," playing Sunday afternoon at the Music Hall in Los Angeles. We decided to spend the weekend in the city, and see what else was going on there.

We were standing in the LA line outside the gate Saturday morning when a military bus drove up. The driver opened the door and announced, "There's a plane leaving for LA in fifteen minutes. It can take twenty of you."

There were less than a dozen of us in line. We all climbed aboard. When we arrived the plane was not yet ready for boarding. I wandered off to look at a small twin engine craft nearby. It had a Plexiglas nose and a Bugs Bunny cartoon painted just below the pilot's window. As I studied the cartoon, the pilot approached. "Want to go to North Island?"

I thought of Graves. "Yes," I answered, "but I'm here with my buddy."

"Go get her."

I hurried back to tell Pellier. She said, "Let's go!"

The pilot was waiting. He looked me over and asked, "How much do you weigh?"

"A hundred and ten."

"Get up in front."

There was a row of seats on either side. The pilot followed me in and I took the front passenger seat. "I mean way in front." I moved up to the co-pilot's seat. "No, get down there in the nose."

I climbed down into the Plexiglas nose of the plane and sat on the small wooden floorboard. It felt like I was looking out at the world from inside a fish bowl.

He motioned Pellier to the co-pilot's seat, and explained to us that soon another WR would enter the plane, accompanied by two MP's. She was a prisoner, and we were therefore not allowed to speak to her. When they came aboard the door was secured. For someone in trouble, she didn't look too worried.

We began moving forward on what was to be my first flight, ever. I tried not to think of all I had learned in Norman about the many things that can go wrong with a plane.

When we picked up sufficient speed, I felt the liftoff. Despite extra weight in the nose, we gained altitude rapidly. We were soon out of the populated inland area, flying south along the shoreline. I was floating high above the sea in a bubble.

Passing over Laguna Beach, I spotted the rambling roof of Victor Hugo's, Kilgallen's favorite hangout. I saw swimmers, waders, and children building sand castles, not aware that they were being watched from above. One man, hearing the plane, looked up and waved. I waved back and wondered. Did he see me?

I didn't join in the conversation Pellier was having with the pilot, but gave my total attention to the panorama spread out beneath me. I wanted to remember it for the rest of my life.

Too soon we were circling the North Island Navy Base, losing altitude. I felt the plane touch down. We had come back to earth and it was time to leave my bubble. How could I tell the pilot how much he had given me? I didn't know how to thank him.

We found Graves' barracks, but she was not at her bunk. Her bunkmate said, "She took off in her slip, so she's still around. Probably trying to scrub grease out from under her nails."

"You mean she's actually working on planes?" I asked.

"Yeah, she pulls engines with me out on the line."

I knew then that I should have transferred down.

We told her about our flight, and the prisoner. "That must have been Wesley. I heard she gave herself up in Los Angeles."

I asked, "What did she do?"

"Her fiancé hit LA. He called her, so she went AWOL and they got married. He had some time there before shipping out again, so she said she would be with him until he left, then come back and take her punishment."

That solved the mystery of the prisoner on the plane, but I was still curious about Graves' marriage. We found her in the laundry room, whistling and ironing a shirt.

When she saw us, she stopped. Her mouth fell open. "How did you guys get here?" Without waiting for an answer she added, "Let's go someplace where we can talk. Freddy, you won't believe what happened!"

Pellier smiled. "So you've joined the ranks of the married. Welcome to the club!"

"But you won't believe what happened!" She turned off the iron, draped the shirts over her shoulder, and led the way back to her bunk. We had to hurry to keep up.

Reaching her bay, Pellier asked, "Where's your husband now?"

"He'll be picking me up in a little while. I had to come back to do some laundry. But wait'll I tell you, Freddy, you're gonna love this."

When she turned to hang her shirts in the closet, Pellier whispered to me, "They must be very lax down here, if an officer can just come in and pick her up."

Graves dressed quickly. Reaching for her hat, she said, "Let's go to the slop chute for a cup of coffee. Everyone around here is tired of hearing my story."

It was close by. We took our coffee to a corner booth.

"Two weeks ago I was walking down the street in San Diego with my bunky," Graves began. "There was this big Marine sergeant in front of us. I saw his face reflected in a store window, and he saw mine at the same time.

"It was Bob! Freddy, it was Bob!"

Pellier looked puzzled. "Who's Bob?"

"He's my husband."

"I thought you married John." Then, smiling her knowing smile, she asked, "How was the honeymoon?"

Graves grinned. "I don't think we ought to talk about it now, in front of Freddy."

Pellier nodded in agreement. I was older than either of them, and they were treating me like a child.

"You asked who Bob is." She told Pellier her story, as she had once told it to me.

"How is Bob doing?"

"He's fine. It turned out the injury wasn't as deep as they first thought. They were able to correct the problem. It took time, and a lot of therapy, but he's okay now. He's stationed at Camp Pendleton, waiting for orders to ship out again."

I asked, "Why didn't he get in touch with you?"

"He planned to surprise me. But when he went home on furlough they told him I got engaged to some major, and ran off to join the Marines."

It didn't seem fair that she had two great guys in love with her, while I had none. I asked, "What will you do about John?"

"Oh yes. John. Well, I thought he was better than nothing."

"How are you going to tell him?"

"I'm coming to that," she laughed. "And this is the part you won't believe."

After what I had just heard, I was ready to believe anything.

"Bob and I caught a flight to Yuma last week to get married. We were so happy I just couldn't think about John. I decided to wait and deal with him after Bob shipped out."

Pellier shook her head. "Poor John."

"Don't feel sorry for him. He's getting exactly what he deserves."

I asked, "What do you mean?"

"Well, when we came back from Yuma there was a letter from him waiting for me. Just seeing it made me sick. His letters were always so affectionate I could hardly stand to read them.

"But when I picked this one up I noticed there were two envelopes that had been sealed together with censor's tape. The one on the front was addressed to me, but the other, behind it, was for some gal named Diane in Boston. It was also in John's handwriting."

Pellier asked, "Did you open them both?"

"Of course! Mine was the usual line he always handed me about how wonderful I am, and how great it was going to be when he came home and we would be married. Hers was about the same, except he didn't mention marriage."

Pellier frowned. "How could such a thing happen?"

"The officers censor each other's mail to make sure there's no military secrets in them. Then the censoring officer seals it and mails it out. Evidently the same man read both letters and decided I should know about Diane.

"I wish I knew who he was so I could thank him."

*   *   *

Toasting the bride and groom, L to R: Mr. & Mrs. Bob Smith,
Bob's buddy, Freddy, Bob's buddy, and Pellier. Paris Inn, San
Diego, April 7, 1945

Graves and crew, on land

"The Checkerboard Squadron" in the air. We were proud of
these.

CHAPTER 38.
I SHOULD HAVE
SKIPPED DESSERT

Laguna Beach was Kilgallen's favorite liberty town. She referred to it as "The center of culture and the hub of the universe." Whenever she wanted to go there she'd say, "I'm going to Laguna Beach and lose my virginity. Anybody want to come along?"

Of course, it was an idle threat. Kilgallen only said it to get a response from Lawson and me. She knew we would join her, if only to try to keep her out of trouble.

She always headed for Victor Hugo's. Marine fighter pilots would be gathered around the grand piano there. At first sight of her the pianist, a dignified, white haired gentleman, would break out in "Clair de Lune." He knew it was her favorite.

Kilgallen could make a bourbon and Seven-up last all evening while she talked with the men and enjoyed the music. The pilots always sang along when he played the Whiffenpoof Song. Once, as they finished, she said softly, "'Gentlemen Rankers,' from Kipling's 'Barracks Room Ballads'."

But there was another side to Kilgallen that could not be nurtured at Victor Hugo's. One evening I became caught up in it when she walked into my bay.

"Freddy," she said, approaching me cautiously, "I've been invited to Laguna Beach for dinner tomorrow night and he asked me to bring a friend. Would you come with me?"

What was this? A blind date? Knowing Kilgallen, I became

suspicious. "That depends. Who is 'he' and what does he have lined up for me?"

"Oh no," she laughed. "It's nothing like that. 'He' is a minister. The Reverend and his wife have invited me to come, with a friend, to dinner in their home."

"A Protestant minister, Kil?"

"Yes." She smiled. "A Protestant minister."

"How did you meet him?"

"Lawson and I stopped at the USO in Santa Ana today. He was pouring coffee. Lawson and I had a cup, and we talked."

I remembered my last Christmas dinner. "Why does everybody think they have to feed us? There's nothing wrong with the chow on the base." I shook my head. "No thanks. They mean well, but it makes me feel like a charity case."

"Freddy, you don't understand. This man is a philosopher. We had a wonderfully uplifting conversation, until Lawson got restless. It's been a long time since I've talked to a really intelligent person."

"Thanks."

"Well, you're okay, Freddy. You're not stupid or anything. But no one here can discuss Plato or St. Augustine with me."

I began to see her problem. "Let me think about it."

"I told him I'd come, and he could expect two of us."

"I don't know anything about Plato or St. Augustine."

"Neither does anyone else around here. But you're a good listener, you won't try to change the conversation, and you're not easily bored."

I looked at her in disbelief, feeling I had just been psychoanalyzed. "Is that supposed to be a compliment?"

She ignored my question. "Look, you're the only one I can count on to . . . well . . . fit in."

"Kil, I haven't been to Protestant services since they made us all go to church that first Sunday at boot camp."

"You'll do just fine," she said, as if it were all settled. "And maybe you'll learn something."

I knew I had a lot to learn. "Okay, I'll go."

"Good!" She started to leave, then turned back to add, "I really appreciate this."

The following evening we arrived at a neat but modest home on the hill. Kilgallen rang the doorbell. A large muscular man in his mid-forties answered. He was dressed casually in a white shirt, grey slacks, and a maroon sleeveless sweater that looked handmade. He had round, soulful blue eyes and blond hair neatly combed to one side. While he gave the impression of being a serious, thoughtful gentleman, his smile was friendly as he greeted us.

"Come in, come in. It's beginning to rain again," he said. "I've been looking forward to your visit."

Turning to me, he extended his hand. "I'm Ken Werner."

He hung our trench coats on a rack by the door and we perched our hats on top of them. The house was filled with the aroma of freshly baked bread.

A small, energetic woman with dark hair combed back entered from the kitchen. "This is my wife, Evelyn."

After introductions, he led us all toward the living room. I noticed an open door off to the right. Glancing through it, I saw a husky teenager in gym shorts, doing push-ups.

"That's our son Roger. You'll meet him shortly." He smiled, adding, "He found some of my old Charles Atlas magazines, and now he's on a body building program."

He didn't look like he needed it.

"Kenneth has told me how much he enjoyed talking with you," Mrs. Werner said. "I'm so glad you could come."

As we entered the living room, Kilgallen was immediately attracted to an extensive library that filled one entire wall. "I see you have Tolstoy's 'War and Peace'."

"Yes, but I'm more impressed with the religious writings he did later, there to the left of it."

Kilgallen eyed him thoughtfully. "Tell me, what's your opinion of his 'The Kingdom of God is Within You?'"

Mrs. Werner excused herself and started to leave for the kitchen.

"Please let me help you," I begged. "This conversation is way over my head."

She let me finish setting the table. Soon Roger joined us, dressed now in a handmade light blue sweater and darker blue slacks. He looked a lot like his father. He had the same blond hair and blue eyes, and he was almost as big. A handsome kid with only a mild case of acne, he was quick to tell me he had just passed his driver's test. He followed me around, adding, "I'll probably join the Marines next year."

His mother frowned. He continued, "I sure hope this war lasts 'til I'm old enough to get into it."

"Roger, don't talk like that!" She turned to me. "He doesn't really mean it."

"Hey, I mean it. I don't want to miss anything."

Mrs. Werner had already disappeared into the kitchen. When she came back out, she was carrying a large bowl full of fried chicken. "We've kept chickens since they started rationing," she said. "At first it was just for the eggs. Kenneth and I couldn't kill them. But Roger takes care of that for us now."

The boy smiled proudly.

Kilgallen and Rev. Werner had to be coaxed to the table. "Come on now, before the food gets cold," she said. "You'll have all evening to talk."

The chicken gravy tasted even better than what they serve in the mess hall, and her Waldorf salad was much like my mother's. Rev. Werner opened a hot bread roll and poured gravy over it.

"This is what's really good," he said.

I tried it. He was right. This was a special treat, and I regretted the comment I had made to Kilgallen earlier. They did not make me feel like a charity case.

After dinner Kilgallen and the Reverend resumed their discussion in the library while Mrs. Werner and Roger sat with me at the table, sharing photos they had taken as missionaries in the Philippine Islands before the war.

The evening went fast. I looked at my watch and went in

search of Kilgallen. "Kil, we have to go. Our last bus leaves in half an hour."

Mrs. Werner frowned. "My, how time flies! I haven't served the dessert yet. Couldn't you stay the night? We have an extra room, now that our daughter is away at college."

"I would really like that," said Kilgallen.

"I can't," I said. "I have barracks duty tonight."

"Oh, I'm so sorry." Our hostess looked crushed. "I baked a lemon meringue pie especially for you girls."

Kilgallen's face dropped. "That's my favorite."

"You don't have to leave now," I said. "You can catch a bus back in the morning and I'll see you in the art department." Expressing my appreciation for a very pleasant evening, I reached for my trench coat.

Roger asked, "What time do you have to be back?"

"I have duty from two to four."

"Hey, could I drive her home later, Dad?"

The Reverend thought it over. "I see no reason why you can't. But be careful, Son. It's a wet night."

The boy grinned. "Sure, Dad."

Later I said good-bye and left with Roger. It had been raining heavily all evening, and water was running through the streets. I thought conversation might be awkward with a sixteen year old boy, but he seemed to have a great deal of curiosity about servicewomen. As soon as we were out of the driveway he began to question me.

"What do you girls do on liberty, anyway? Do you date a lot of guys, or do you have a steady?"

While I pondered the question, he continued. "You know, at school we hear a lot of stories about you women in the service. They say you're all alike."

"Who told you that?"

"A lot of guys. You know, they've been out with 'em. They know how it is."

"Do you believe everything they tell you?"

"Sure, why not? They're seniors, after all. I'll be a senior next year. I can hardly wait."

Roger began to slow down. We were still a ways from the turn-off to El Toro, but I could already see the lights of the guard's station at the gate.

"There's a little side road here somewhere. I don't think I've passed it."

"There's no short cut," I said. "There's nothing but bean fields between here and the main road to the gate."

"No, I mean on the other side," he said. "I think it's right here."

He made a sharp left turn into a narrow muddy road bordered by orange groves on both sides. Then he stopped the car, turned off the lights, and lunged for me.

I grabbed the handle on the door. It flew open when he pushed me against it and we both fell out, into the mud.

"Hey watch it," he said. "My mom just finished knitting this sweater."

He stood up and checked to see how badly it had been soiled, though it was too dark to tell. That's when I made a run for it.

"Hey come back here," he yelled. "What's the matter with you?"

I reached the street and crossed over to the other side. I started running across the bean fields, directly toward the lights of the gate. Roger was coming up behind me yelling, "What are you doing? Come back here!"

My heels kept sinking into the soft mud, slowing me down. I was no match for him in his tennis shoes. I was winded and short of breath when he caught up, but he was still breathing normally.

He locked his arms around my chest so that I couldn't move. I was completely helpless.

"What's the matter with you?" he asked again. "What did you expect?"

"I expected you to take me home."

"Is that what you want? You want to go home? Well then, why didn't you say so? Okay, I'll take you. Get back in the car."

I followed him back, feeling very confused. This kid was definitely in charge of the situation, and he had the physical strength and energy to back it up.

When we reached the car he opened the door for me. I stepped in and he slammed it shut. "Now stay there!"

He backed the car out to the street and squealed the brakes. Then he shifted gears and tromped on the gas. I hoped the guard at the gate didn't hear him.

We rode in silence until we neared the base. Stopping a short distance from the gate, he buried his face in his hands. "Wait a minute," he pleaded. "If my dad finds out about this, I'm in trouble. I didn't expect you to . . . well, how was I to know you were different from the others?"

"Every one of us is different from the others."

"Aw, come on, I didn't hurt you or anything. My father will kill me if he finds out about this. You're not going to tell him, are you?"

I started to leave. "Thanks for the ride home. I'll never forget it."

"He's really gonna kill me."

We had switched roles. Now I was in charge. I tried to understand the hormonal pressures of a sixteen year old boy.

"Did you learn anything?"

"Yeah. Yeah, I learned plenty. I learned not to mess with Women Marines."

"Then I won't tell your father."

I got out of the car, but probably not completely out of his life. He would still have to explain the soiled sweater to his mother, and his father would surely ask how all that mud got on the floor of the car.

*   *   *

CHAPTER 39.
THE CHILD

Kilgallen and I had stopped in Los Angeles for lunch. She suggested we take a quiet table off in a corner "where we can talk," seeming to have something on her mind.

She never had trouble talking anyplace, but I followed her to a corner table. She motioned me to the seat against the wall and sat facing me.

I ordered a ham sandwich on rye and a glass of buttermilk. Without looking at the menu she said, "I'll have the same." Then, leaning over close to me, she lowered her voice and asked, "What do you hear from Mike?"

She had often asked me that question. His letters were always interesting and impersonal, so that I sometimes shared parts of them with her. But now she seemed to want more than just a brief run-down on the living conditions of the checkerboard squadron on Okinawa. I didn't understand.

"Why do you ask?"

"Freddy, do you like Mike?"

"Sure I like him. Why?"

"I mean, do you really like him? Do you think you'll marry him?"

"Kil, we only dated for a month, and most of that time was spent dodging the MPs. I have no idea what might happen if we ever meet again."

"But you like him?"

"Yes. I like him."

"Casey. That's Irish, isn't it?"

"Yes. Mike is Irish."

"Irish Catholic?"

"I told you he took me to Mass one Sunday."

"Yes. I remember. It sounds like this could get serious."

She paused to add impact to what she was about to say. "I want to help you with your catechism."

"My what?"

"Catechism." She smiled. "You're so uninformed. You can't be married in a Catholic church unless you're a Catholic, and you can't join until you've taken your catechism. If I help you with it now, you can have that behind you when Mike comes back."

"We're not engaged."

"You will be, and you'll make a good Catholic."

"I'm not even much of a Protestant."

"That's why you'll make a good Catholic. You don't have a lot of preconceived ideas."

"Kil, if I married a Catholic, in ten years I could have ten babies, and I don't even know how to take care of one."

She thought that was funny. "That's not true." She laughed. "My parents are good Catholics and they only had six children. You just have sex when you want a child. That's what it's for. Then, when you have all the children you want, you simply stop having sex."

The conversation was making me uncomfortable. "Why did we get started on this?"

"Don't change the subject. You have a good thing going here with Mike, and men like him don't come along every day."

We were silent for a while. I had almost finished my sandwich, but Kilgallen had hardly touched hers.

Straightening up, she raised her voice and said, "Listen, I've made up my mind about one thing." Even louder, she added, "I want to have a child."

I was shocked. The ladies at the next table looked up. What can they be thinking of her? Such a remark, overheard, could give all of us who wear the uniform a bad name. What one of us says reflects on us all. They didn't know Kilgallen. They wouldn't understand.

"You can't mean that."

"I mean it. I'd like to have a child with a husband, of course, but it's beginning to look like that isn't going to happen. I think men are afraid of me."

The ladies stopped talking. I sensed they were listening intently.

"Nobody plans to have a baby alone, Kil," I pleaded. "What will people think?"

"I don't care what they think. They can love me, or they can hate me. It makes no difference. I want a child, and I'm going to have one. That was one of the reasons I left the convent, and I'm running out of time."

Running out of time? I had never thought of it in just that way, but since my twenty-third birthday, with no marriage prospects in view, I had begun to suspect I was well on my way to being an old maid.

"I've been out of the convent for a while now. And do you know what I've learned?"

"No. What?"

"All of the intelligent, well educated men my age are either married or divorced. If I'm ever going to have a child, it will have to be on my own, alone."

She couldn't be serious. "But you're Catholic. What would your church say?"

"I'll really have to do penance for it, but I'm used to that." She paused. "When you go to confession, you're sitting in a little box, about the size of a phone booth. The priest is on the other side of this screen. "Sometimes, if the light is right, you can see his profile.

"Once I saw him turn around to try to get a good look at me. I guess he couldn't believe what he was hearing."

I couldn't believe what I was hearing either.

"I'll have to say a lot of Hail Marys for this one."

If Kilgallen goes through with her plan, I thought, her penance won't stop with the church. Society will surely pass judgment on her as well.

"So think about what I told you."

"About the child?"

"No. About letting me help you with your catechism."

She was back on that subject again.

I was still thinking of the child.

*   *   *

CHAPTER 40.
THE PACIFIC THEATER,
THE EL TORO THEATER,
AND THE END OF THE SHOW

In Mike's first letter he was able to say he was on Okinawa with his squadron. "Two of us share a room in the BOQ," he wrote. "We each have a bed and chair, and we share a dresser, desk, and lamp. There's ample closet space for our limited wardrobes and even a radio to pick up Tokyo Rose. I'd say we have all the comforts of home.

"There's only one thing I miss. Terry and the Pirates. I guess I'll never know if Terry survived his latest daring adventure."

I could take a hint. The next morning I dropped a nickel in the slot machine at the chow hall and picked up the Los Angeles Times. After cutting out the comic strip, I began reading the rest of the paper. I wanted to keep a closer watch on the war in the Pacific Theater, now that I had a good friend fighting there.

I liked having someone overseas to write to again. Mike always enjoyed hearing stories of my adventures with Kilgallen. Now he would read about them.

He, in turn, sent a running account of his observations as he pursued his newest hobby, gooney bird watching. He said those large albatross seemed to think the runways had been built especially for them. They would race into the wind the entire length, desperately flapping their wings in a comic attempt at takeoff. If

240   INGA FREDRIKSEN FERRIS

they didn't succeed they waddled back and tried again. Once airborne, he said, they were very graceful in flight.

While opening one of his letters, something fell out. I picked it up and saw a photo of an F4U Corsair with checkerboard cowling, lying upside down in a ditch. I feared his base had been attacked. But on the back he had written, "Typhoon did it."

Mike's letters were generally upbeat and rich with humor. He mentioned the war only once, describing combat with the enemy somewhere over the Pacific.

His squadron had encountered a number of Japanese Zeros. One of them was coming up from behind, gaining on a Corsair. It looked like the end for our pilot. But a member of their squadron came down and attacked the Zero from behind, shredding its tail assembly with his propeller. The Zero circled down into the sea, and both our pilots made it back safely, suffering only scratches on the powerful propeller.

Mike concluded, "He'll get a silver star for that."

Sending Terry and the Pirates to Mike gave me a record of the date I had last written so that I didn't repeat my stories. And reading the news, as the war continued, I became even more engrossed in it.

On April 12th knowledge of President Roosevelt's death spread across the base quickly. Flags were immediately lowered to half-staff. But the loss became a stronger reality for me when I read the headlines the next morning: "PRESIDENT ROOSEVELT DIES." In smaller print just below, "Harry S. Truman Sworn in as Chief Executive." We had a new boss.

On May 2nd there were more bold headlines. "HITLER KILLED IN BERLIN! Adm. Doenitz Takes Power as Fuehrer. New Leader Gives Pledge He Will Continue Fight Against Bolshevism!!"

That fight was short lived. The May 8th headline read: "FULL VICTORY IN EUROPE. Allies to make Formal Announcement Today. War's Greatest Triumph Comes at Reims School, Quarters of Eisenhower."

While it brought an end to the fighting in Europe, for many

of the men there it meant just moving on to the Pacific Theater to face a different enemy. I wondered. How long could Japan hold out now, with all the Allied forces concentrated on them?

But peace in the Pacific was not to come easily. The Japanese military had inherited a philosophy from the Samurai that prized honor above life. Death held no fear for them. Rather, they took pride in sacrificing their life for their emperor. They worshipped him as a god, convinced it would be a privilege to die for him, for they would be richly rewarded in the hereafter.

Countless numbers of young Japanese volunteers were briefly trained to become kamikaze pilots. They flew aging, expendable planes heavily loaded with explosives and only enough gas for a one-way trip. Their target was the heart of our battleships and aircraft carriers maneuvering in the Pacific.

We would not match that.

Yet from all reports we were winning the war. On July 27th the headlines read: "ALLIES GIVE JAPAN TERMS."

The next day brought "JAPAN'S FALL IN BALANCE—TO-KYO JAP CABINET DECIDES TO FIGHT ON DESPITE DESTRUCTION ULTIMATUM."

I was completely involved in the war now, wishing I could play a more active role in it. ABG-2 personnel had moved up from San Diego, but they weren't yet ready for us to join them.

Three days later: "60 JAP SHIPS 138 PLANES WRECKED BY HALSEY FORCE."

August 2nd: "JAPS GET WAR'S GREATEST AIR RAID . . . Forts Drop 6632 Tons of Bombs."

What will it take to convince them they must surrender?

On August 6th: "B29'S ATTACK JAPAN; FOUR CITIES ON 'DEATH LIST' HIT . . . Superforts Shower 3850 Tons of Bombs on Vital Nippon Industry Centers."

Still they would not give up. They seemed to have an endless supply of young pilots anxious to be blown to bits on our ships' decks.

The next day's headlines shocked the world.

August 7th: "ATOMIC BOMB HITS JAPAN . . . Man's Most Destructive Force, One Equal to 2,000 B-29 Loads, Blast Nips."

Reading on, "The most terrible destructive force ever harnessed by man—atomic energy . . . Japanese face threat of desolation . . .

"Existence of the great new weapons was announced personally by President Truman . . . (it) had been dropped on the Japanese army base of Hiroshima."

Mankind had discovered a means of destroying itself.

I paused at the door to the mess hall, feeling exhilaration at the possibility that the war would soon end. But at the same time I was fearful, knowing so much destruction could be possible in one blow. I wondered. With knowledge of this weapon, could the world ever know real peace again? And why were we destined to be first to use it?

I thought of our men out on those ships, sailors I had gone to school with, and drank beer with, at Norman. We couldn't deny them the strongest protection we had at our disposal. No wife, mother, or child of one of them would question the wisdom of its use.

On the other hand, does any country have the right to wreak so much loss on another? I felt certain that if the enemy had it first, they would not hesitate to use it on us. President Truman had my sympathy. New on the job, he had inherited full responsibility for a tremendous decision.

There was more the next day. Aug. 8th: "FLYERS REPORT ON ATOMIC BOMB . . . 60 Per Cent of City Wiped Out."

Aug. 9th: "RUSSIA ATTACKS JAPAN . . . SECOND ATOMIC BOMBING! . . . New Missile Hits Nagasaki, Great War Plant Center."

Aug. 12: "PEACE TERMS PUT TO JAPAN: HIROHITO MUST OBEY ALLIED BOSS."

The next morning's headlines read: "SURRENDER NOTE ON WAY, TOKYO RADIO ANNOUNCES."

Later that day I was in the north wing of the chow hall running their dishwasher when I heard a lot of shouting in the galley.

While they banged pots and pans together, a cook rushed out to the mess hall shouting, "The treaty has been signed! The war is over!"

The historical significance of that moment overwhelmed me. I wanted to go back to the squad room and be with my buddies. The killing had ended, and our men would be coming home. I paused to reflect on the news.

"Hey, there's no room on this rack for my tray!"

Automatically I moved up an empty rack, shoved the full one on to the moving belt, and checked the temperature gauge. My mind was not on my work.

Liberty that night was not an option for me. I had the first barracks watch. While others were getting ready to leave the base and celebrate, I got out my stationery and started a letter to my mother. I reported for barracks duty shortly before lights out.

When the first WR came in off liberty her cheeks were a brilliant red, almost raw. "I had to come home." She giggled. "My face was wearing off. The streets out there are swarming with servicemen. They're drinking, dancing, and kissing every female who'll hold still for it."

As I started on my rounds, I heard joyful shouting from every direction. Marines aboard the base celebrating their victory made it impossible to obey rule #2, and observe "..everything that takes place within sight or hearing."

One WR came in and said, "Too bad you can't go over to the theater. Someone brought in a record player and everybody's dancing. I came back to change my shoes."

Later one showed up dripping wet, and it wasn't raining. "You should see the pool," she said. "A bunch of the guys climbed the fence and opened the gate. Now everybody's jumping in."

She had lost her hat somewhere, and she was making puddles on our carefully waxed hardwood floors, leaving a trail of water as she went in to change.

But the one who topped them all rushed in completely out of uniform. Boondockers in hand, her dungarees and overseas cap were draped over her arm. Soaking wet and wearing only panties, bra, and skivvie shirt, she tried to defend her conduct. "The men were stripping to their shorts to go for a swim," she explained, "so why couldn't we?"

She paused. "But a couple of them went too far when they took off their shorts. We had to leave."

The two-hour duty went fast. I recalled General Order #5— "To quit my post only when properly relieved."

My relief came late, and I noticed her hair was wet.

*   *   *

CHAPTER 41.
FOR A STRAWBERRY WAFFLE

Shortly after the war ended, every Marine on the base was given a seventy-two hour pass. They were to be divided over two weekends, to maintain adequate staffing. We discussed our options in the art department. Kilgallen suggested to Lawson and me that we take the first weekend and get as far away from El Toro as we can.

Billie, who sometimes helped out in the art department, suggested, "We could go to Bunny's for a strawberry waffle."

Lawson frowned. "Where's Bunny's?"

"San Francisco."

Kilgallen was interested. "I've always wanted to see San Francisco. Let's go."

"But Kil," I tried to reason with her. "Do you know how long it would take just to get there?"

"Let's not worry about train schedules or buses. We can hitchhike faster, and it's free. We might even meet some interesting people who are driving up there from LA."

Billie added, "We could stay at the Sir Francis Drake. They've turned their penthouse over to servicewomen."

Sgt. Baker glanced at Paula and Punchy. "We can handle things here by ourselves Friday, and take the second weekend. That will give us another payday."

I hadn't thought of that.

My objections were overruled. Friday morning, shortly after 0800, the four of us, Kilgallen, Lawson, Billie and I, were standing outside the gate behind the LA sign.

The line for rides was long but it moved quickly until it was our turn. Then we were stuck. Drivers said, "I can take two," or "Room for three," but nobody could take four. Smaller groups behind us got the rides instead.

When a civilian in an old pick-up pulled over and said, "I can take all of yuh," Lawson and Billie climbed in the cab. "The rest will hafta ride in back with Kelly."

Kelly was an exuberant Irish setter. When he wasn't chewing on our hats or licking our faces, he was rubbing his back against us and he smelled like he had been rolling in manure. When I pushed him away he reared up. If I hadn't grabbed his collar, he would have gone over the side.

I ordered, "Sit!" He sat. But Kelly had a short memory. I had to keep reminding him all the way to Los Angeles.

He dropped us off on the Pacific Coast Highway. Progress was slow from there. The rest of the day was spent in long waits between short rides.

It was getting dark and we were still a long way from San Francisco when two teenage boys in a four-door sedan pulled over. One jumped out and opened the back door. After Billie climbed in, the kid darted into the middle seat. Lawson followed him in so Kilgallen and I sat in front.

The driver had a heavy foot. When he stepped on the gas, it felt like I was being pushed down into the seat. The kid in back talked continually. "How about this, Mack? There's two for you, and two for me. I got me a blonde and a brunette female Marine, and you even have yourself a red head. What do you think of that?"

"Where'll we take 'em, Dave? How about that road house south of town?" He turned the car around and headed south.

"Naw, they check your age there," said Dave.

"Yeah, but these babes look old. They could swing it."

He was picking up speed, making me nervous. I wondered how we could get away from them.

Kilgallen put her hand on my forehead. "Freddy, do you think you might vomit again?" She turned to Mack. "She's been sick all day. Really made a mess in that last car."

Mack took his foot off the gas. "She's sick? Is she gonna to throw up? God, she better not do it in here. My dad would kill me!"

He slammed on the brakes so fast I almost went through the windshield. I jumped out and Kilgallen followed, while Lawson and Billie abandoned Dave. He climbed back in the front seat, Mack made another U turn, and they sped off into the night, leaving us further from San Francisco than when they picked us up.

By the time we dragged into the lobby of the Sir Francis Drake Hotel, it was beginning to get light. The lady at the desk looked surprised. "The penthouse is still full, but wake-up calls start soon for the scenic trip. It shouldn't be long. You can just relax in the lobby.

"My, you're certainly early."

"We're not early," said Kilgallen. "We're late."

"Oh my," she said. "Oh, my."

Kilgallen and Lawson relaxed so much that when the lady came to tell us there was room for two, they were already asleep. "You'd better go up with them, and let them have those first beds," she said. "They can't sleep here in the lobby."

Kilgallen had trouble waking up. She leaned on me in the elevator all the way to the top floor. Billie made her bed while I took off her shoes. A couple more cots became available, and soon we were all asleep.

Around noon I heard Lawson's voice. "Hey, I slept all night with my shoes on." We woke up Kilgallen and Billie, and we tried to make ourselves presentable.

Kilgallen was at an ironing board pressing her skirt when she noticed something strange. "This is supposed to be a clean towel, but it smells terrible."

I took a whiff. "That's Kelly's manure."

"I can't go out smelling like that!"

I sniffed my blouse. It was no better.

Kilgallen said, "We can't afford room service. We'll have to take them to the cleaners ourselves."

"Wearing what?"

Lawson and Billie dropped off our uniforms on their way to have that strawberry waffle at Bunny's. They brought back coffee and rolls for us. Then they went out to see San Francisco while we took a birds' eye look at the city. We read a San Francisco Chronicle someone had left. Kilgallen worked the crossword puzzle. She finished it, and she did it in ink.

By the time Billie and Lawson got back with our uniforms I was hungry again. "Sorry it took so long," Lawson apologized. "They had to run them through twice to get rid of the smell."

Kilgallen looked at the bill. "That much? I'll be broke before we get home."

We both dug into our reserves, but she had to dig a little deeper than I did. Lawson asked, "Gonna make it, Kil?"

"I hope so. Let's go get some lunch."

"Lunch?" Billie asked. "It's almost time for dinner."

Kilgallen gave a weak smile. "Well, we saved some money there."

We each spent a nickel for a ride on the cable car. Then Kilgallen asked me if she could borrow some money for dinner at the Top of the Mark.

"Kil," I said, "I can't even afford one meal up there."

"They say the view is beautiful, looking down over the city from the Mark Hopkins Hotel. I don't want to miss that. Let's just go up and take a look anyway. They can't kick us out."

The civilian women going up in the elevator with us were dressed so expensively it was hard to believe that we, not they, were the best dressed women in America. When we reached the nineteenth floor, Kilgallen led the way out and went to ask the hostess for a menu.

I felt uncomfortable being there. I took a few steps to the left and glanced out through the expanse of glass on the other side of the room.

There were two gray-haired Army officers seated in a booth by the window. They waved, and beckoned me to come over for a better view. I smiled and shook my head, but they persisted. "Come on, just take a look," one said. "You've never seen anything like this in your life."

I supposed there was no harm in that. I approached their table. One got up and said, "Here, sit by the window for a minute where you can see it better."

I hesitated, then sat down and slid toward the window. The maitre 'd was there in an instant. "You can't do that here," he said. "I must ask you to leave at once."

The officer shook his head. "I'm sorry," he said. "I just wanted you to see it."

I didn't see it. As I joined the others, Kilgallen shook her head. "This is just a bar."

"I've been asked to leave," I blurted. My heart was pounding now, and I felt so humiliated I was barely able to speak. Would they have treated me this way if I were dressed as elegantly as those civilian ladies who rode up with us?

Choking back tears, I followed them to the elevator, feeling I was already at the bottom of the Mark.

Once outside, the fresh cool air felt good on my face. Kilgallen stayed close by. "Freddy, what happened? What has upset you?"

When I blurted it out they, too, felt my pain and my anger. We wandered aimlessly down the streets of San Francisco for a while, not caring where we went.

Billie broke the silence. "I'm hungry."

Lawson spotted a hamburger sign. "The price is right," she said. "Let's go in there."

This was not the best part of town, but four Marines ought to be able to take care of themselves, and we could be reasonably sure they wouldn't kick us out. We went in.

The restaurant was dimly lit, with red and white checkered tablecloths, slightly soiled. We found a table and a waitress dropped off menus as she passed. Lawson glanced up over the top of hers.

"Some civilians are staring at us from across the room, trying to get our attention. They're making me nervous."

I turned to see four able bodied young men dressed in sport jackets and ties. They smiled and waved.

Lawson frowned. "Don't look at them or they might come to our table."

Kilgallen answered, "Lawson, if you look at them, you can probably get them to pay for our dinners." She ignored Lawson's glare and went on. "Civilians have plenty of money. Why shouldn't they buy us a meal? It's the least they can do for their country." She eyed them, smiled, and said "Hi."

They came right over. The three younger men, almost boys, held back, letting the short, dark, mature one come forward. He had a scar on his left cheek, but he didn't look like he had lost many fights.

"You Marines, yes?"

"Yes," Kilgallen answered, smiling again.

"We Marines too. Merchant Marines. We talk to you. Is okay?"

"Is okay," she answered cheerfully.

They went back for their chairs and joined us, crowding closely. The man who had spoken placed his chair next to mine.

"Me Joe," he said. "Me boss."

He motioned to the other three scattered around the table. "These men work for Joe, do what Joe say. These Richard, these Jack, and these Steve. All do what Joe say."

Richard, sitting next to Lawson, agreed. "That's right, Joe. You're the chief."

He had the start of facial hair, but hadn't yet begun to shave. Lawson asked him, "How long have you been in the Merchant Marines?"

He cleared his throat. "This is my first trip out. We sailed from New York, to take our ship to the Pacific Theater. But on the way, we learned that war is over too."

He looked relieved.

Jack wasn't much older than Richard. His shiny black hair

had been oiled down. Resting an arm behind Billie's chair, he boasted, "We make good money."

Steve smiled at Kilgallen. "That's the truth." His brown curly hair was overdue for a haircut. Certainly it wasn't military, but neither was the Merchant Marines. "When I get out, I'll have a nice little bundle to take home," he said. "I can do something with it, you know?"

Kilgallen nodded. She already had plans for what he could do with some of it this evening.

The waitress came to take our orders. Billie, Lawson, and I stuck with hamburgers, but Kilgallen ordered a steak, medium rare.

After the waitress left, Joe spoke. "Joe in Merchant Marine long time, save lots money. I go home, be rich man."

As he pounded his chest with pride, a confused waitress approached our table. She turned to Joe. "Your dinners are ready, Sir. Shall we move you all to a larger table, or . . ."

"You put dinners over there. We sit at our table." Then to me he said, "After dinner we show you town, okay?"

Kilgallen answered for us all. "Okay."

Joe picked up his chair. "Come, we go eat." The others followed, each taking his chair.

"Why did you say it's okay?" I asked. "I don't want Joe to show me the town."

Lawson and Billie agreed.

Kilgallen spoke softly. "Listen, these guys are loaded, and we could all use a free meal."

Lawson crossed her arms. "Who said we're getting a free meal?"

"If we don't, I'm in trouble. This might have to last me until I get home."

She relished every morsel of her steak while she tried, without success, to reestablish communication with the men across the room. As they passed our table on their way out, Joe winked at me. "We see you girls later."

Lawson said, "I hope we've seen the last of them."

Billie bit hard on a French fry. "Don't count on it."

"I can't believe I'll have to pay for this steak. What ever happened to all of the gentlemen?" But Kilgallen did pay for her steak. She even left a modest tip.

They were waiting for us outside. Joe took a firm grip on my arm. "You come with me," he said. "I show you town."

It did no good to protest. The part of town he showed us was not what we had in mind for our one night in San Francisco. It was dark now, and we were walking down a dimly lit street.

It wasn't much lighter in the bar he chose. As soon as we were seated Lawson said, "We can't stay long. We have to go back and wash and iron our shirts for tomorrow."

Joe laughed, and the others joined in. "Drinks all round. When Joe drinks, everybody drinks."

"I tell story," said Joe. The young men listened politely, though they had probably heard it many times before. "My father Hawaii," he began. "He go out on boat to Japan, buy my mother for fifty dollar. She good woman for fifty dollar."

He paused to light a cigarette. "Take mother to Hawaii, I born there. Father go out to sea, no come back. Mother work hard, no learn good English like Joe."

He paid for the drinks, then continued. "Joe grow up on street, learn how to fight, then go out to sea like father."

He took a gulp from his glass. "But I no kill nobody unless they deserve it. You be good to Joe, Joe be good to you. Anybody double cross Joe, Joe give 'em this!"

He whipped out a knife so fast I couldn't see where it came from. Its blade reflected the lights from the bar, and I wondered whose blood had been spilled on it.

We had to get away from these men. "I need to powder my nose," I said. "Anybody want to come along?"

All three followed me to the head. Once there I asked, "How can we get out of here?"

Kilgallen opened a window and looked down. "It's only about five feet. We can make it."

I pulled a chair over to the window. It didn't seem too far down to the alley. I climbed out on the sill and slid off. Just a few scratches from the bricks, I thought. I wouldn't discover the run in my precious nylons until later.

Kilgallen followed, then Lawson and Billie. It was dark down there. We ran to the end of the alley. Then, walking as fast as we could without attracting attention, we headed for the hotel.

The same lady was at the desk again. "You're getting in earlier tonight," she said. "Did you see San Francisco?"

"Well, yes," Kilgallen sighed. "We saw a part of it."

*   *   *

CHAPTER 42.
LOST ALMOST

Billie was first up Sunday morning. She got the rest of us on our feet in a hurry.

A fog had settled over San Francisco during the night. It was so heavy that it was difficult to make out the streets below. Not a good day to be hitting the road, I thought, but we had to get back to the base. With two irons available and plenty of showers, we were able to get dressed and check out fast. Kilgallen left for early mass and I went to the USO with Lawson and Billie to get something to eat.

When she joined us later she quickly finished off three doughnuts and two cups of coffee. Wrapping another doughnut in a napkin, she stuffed it in her purse and we left to catch a bus to the edge of town.

The fog was not as heavy at the end of the line, but it was thick enough to make hitchhiking difficult. By the time they could see us, it was too late to stop. Progress was slow all morning. Even after the fog lifted and more cars took to the highway, there were too many of us to fit into most of them.

Well along in the afternoon, Kilgallen spotted a soldier hitch-hiking just ahead of us. She went down and talked to him.

Billie was soon getting impatient. She called, "Kil, we're trying to work our way home here."

She returned, bringing the soldier with her. "This is Walt," she said. "He's going as far as Los Angeles with us."

Walt was tall and slim, with a wide smile. Billie leveled with him. "You'll never get a ride if you come with us, and neither will we. It's hard enough with four."

"After what happened last night," said Kilgallen, "I'd feel a lot safer with a man along. It'll be dark before we get home."

We couldn't talk her out of it. Walt seemed like a nice guy who felt we might need protection. Too bad for him, I thought, that he got involved with us. He would make better time alone.

Now we were five. We needed a six passenger car with a lone driver. Not too many of those out on Sunday. One came by and took us a ways. Then there was a short ride in the back of a pickup.

The sun was setting and I was getting very hungry when a driver went beyond his turn-off to bring us to a combination grocery store and gas station. We bought a small jar of peanut butter, jelly, and a loaf of bread. Walt supplied cokes and shared his pocketknife to make sandwiches. We sat on the steps in front of the store to eat. After making use of the facilities at the gas station we hit the road again.

It had been dark a while when we were dropped off in front of a roadhouse. "Let's not stand here," said Lawson. "I don't want to ride with some drunk coming out of the bar."

We walked down the highway until the roadhouse was out of sight. A lone man in a six passenger four door sedan stopped and rolled down his window. "Where ya headin'?"

Walt answered. "We're going to LA."

"Climb in. I'll take ya there."

It seemed to be a lucky break, but the driver looked disreputable. Kilgallen whispered, "Walt, sit next to him, will you? There's something funny about him."

I sat in back between Billie and Lawson. The seat was lumpy. I could put up with that for a ride all the way to Los Angeles, but the driver made a U turn and headed north.

Walt asked, "Did you say you're going to LA?"

"Yeah, yeah, I'll take you to LA. But first I gotta get some money." He drove us back to the roadhouse. "I'm going in here and get some more money. Now all of you wait right there, and when I come out I'll take ya to LA."

After he left Lawson frowned. "That's strange. Why is he going in a roadhouse for money?"

I reached down to investigate one of the sharp objects I had been sitting on. It was the fastener on an empty purse. I held it up. "What's this doing in here?"

Billie started feeling around. "Here's another one, and another!"

Lawson picked up two from the floor. "They're everywhere!"

"The guy's a purse snatcher," said Walt. "We have to turn him in."

Kilgallen objected. "Let somebody else do that. We have to keep moving."

"I guess you're right," he agreed, "but we can't stick around here or we'll get involved. He'll be coming out."

We abandoned the car fast.

Looking up the road, Billie shouted, "Here comes a bus! Flag it, everybody, flag it!"

We waved our arms frantically until the bus pulled over. It stopped in front of Billie, and we all climbed aboard. The driver asked, "Where you heading?"

Kilgallen rummaged through her bag until she found her coin purse. "How far can you take us for a quarter?"

He took a quarter from each of us and got back on the road. "What are you Women Marines doing out here in Lost Almost?"

"Lost Almost?" I asked. "Is that the name of this town?"

The driver smiled. "Folks around here call it Los Alamos, but we drivers have our own name for it."

He gave us a long ride for our quarter, dropping us off in front of a well-lit gas station. An attendant was filling the tank of a model A single-seater. The driver, a stout man with graying hair, approached us.

"I can take two of you as far as LA," he said.

That was a break. No matter which two he took, we'd all be better off if we split up.

Kilgallen said, "I'm not leaving without Walt."

Lawson shook her head. "I'm staying with Kilgallen."

"So am I," said Billie.

I couldn't understand their attitude. Kilgallen seemed to have a master's degree in trouble. She had led us into this mess, and now Lawson and Billie seemed to think she was the only one who could get us out of it.

"You can take me to Los Angeles," I said.

A sailor came out of the head and walked up toward the highway. The driver approached him. "Need a ride to LA?"

"Boy, do I!" he answered. "I gotta get to Long Beach."

"I'll take you and this young lady Marine here."

I expected him to drop us off at a bus stop somewhere in Los Angeles where I could catch a red car, but instead he pulled over at a cross street out on the Highway.

"I'm not going much further," he said. "This is a good place to leave you. You can both get rides from here going in opposite directions. Sailor, you'd best stand over there on the north corner by that stop sign."

He turned to me. "You stay here because you'll be going east. These cars have to stop too. Be careful who you take a ride with." And he was gone.

The sailor offered to wait with me. The blackouts had been lifted, and the corner was well lit. Soon a car came along. A nice little old man opened the door and said, "You folks need a lift?"

"The lady does, but I'm going the other way. I'm just staying with her until she gets a ride."

"Oh, I know. You can't be too careful."

The car was still in second gear when he said, "I'm only going a couple blocks, but every little bit helps, eh?"

This was help I could have done without. He dropped me off

and turned down a long, dark lane. There were no houses around, no street lights, and not even a star in the sky.

Starting to walk back toward the lighted intersection, I was blinded by the headlights of an oncoming truck. It pulled over and stopped beside me. The cab door flew open and a friendly voice asked, "Need a ride, Lady?"

I climbed up to the seat beside him and flopped down, totally exhausted. My body felt numb.

The driver was wide-awake and cheerful, despite the late hour. "You're getting an early start, aren't you? Where are you going?"

"I'm trying to get back to El Toro. I've been on the road since eight o'clock this morning."

"Since eight o'clock? But it isn't even six yet."

I couldn't see my watch. "What time is it?"

He turned on the light in the cab. "It's 5:35," he said. "I'm right on time. I'll drop you off at the road leading into Santa Ana. I pick up my load just beyond that. It'll be easy to get a ride from there."

This man was just starting his workday and I was still working on yesterday. Sinking down into the comfort of the seat, my body yielded to extreme fatigue.

"My friends call me Tex. What's your name?"

"Fred. They call me Fred."

He began to talk about his wife and children. His soft voice soon lulled me to sleep.

A sudden loud blast shook the cab of the truck. I bolted up, bumping my head against the roof. "What was that?"

Tex smiled. His left hand loosened its grip on the cord above the door. "We just passed my house. That's how I say good morning to my wife. She's still asleep when I leave for work."

I stayed awake for the rest of the trip. He could blow that horn again.

It was light and traffic had picked up when he dropped me off at a familiar corner. There was grease on my right thumb. It was probably from something in the truck. I wiped it off with a hanky.

How did my hair look? Was my hat on straight? Were my eagles flying high?

A car drove up and stopped in front of me. A mature man in a Marine officer's uniform stepped out and motioned me into the car. I don't remember if I saluted or not.

I turned to thank the driver, a kindly looking gray haired gentleman, but his rank overwhelmed me. In no condition to confront a full colonel, I glanced at the other officer. Silver eagles perched on his shoulders as well.

The driver broke the silence. In a friendly, fatherly voice he said, "What in the world is a little girl like you doing out here hitch-hiking by yourself?"

Before I could answer the other colonel added, "I would be worried sick if I thought my daughter was out alone, hitching rides. How did this happen?"

I told my story briefly, and not altogether coherently. They were understanding and sympathetic. As we neared the El Toro turn off, the driver began to slow down.

"We're on our way to Camp Pendleton, but I don't want to drop you off here." He turned to his companion. "What do you say we take her all the way home? This little girl's been through enough for one weekend."

"Good idea."

He drove up close to the gate. The other officer stepped out and held the door open for me. I said, "Thank you, Sir," saluted them both, and turned to enter the base.

The guard on duty whistled. "You travel in class."

"You didn't see the rig I was riding in earlier."

"No, but it might account for the smudge on your nose."

I had time to shower, change into dungarees, and go to chow before reporting for work. The others were not so lucky. Kilgallen called the base just before 0800 to report the three were "unavoidably delayed." Later they stumbled up the theater stairs, still in uniform and looking disheveled.

Paula had been asked to design a pair of masks to be painted above the theater entrance. When she asked for a model, Kilgallen quickly volunteered to pose. I helped her drag in a comfortable chair from the projection room. She sank into it and promptly fell asleep.

*   *   *

CHAPTER 43.
WELCOME HOME THE BOYS

I requested a furlough to see my mother once more before my discharge. Roth was leaving for Colfax, Washington, the same day, so we planned to travel together. When she learned of a military plane taking off from El Toro for San Francisco on the morning of our departure, we cashed in our train tickets and took the flight, knowing it would save us both time and money.

Leaving the base right after morning chow, we were off to a flying start. We had lunch at the Southern Pacific Depot in San Francisco. The station was jammed with servicemen on their way home. Roth said, "Looks like the war is really over."

"Yeah, and the troops are all coming through here. Now, where do we buy our tickets so we can get moving again?"

We found the end of one of the ticket lines and fell in behind some servicemen. It was quite a distance from the window, but waiting in line was something we were good at.

The soldiers ahead of us were very friendly. One turned to me. "You're the first woman I've stood close to in three years. Can I hug you?"

Of course. "Welcome home," I said. "Welcome home!"

From behind we heard, "Hey, how about a hug for the Navy?" They started coming over from the other lines. Roth and I were so busy trying to hug them all, we almost missed an announcement blasting out over the loud speaker.

"ATTENTION! TICKETS WILL BE SOLD ONLY TO MILITARY PERSONNEL RETURNING FROM OVERSEAS

DUTY. EVERYONE ELSE WILL HAVE TO FIND OTHER
MEANS OF TRANSPORTATION."

Roth nudged me. "Hey, they means us."

One sailor offered to slip her in his sea bag. She declined the
offer, and we left to find a phone.

I called the bus depot. They wouldn't sell us a ticket either.
We went out to the street and started walking, unsure of our direction. My luggage was getting heavy when we spotted a USO. It
was crowded. We found a lady in the back making coffee, and took
our problem to her.

"It seems to me," she said, "there used to be a place near here
that found rides for people who were stranded during the war. It
was a share the ride thing. Let's see . . ."

She got out the phone book and wrote down a number. When
she finished with the coffee she went to the office and called. "They
need a ride north," she said. "Yes, two lady Marines." She covered
the mouth piece and asked, "Portland and where in Washington?"

"Colfax," said Roth. "Just say Seattle."

She jotted something on a piece of paper and said, "They'll be
right over."

She handed me the note. "Here's the address. He has room for
two more on a ride going to Seattle, but he won't hold it for you."

It was a few blocks away. As we neared the address, a drunk
began to follow us, making suggestive remarks. I found the neighborhood intimidating. From the outside, the place looked like an
old, abandoned store. A poorly made sign above the door read
WYLIE'S TRAVEL INFORMATION.

Entering, I saw one deep room, thick with smoke. There were
a couple of shabby couches near the front, with smelly ash trays on
stands nearby. Old wooden chairs were scattered about for extra
seating.

The desk, off to one side, was missing a leg. A coffee can supported one corner. A wizened little man sat behind it. A cigarette
dangled from a corner of his mouth and his eyes seemed accustomed to squinting from the smoke.

"You girls goin' to Seattle?"

"I'm just going to Portland, but my buddy needs a ride to Seattle."

"Makes no difference. You pay through to Seattle, 'cause that's where the car's goin'. He can take five. He already has three so you two 'll fill it up. Pay me now."

His price amounted to more than my refund on the round trip train ticket from Los Angeles, but it would get us moving again.

"When do we leave?" I asked.

"Aw, he ain't even come in yet. He's due in from Salt Lake, and he'll need some sleep. Be here ready to go though, eight AM sharp tomorrow morning."

He took our cash and made some entries in a ragged black ledger, putting the money in his pocket without offering a receipt. "Make sure you're here on time. If you're not, Jed will leave without you."

I wondered if the nice lady back at the USO had ever checked this place out.

We went back to a better neighborhood to find a hotel room. The servicemen returning from war had filled them all. Even the chairs in the lobbies were taken.

I called the Sir Francis Drake. Their pent house was packed with servicewomen returning from overseas. We went back to the USO. The lady we had talked to earlier called every hotel in town and the YMCA. There was nothing available.

"I wish I could help you, but I've already promised our fold down bed to two servicemen for tonight."

I looked at Roth. "Remember those couches back at Wylie's?"

"We're not that desperate, are we?"

"I think we are. Let's go ask."

We went back. I was glad to see the couches still there, but I hadn't noticed the lumps before. Roth approached Wylie at the desk. "Do you know where we might find a room for tonight?"

"No way! This town's sewed up tighter'n a drum." He motioned toward the man standing next to him. "My driver here can't even get a room. He'll be sleepin' on one of those couches tonight."

"I'm Jed," he said, extending his hand. "You ladies going to Seattle?"

"Yes." I shrugged. "We're going to Seattle."

Jed was short and stocky. He wore a chauffeur's cap perched jauntily to one side, and had a thin black moustache nestled up close to his nose. "Ought to be a good trip. No sign of rain. Nice to have you ladies along." He paused. "You'll be back here at eight tomorrow morning?"

Roth shook her head. "We can't find a room, so I guess we'll spend the night sleeping here in the doorway."

"Hey look, why don't you take these couches? Wylie here won't mind. At least, you'll be inside."

Wylie took the cigarette from his mouth and leaned forward. "I wouldn't mind, Jed, but where you goin' to sleep? My drivers need their rest."

"Could we sleep in the car?" I asked. "That way, we could be sure you wouldn't leave without us."

Jed shook his head. "I'll sleep in the car. I've done it before. Even have a pillow and a blanket out there. No, I'll be fine. You ladies take the couches. I'm going out to eat. I'll be parked out back later."

I turned to Wylie. "What time do you close?"

"Whenever I've filled all my cars for their next trip. I'm through now, so I'm leaving."

"Then how will we get back in?"

"Just come in the back door. It's got no lock on it."

Roth frowned. "Aren't you afraid someone will break in?"

"What the hell fer? Nothin' here anybody'd want." He pointed to the black book. "I keep my records with me." Reaching for his coat, he added, "Make yourselves to home."

He lit another cigarette, picked up his ledger, and left. I looked at my watch. "Let's go eat. We need to be back before it gets dark."

Roth locked the front door while I put our luggage out of sight behind the desk. We slipped out the back way, into a small parking lot next to the alley.

Roth said, "I remember seeing a lunch counter in that Woolworth's down the street."

We each had an egg salad sandwich and coffee there. When we started back, returning servicemen were everywhere, wandering aimlessly through the streets, waiting for their train time. They greeted us with whistles as we passed. I was thankful Lawson wasn't with us, or we never would have escaped them.

We got back in the same way we had left. It was getting dark. A light bulb dangled on a cord from the ceiling. As soon as I turned it on, servicemen began lining up at the front window.

"Hey," one said, "there's gyrenes in there!"

"No kidding. You mean BAMs? Where?"

We were clearly visible from the street. Encounters that had seemed friendly earlier in the station took on a different meaning here now. We were in an empty building with big front windows, no lock on the back door, and streets teeming with virile young men who had not been near a woman in years.

Roth whispered, "Turn off the light."

I turned it off and we pretended to go out the rear door.

"They left," said one.

"They went out the back way. How can we get to 'em?" said another.

A strong voice ordered, "Hey, leave 'em alone."

They moved on, and we spent the rest of the evening in darkness. Still, neon lights flashing from the bar across the street made hiding difficult.

I found my toothbrush. "How can we see to brush our teeth?"

"Just make sure you close the door before you turn on the light in there."

The head was filthy. I gave my tube of Ipana a squeeze and started to brush before I turned on the faucet.

"Hey, there's no water in here!"

Roth opened the door. I turned off the light. She stepped in and closed the door. I turned it on again and looked in the mirror. I was foaming at the mouth.

"No water?" she asked. "Does the toilet work?"

It looked dry. Pulling the chain did nothing. The wooden water chamber above was empty too. And I still had a mouth full of foam. I spat what I could into the toilet and swallowed the rest.

There was a gas station on the corner. We decided to go there. Slipping out the back door, we noticed a '39 Ford sedan in the parking area. Roth peeked in.

"Jed's already sound asleep," she whispered.

The gas station attendant was sympathetic. He offered to leave the ladies room unlocked for us that night. "Wylie's been using my men's room for months," he said. "Claims he's got a leak in his water line somewhere. Always saying he's going to get it fixed. I doubt he ever will."

When we got back there was nothing to do but go to bed. There was no argument for the couches. One was as lumpy as the other. We arranged them so their backs were toward the street. Then we propped a wooden chair against the back door and snuggled under our trench coats, confident we could not be seen.

The streets still swarmed with servicemen with no place to go, but I felt safe from them until I heard voices at the window again. "Hey, there's BAMS in there!"

How could they see us? Anger welled up in me, as it always did when I heard their offensive name for us. Groups of them kept tapping on the window, calling to us throughout the night.

Roth whispered, "How do they know we're in here?"

The next morning she discovered how. "Freddy, you left your hat on the desk!"

"Gee I'm sorry," I apologized. "I just figured it was the cleanest place to put it."

She gave me a dirty look.

Jed was getting out of his car as we left for breakfast. He joined us. Over coffee he said, "Sorry, I forgot to tell you girls about the water. Wylie won't do anything around the place. He says it's not his. I don't think he knows who owns it. He just uses it."

Roth asked, "Does he own the cars?"

"No. I drive my own. We all do. He only makes the connections, collects the money, and takes his half."

"How did you get gas during the war?" I asked.

"Wylie found loopholes. He said if we justified the trip and took riders, he could get the gas for us.

"We'd use stories like going back to school, visiting our ailing mother, you know . . . things like that. We got away with it. Civilians were having trouble getting tickets to go anywhere, so they kept us busy. It's been a good living for me since I was discharged from the Army."

It must have been an even better living for Wylie.

When we got back to the office the other three riders were waiting. The tall slim one in uniform was Dan, a young Coastguard lieutenant. The other two were like a pair, though they had just met. Both were short, round, and middle aged. Carl had straight blond hair and an eye for the ladies. Arnie wore a felt hat down over his forehead. We would later learn he had an inside pocket in his coat that held a small, flat bottle of whiskey.

Jed secured our suitcases on the luggage rack above. Then he started the engine. "Climb in," he said.

It was exactly 0800. We were right on schedule.

Carl was already in the middle seat in the back. He called, "C'mon, ladies, climb in."

We slipped in on either side of him. Dan and Arnie would ride in front with Jed.

Soon after we were underway, Carl became very friendly, sharing a few off color jokes that we didn't appreciate. A little further up the road, Roth let out a yell.

"Hey, quit that!"

Carl grinned sheepishly.

Jed looked in the rear view mirror. "What's going on back there?"

"He pinched me!"

Jed pulled over. "I want Carl up here with me."

Arnie traded places with him and we were on our way again. At first the change seemed an improvement, but Arnie soon became a problem too. As the liquid in his bottle diminished, so did his judgment. I was sitting in the middle now. He began to insist that I imbibe and when I refused he became belligerent.

"Whatcha matta witchu Lady Marinsh? Think yer too damn good to drink wif me?"

Jed stopped again. "I want both Carl and Arnie up front. Dan will sit in back for the rest of the trip." He turned around and added, "I'm sorry. I don't usually have young ladies on these runs." He smiled. "If Dan gives you any trouble you two can ride up front with me."

He took the bottle from Arnie and got back on the road. We spent the rest of the day with Dan, reading Burma Shave ads and swapping sea stories. That night Jed pulled over in the outskirts of a small town and we all slept in the car until dawn.

We reached Portland the following afternoon. I declined Jed's offer to deliver me to my door, asking instead to be dropped off at the railroad station. As soon as Jed got my suitcase down from the rack I said good-bye and dashed inside, bracing myself to compete with a crowd for a ticket back to Los Angeles. But the station was almost empty and there was no line.

An elderly man at the ticket window said, "Hey, what's the hurry? Ain't another train due yet for a half hour."

"Can I buy a fare straight through to Los Angeles for next week?"

"Ain't no reason why you can't."

"Are you sure I won't get bumped off in San Francisco?"

"Not if you got a ticket clear through to Los Angeles."

I buried the ticket deep in my purse and pressed it shut before moving away from the window. It was a comfort to know I would not have to spend another night at Wylie's Travel Information Hotel.

*   *   *

CHAPTER 44.
AIR BASE GROUP TWO

When the hangars were finished, Air Base Group Two (ABG-2) began the transfer up from North Island. However, by the time they were ready for us to join them, peace had been declared. We discussed our options in the art department.

Sgt. Baker said, "You don't have to go out there. The war is over. You can remain here until you are discharged."

Kilgallen beamed. "I'm staying here. They wouldn't want me working on those planes."

Lawson agreed. "If Kilgallen doesn't go, I won't either."

Punchy and Paulson were not a part of ABG-2. They, like Sgt. Baker, were permanently assigned to the art department. The sergeant looked at me. "Well, Freddy, you're not going to leave us, are you?"

I thought about the money the government had spent on my training. The art department certainly didn't need me. Maybe I could still be of some use to ABG-2.

"I think I should go out to the hangars."

Kilgallen shook her head. "Freddy, I'll never understand you."

I knew I had made the right decision when I was issued two sets of men's dungarees with matching overseas cap. I hooked my Dzus key to the belt and ran the dungarees in the washing machine for an hour to make them look salty.

We squeezed into big rigs with open double trailers for the ride to the hangars. We called them cattle cars. They had a canopy cover, with protective railings around the sides.

If we couldn't get inside we stood on an outside step, clinging to the poles that supported the roof. Those who couldn't reach a pole grabbed the nearest body that could. Fortunately, the ride was gentle, and the turns were taken cautiously.

A sergeant was there to meet us. "All of you in this car follow me," he said, and he led us to hangar A. He began reading a list of available jobs. When he said, "We need two people for the plastics department," it sounded interesting. I raised my hand. Another hand went up on the other side of the crowd.

He motioned to a Marine at his side. "This is Sgt. Daily. You two go with him."

Sgt. Daily appeared to be a weathered, Old Corps Marine in his middle thirties. He was a quiet man of average height, slim, with thick brown curly hair.

The other WR reached him first. "I'm Rudkin."

"Rudkin!"

I hadn't seen her since she graduated in the top three of the class ahead of us at Norman. I noticed she made PFC.

"Freddy!"

"Uh . . . you two know each other?"

"We went through boot camp together," said Rudkin.

"Oh. Well. Why don't you both follow me?"

We followed Sgt. Daily the full length of the hangar and back almost to the coffee shop in the corner. The plastics department was spacious and empty, save for a few work tables. Nobody was working at them.

A tool cage by the coffee shop contained several rows of metal shelving. The shelves were empty, except for a couple boxes of Phillips head screwdrivers and box wrenches. The office, this side of the tool cage, was enclosed in a partition about three feet high. A low swinging door led into it from the shop. Inside was an empty filing cabinet, a couple chairs, and two desks, both bare save for a racing form on one.

The sergeant went into the tool cage and brought out a screwdriver and box wrench for each of us. Then he went outside to get a weathered sliding enclosure that had been removed from a Corsair. He set it on a worktable and placed a new Plexiglas covering nearby. I could hardly wait to get started.

"You'll take off the old Plexiglas and replace it with this new one," he said. "But don't remove the protective coating on it because the plane's going into moth balls."

"They're mothballing our beautiful Corsairs?" I asked.

"Better they end up in the moth ball fleet than at the bottom of the ocean with a dead pilot inside."

I couldn't argue with that.

The nuts and bolts on the metal strips, holding the Plexiglas fast to the frame, were spaced close together. They ran the full length of the enclosure, across the ends, and both sides of the two reinforcing strips at the top.

There must have been a hundred of them. I couldn't begin to guess how long it would take us to remove them all. We picked up our tools and went to work. I was anxious to get this boring job over with. But the sergeant dashed my hopes for that when he added, "When you finish this one, there's a lot more out there." He took the racing form from the desk and disappeared into the tool cage behind some shelving.

About an hour later PFC Billingsly appeared and introduced himself. He was younger and taller than Sgt. Daily, and seemed rather arrogant. I heard a rumor later that he came from a wealthy San Diego family.

Billingsly did not replace sliding enclosures. He seemed to have no job at all, though occasionally he did make a plastic nameplate for an officer, or laminate pocket-sized copies of discharge papers for his friends. Much of the time he moved about the department singing "Tampico," like he vacationed there often.

In the weeks that followed, Sgt. Daily began each morning hiding out in the tool crib with his racing form. He filled large sheets of paper with numbers, and studied his mathematical computations until his bookie came around.

After placing his wager he moved on to the coffee shop. He never lost a bet. He promised to reveal his system when he was sure it worked, but that day didn't arrive while I was there. When the Marine bookie arrived, the other men could only say, "Which horse is Daily betting on? Put two on that one for me."

The work was tedious, and it didn't take long for our fingers to become sore from the constant friction. But Rudkin was a great story teller. Her jokes and anecdotes kept us both laughing while the work continued without conscious direction. Once I tried to contribute a joke my brother-in-law had told, but I forgot the punch line.

"Freddy," she said, "you're much funnier when you don't try to be."

As we sought escape from boredom, our laughter got stronger and it lasted longer. One morning Rudkin was starting her second or third story when I reached the breaking point.

"There was this man," she began. "He had an ugly dog he didn't care much for. He called him Flea Bait . . ."

I never found out what happened to Flea Bait. Unable to wait for the rest of the story, I burst out in uncontrolled laughter.

Rudkin couldn't go on. She started a quiet snicker that grew, slowly, to a full-blown side splitting roar. We stood for a while, trying to regain our composure. It wasn't working. We put down our tools and headed for the office.

Rudkin, entering ahead of me, clasped her hands behind her head and bumped open the low swinging door with her hips just as Sgt. Daily returned from the coffee shop. He was only mildly amused. "Why don't you two take a long break?"

It took a lot of coffee to sober us. It was time to take a look at our problem.

"Freddy, have you noticed we're the only ones working?"

"Yes. Maybe we ought to change our attitude."

We continued to start each day working on the sliding enclosures, and we stayed with it as long as we could. But we began taking longer breaks. Sgt. Daily didn't seem to care. We left earlier for noon chow and returned later to the hangar. That didn't bother him either. We took a tour of the other hangars, visiting buddies along the way. They weren't busy. I spent some time at hydraulic fittings chatting with Roth and Tierney. They had nothing to do. Neither did a few civilian workers who were still there on payroll.

Rudkin took stationery to work. I started bringing along the Los Angeles Times. Billingsly complained when he found that Terry and the Pirates had been cut out.

Kilgallen insisted I read *The Fountainhead*, by Ayn Rand. She loaned me her copy and I took it to the hangars. Then I went to the library and picked up *The Black Rose* by Thomas B. Costain, and I had discovered the enchantment of books.

The only busy people in ABG-2 now were the WRs in motor transport who drove the cattle cars back and forth between the hangars and the barracks. But when we got a new transportation officer, even their jobs were threatened.

"Steering and braking those heavy rigs takes a lot of strength," he said. "That job is too hard for a woman. Starting tomorrow, they will all be replaced by men."

The next day a number of Marines were thrown out on the turns, sending many to sick bay with broken bones.

The women got their jobs back.

I was glad I went to work in the hangars. Otherwise I wouldn't have my men's dungarees. But I thought it was time to volunteer for another tour of mess duty.

It was hard to get excited about the moth ball fleet.

*   *   *

For dress-up in the summer, we could wear our whites . . .

. . . but we felt more at home in dungarees and boondockers

At hydraulic fittings, Roth and Tierney had nothing to do . . .

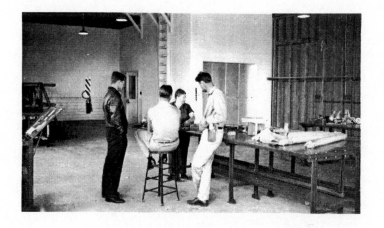

. . . neither did civilian workers still there on payroll

CHAPTER 45.
THE SANDWICH MILL

One Saturday afternoon, Kilgallen and I were sitting on a bench that overlooked the ocean at Laguna Beach when she clasped her hands. "I have to get some money fast."

"Money? What do you need money for, Kil? You have a place to sleep and plenty to eat."

"You know, we're not going to be here much longer. The war is over, and we have to start thinking about our future."

I shook my head. "I'd rather not think about it. The idea of going back to civilian life scares me."

"I can hardly wait to get my freedom," she said. "Do you remember that afternoon last week when I got special permission to leave the base?"

"Boy, do I! We were looking all over for you."

"Well, I had an appointment with Jerry Giesler. He's an attorney in Los Angeles."

"An attorney? Kil, are you in trouble? You know we have free legal services on the base."

She laughed at my suspicion. "No, Freddy, I'm not in any trouble. Not this time."

That was a relief. I could never be sure with her.

"I heard he's involved in some land deal around Las Vegas. I was curious about it so I called him and asked if we could talk."

"You're interested in land in Las Vegas?"

"Yes. This property should be a good investment. I went to his home. It was lovely, with white carpeting. He talked to me all afternoon and didn't charge me anything. He said there's an eighty-acre strip along Highway 91 selling for $12,000. They're going to bring in water and electricity, and build a new airport so people can fly out from California to gamble. It's legal there. They plan to put up a big hotel with a swimming pool and gambling room. They may even have entertainment."

What kind of a crazy scheme was Kilgallen getting herself into now? "Isn't Las Vegas in Nevada, out by Boulder Dam? There's nothing out there but desert."

"It won't be when they get through with it. But I'll need some money for a down payment."

"How much will it take?"

"A lot. I think I can convince my father to help me out and co-sign, if I show him I've made a start. But I'll need some money first."

We got up and continued our walk down Main Street. I began thinking about money. I would need some too. All the clothes I'd left in Portland were out of style. Wartime skirt length was just below the knee. Now that more material was available, we would wear them at mid calf.

"I guess we'll both need money when we get out," I said, "but there's a regulation against working without a work permit, and you have to prove a hardship for that."

"I thought you might have some ideas. You seemed to be doing pretty well when they were taking out for your dependent mother."

"Well, she doesn't need my help now. I get along just fine on what they pay me. Besides, nobody wants their uniforms altered anymore."

We walked in silence for a while, each deep in our own thoughts. As we approached the Sandwich Mill, I noticed a sign in the window. It read DISHWASHER WANTED.

"There's a job for you," I teased.

"Let's go in."

I hadn't expected her to take me seriously. She started for the door, so I followed. Somebody had to watch out for her.

The waitress was a pleasant, blonde, middle-aged woman with a pencil over her right ear. Kilgallen approached her.

"I'd like to speak to the manager."

"Frenchy is busy in the kitchen now. Can I help you?"

"We saw your sign in the window. We'd like to apply for the job."

Where did she get that "we" stuff? I didn't want to get in trouble.

The waitress looked surprised. "You want a job? Don't you already have a job?"

"I'd like to talk to him about it. If he's busy we can wait, or come back later."

The waitress disappeared into the kitchen. I glanced at the pass-through window and Frenchy's eyes met mine. He smiled.

A moment later she returned. "Just go on back," she said.

Reluctantly, I followed Kilgallen into the kitchen and watched as she talked to him.

A gray haired man, I would guess Frenchy to be in his middle fifties. He wore a white apron over his round belly. It had long strings that crossed in the back and returned to tie in front. The knot shook when he laughed.

"What can I do for you gyrenes?"

Kilgallen greeted him pleasantly. "We saw your sign for dishwasher. We can work weekends."

She was using the "we" word again.

Frenchy reached for a towel and wiped his balding head. He pointed toward the dishwasher on the other side of the kitchen. Dirty dishes were stacked high around it. "My wife is coming in pretty soon to help out," he said. "Do you think you could run one of those machines?"

"We have one on each side of our mess hall," Kilgallen explained. "Freddy here just finished running one for a month on mess duty."

I added, "Yeah, and forty-five women on the base got trench mouth last month."

My remark irritated Kilgallen. "They traced it to the dish-washer on the south wing. Freddy was working the north wing. It wasn't her fault."

"So you figure she can read the temperature gauge, eh?" He laughed again. "That's good. I wouldn't want an epidemic of trench mouth to break out here in Laguna Beach because I'd hired gyrenes to wash the dishes.

"By the way, what's trench mouth?"

We both got the job. We would start the next day, working Saturdays and Sundays from 1200 to 2000. It paid a dollar an hour plus one meal and all the coffee we could drink. That was hardly enough to risk getting a deck court for. I reminded Kilgallen of that on the way home.

"Don't worry about it, Freddy. They have to catch us first. Who's going to be snooping around in that kitchen anyway? We'll be wearing skivvies and Frenchy can give us one of those long white aprons to cover our dungarees. We'll pass for civilians."

By the time we got back to the base I was feeling better about it. I could use the money, and Kilgallen was really enjoying the idea of breaking another regulation.

The next morning we arrived at the Sandwich Mill well before noon with our dungarees in a bag. We changed in the employee's head, and Frenchy gave us each a long apron. I had to admit Kilgallen was right. It pretty much covered the pants.

Stella, the waitress, knew we must not get caught. "Warn me before you come out for the dirty dishes," she said, "so I can make sure there's no MPs out there."

"Or women officers," Kilgallen added. "Those little second lieutenants with their bachelor degrees in domestic science would turn us in quicker than the MPs."

"Now how would I know a woman officer? You all look alike to me." Stella didn't wait for an answer.

The breakfast dishes were waiting so there was plenty of work to keep us busy, and the time went fast. By the middle of the afternoon we were caught up. Frenchy asked, "You girls getting hungry? I can't give you filet mignon, but you can have any of the sandwiches on the menu, or abalone steak. We sell a lot of those."

Kilgallen asked, "What's abalone?"

"We'll take two," I said.

"Cheapest thing on the dinner menu," Frenchy went on. "And I know how to cook 'em. They just cut 'em off the rocks when the tide's out. It's a lot easier than catching fish. They're everywhere out there."

When our meals were ready, Frenchy set them up on the pass through. "We can't eat out there," I said. "We might be recognized."

Frenchy started looking around the kitchen. "I'll tell Stella to bring a couple chairs in from the dining room."

"We don't need chairs," said Kilgallen. "There's plenty of room here in the corner."

We took our plates there and sat down to eat.

"Hey, what are you doing?" Frenchy asked. "You don't have to sit on the floor!"

Kilgallen smiled. "We always sit on the floor."

Frenchy laughed. "Stella has to see this." He stuck his head through the window. "Stella, can you come back here a minute?"

She stepped into the kitchen and Frenchy pointed to us. "Look where they're eating their dinner!"

I couldn't understand all the fuss. It seemed to me we were behaving normally.

"They're sitting on the floor!" She giggled. "Get up, girls. I'll get you some chairs."

Kilgallen shook her head. "No, this is fine. The floor is clean, and we like it down here."

"Yeah," I added, "it's cooler."

Stella giggled again. "But you look so funny."

I couldn't see the humor in it now, but two years ago I might have laughed at the sight of us too. Would I be able to change back? And did I really want to?

"Freddy, this stuff is great. How come you're not eating?"

Her question brought me back from my thoughts. No use letting good abalone get cold.

I suspect that Kilgallen would have washed those dishes whether she got paid for it or not, just for the thrill of breaking another regulation. We seemed to be getting away with it, but I always felt a little nervous when I went out to get the dirty dishes.

About the third Sunday, as I headed for the dining room I met Stella coming in. She looked terrified. "Don't go out there, Freddy!" she said. "There's some women officers sitting in a booth right by the counter where you pick up."

Kilgallen was disgusted. "Take their orders quickly so we can get them out of here." She poured herself a cup of coffee, went to our corner, and sat.

I was curious. I peeked out the pass through.

"Gilda! That's Gilda!" I was excited. The one sitting on the end looked up at the mention of her name. "She's not an officer, Stella. She's an enlisted WAC!"

I ran out to greet a girl who had graduated with me from Marshall High School in Chicago five years earlier.

Kilgallen got up and dumped the rest of her coffee in the sink. Then she picked up the dirty dishes and went back to work, while I took a moment to talk to an old friend.

When I came back to the kitchen Stella remarked, "I can't understand why any girl would join the WACs when they could be a Marine. Your uniform is so much cuter."

"Funny you should say that," I replied. "Gilda said she tried to join the Marines first, but in Chicago the waiting list was so long she was afraid the war would end before they got around to calling her."

"I didn't have any trouble enlisting in Chicago," said Kilgallen. "I just started talking, and I was in before they knew what hit them.

"My trouble came later when I applied for OCS. Imagine! I have a master's degree, but they didn't accept me for Officer's Candidate School."

Frenchy laughed. "You mean to tell me I have a dishwasher working for me for a dollar an hour, who has a master's degree? I'll have to tell my wife about this."

Putting money in the bank was a new experience for Kilgallen, but with her weekends filled she had little chance to spend it. When she felt she had saved enough to confront her father with her plans, she wrote him requesting a loan to "help cover" the down payment on the Las Vegas property.

"I hope he will agree to co-sign," she said.

But when the answer came, she was disappointed. "He thinks real estate out here is a shaky investment." She looked up from the letter. "He insists that all this development out here was due to the war, and now that it's over everybody will go back home to a more stable economy.

"I still think Jerry is right, but I'll never convince my father of that, and it's impossible for a single woman to get a real estate loan without a man to back it up. I'll just have to return to Chicago and go back to teaching school."

Kilgallen lost interest in the Sandwich Mill. She started spending more time with her sisters in Long Beach, and Lawson took her place. By the time she had enough points for discharge, Lawson and I were keeping Frenchy supplied with dishwashers.

He now had two WRs working every evening during the week as well. Frenchy and Stella were amused to learn that they, too, sat on the floor.

All of the dishwashers were from our Norman, Oklahoma, class of 52-44, so we were eligible for discharge at the same time. Eventually it became necessary to give Frenchy two week's notice. Sunday night, after finishing our work, we I told him.

"I don't know what I'm going to do without you girls," he said. "I'm really going to miss you."

Lawson looked surprised. "You will?"

"Yes, I will. You've always been dependable, and you just take over and train each other. Besides," he admitted, "I like you gyrenes."

Lawson smiled thoughtfully. "Frenchy, I'm getting out in two weeks." She bit her lip. "Can I stay on working here until school starts in September? I can wait tables too."

Frenchy beamed. "I'd be glad to have ya, Lawson. Stella's always complaining about not getting enough good help out there."

It was time to go. Lawson hesitated before going in to change. "By the way," she said, "my first name is Vera."

As we dressed, I could tell she was excited. "I did it! I made some plans for my civilian life!"

"What school are you going to?"

"I don't know. I just now thought of it. You know, we have this GI bill."

We dressed quickly and waited for Frenchy to unlock the front door. On his way he picked up something from beneath the counter. He placed it carefully in the window before letting us out.

As we walked away, I glanced back. I had seen that sign before. It read DISHWASHER WANTED.

*   *   *

CHAPTER 46.
UPSTAIRS LOUNGE

Shortly after the war ended, I began to notice that some of the men waiting in our downstairs lounge looked familiar. Where had I seen them before?

Ah yes. It was their photos that had been smiling out from open locker doors. These were the men the women had waited for. Now they were waiting for the women who had waited for them.

Diamond rings that had been sent home from boot camp to accommodate uniform regulations were back, worn now in defiance of the rules. No one was punished for it. That war seemed to be over too.

Chaplains were busy performing long-postponed weddings. Most WRs chose to keep them simple, taking place in the chapel on the base, with both bride and groom in uniform. Some families were present, many were not. Always a few good buddies were there.

It wasn't the ceremony every little girl dreams of, but these girls grew up just in time to experience the most devastating war the world had ever known. Dreams changed.

Still there were a few who would cling to tradition. One Saturday morning I saw evidence of it when I strolled into the upstairs lounge. A sergeant and two assistants were cutting into a large piece of lovely white satin. They had covered the Ping-Pong table with a clean sheet and the long pattern pieces were already pinned down.

That had to be a wedding gown. I picked up the pattern envelope to study it.

The sergeant asked, "You sew?"

"Yes."

"I'm Sully. There's several yards of lace to be hand stitched. If you want to help, go wash your hands."

It would be a couple hours before Lawson and I left for the Sandwich Mill. I had just washed my hands, but there was no use arguing with her. I washed them again.

The bride-to-be was in another barracks. I didn't know her, but no matter. She was one of us. In the days that followed, I spent much of my spare time stitching lace in the upstairs lounge. When Peters noticed what I was doing, she sometimes joined me.

The work had taken over the sewing machine, the Ping-Pong table, and several chairs at one end of the room, but for the rest of the lounge it was business as usual. The hair dryer was always in use, and usually there was a card game going at the coffee table.

I enjoyed listening to a small group of WRs who often hung out on the couches nearby. Their lively talk and laughter helped the time pass as my needle fastened delicate lace to satin edges.

Once I mentioned to Pellier that it would be fun to join them. She told me they were lesbians. I didn't have a dictionary handy, but the word sounded to me like it referred to the performing arts. That didn't interest me, so I made no effort to get to know them.

Conversations had changed. Instead of planning the next weekend liberty, they were talking about the liberty that was going to last them for the rest of their lives.

Many were looking forward to going "back home" to pick up where they left off. Others were still caught up in the excitement of the homeless, gypsy lifestyle we enjoyed in the military. A group that sometimes met on the floor in the corner made plans to buy a car together.

"I know these people in town who have a car that's hardly been used," one said. "It's a '40 Chevy coupe, and they didn't drive it much because they couldn't get gas. Maybe they'd sell it to us, if we offered them enough money."

I nudged Peters. "That sounds like fun. Wish I knew how to drive."

"Maybe we could learn."

I never thought of that.

Near the center of the lounge, one of the WRs playing cards at the coffee table said, "I still have my car back home in New Jersey. I'm leaving on furlough Monday to go get it. I'll push that pedal to the floor and have it out here in no time. Then we can take off and go wherever we please, never have to worry about bus schedules or hitching a ride."

She shook her head. "You won't believe what my mother did. She called me last night and begged me not to drive it out here." Smiling, she added, "She thinks I'm going to kill myself."

Everybody laughed. We all had mothers.

It looked like many were planning to hit the road, and they wouldn't need a man to drive them. The world was changing. We would change with it.

After evening chow one Friday, Erickson came into the lounge where we were sewing. She asked Peters to go with her that night to the dance in Santa Ana.

I was interested. "Is that the weekly dances everyone's talking about, over at the Army Air Force Base?"

"That's it. They send a bus over for us. Those Air Force men aren't like some of the Marines around here. They treat us with respect, and don't refer to us as BAMs."

I was thinking of going, but Peters shook her head. "I don't know how to dance."

That seemed to settle it. Erickson left, and the subject was dropped. I never did attend the dances. Instead, I continued to spend my evenings in the head, where we would call meetings of the All Men Are Bastards club to complain about how they were treating us. I should have gone to the dances.

After the hand stitching was completed on the gown, we went to work on the veil. By the time that was finished, the gown was almost ready.

The next time I went in to use the hair dryer, the cover was back on the sewing machine, and WRs were playing Ping-Png at the table. The upstairs lounge was back to normal.

I never did meet the bride.

*   *   *

MEMORIAL

Taken from the Los Angeles Times, Tuesday, October 2, 1945:

Four Women Marines Die in Auto-Train Collision
SANTA ANA, Oct. 1.—Four members of the Marine Corps
Women's Reserve were killed in a train-auto crash at Irvine, near
their base at El Toro, Coroner Earl Abbey reported today.

Anna McDougall and Nancy Engwall were killed instantly
while Virginia Ruth Spaulding and Shirley Kilian died later in
Long Beach Naval Hospital, the Coroner said. Edith M. Behnke,
another woman marine, suffered critical injuries and is in the same
hospital.

Authorities at El Toro Marine Air Station refused to disclose
home addresses of the women until next of kin have been notified.

Signals Said Functioning

The Coroner and California Highway Patrol officers said that
warning signals were functioning at the Sante Fe crossing on Cen-
tral Ave. near Irvine when the accident occurred. It could not be
learned which of the women was driving the automobile, which
was demolished in the crash . . .

*   *   *

Whalen accompanied one of the bodies back home to New
York.

Edith Behnke recovered and remained in the corps until her
discharge.

Our flags were flown at half-staff, and their empty bunks were
a constant reminder to us of our great loss.

CHAPTER 47.
MUSTERING OUT AT
EL TORO

The Marine Corp went into action quickly to discharge all of the women. One entire squad room in another barracks was emptied for orientation. We would spend our last days in the Corps there, being oriented back into civilian life. I certainly needed that.

A rumor was going around that we may later have the option to sign over into the regular Marine Corps, but the idea met with heavy opposition. In A HISTORY OF WOMEN MARINES, 1946-1977, by Col. Mary V. Stremlow, on page 1 she writes:

. . . In these words, Brigader (sic) General Gerald C. Thomas, Director, Division of Plans and Policies in October 1945, stated the basic Marine Corps case against women on active duty. He elaborated his stand with the contention, "The American tradition is that a woman's place is in the home . . ." and, "Women do not take kindly to military regimentation. During the war they have accepted the regulations imposed on them, but hereafter the problem of enforcing discipline alone would be a headache."[1]

The general would later have need of a large bottle of aspirin.

We had the option to postpone our discharge as long as there were others waiting to take our place in orientation. I was in no hurry. I would wait.

Women Marines from other western bases soon began arriving at El Toro for discharge. The first of these groups to arrive were salts from the early platoons that had gone through boot camp at Hunter College. I recognized my recruiting sergeant in the chow

---

[1] General Gerald C. Thomas, memo to CMC, dated 30 October, 1945 [Postwar MCWR 1 file]

line when Kilgallen pointed her out to me. She was envious of the way her red hair touched the collar. On my way out, I stopped at her table to thank her for making the Marine Corps experience possible for me.

"You were lucky," she said. "For every hundred applications we had in Portland, we could only take seven. I liked you because you were tall and thin. I told my officer I thought the uniform would look good on you."

She glanced at my soiled dungarees and frowned.

"But," she went on, "the lieutenant favored women with at least two years of college. She made an exception in your case because of the recommendation from your boss."

I had no idea competition there was so keen, but I did wonder why so many of the other boots in my platoon had college in their background. Ken Johnson, the plant manager at Radio Specialty, had come through for me.

After the Hunter College WRs had gone through, a very salty looking group arrived from Hawaii. Their overseas service had given them extra points toward early discharge.

They had been closer to the war, and it showed. The sun had bleached their hair and darkened their skin, causing teeth to look whiter by contrast. They wore men's salty dungarees, topped with the women's fatigue bowler hats, each individually shaped, as if to make a statement. They swaggered confidently into the chow hall together. Their appearance created a curious response from the permanent base personnel.

Once Rudkin and I were observing a group of them at the next table when she stopped in the middle of a sentence. "Hey," she said. "That looks like Thompson!"

I noted some resemblance. The sergeant sat tall enough to be Thompson, and she had similar features, but the air of dignity was not there. This WR's hair was almost white, her complexion a solid mass of freckles. Thompson's hair was golden brown, and her skin was fair. It couldn't be her.

"It's her!" Rudkin stood up. "Come on, let's catch her before she gets away."

A look of recognition spread over the sergeant's face as we approached. "Thompson, old bunky buddy!" Rudkin shouted. "What are you doing here?"

"I'm getting out, like everyone else." When she smiled, I knew it was Thompson. She had the straightest, whitest teeth in platoon E-5.

The very salty little corporal sitting beside her added, "Haven't you heard? The war's over!" I glanced at Thompson's buddy. It was hard to tell where one freckle ended and another began. Her sun bleached, short cropped hair stuck out straight from beneath the bowler, and the hat, perched precariously on the back of her head, looked like a jeep had run over it. She kept rambling on. I wondered why Thompson hadn't introduced us.

"I just loved Hawaii," she said. "The sunsets are beautiful, and the beaches . . ." She paused. "Hey, don't you guys remember me?"

I stared at her. "Are you Gordy?"

She nodded. This was the feather merchant who had been the only one to hear the DI's order, "To the rear, Harch!" The one who tripped on her wardrobe as we double-timed it back from the Tailor Shop in a rainstorm. It was Gordy.

"I wanted to drive, but Thompson got to do that, and I had to work on the jeeps."

Thompson grinned. "But you loved it."

"Yeah, I loved it."

Each had lived the other's dream, and neither seemed unhappy about it. They were discharged the next day. They went home together, the right guide and the feather merchant, back to Oregon to begin the next phase of their lives.

There was a notice on the bulletin board. El Toro was mustering out their NCOs, leaving too many privates and not enough sergeants. Beginning 1 Dec 45, all enlisted WRs remaining on the base would be awarded a stripe every four months.

It took me twenty-one months to make PFC. Before I sewed

the stripe on my dungarees, Murdock came to El Toro for discharge. I spotted her as I was leaving the chow hall after lunch. She had been on my mind since the day we received orders out of boot camp, when she had inferred that I lacked the qualifications to be sent to a school.

I hurried over to let her know she was wrong. I needed to explain to her that Battalion Area turned out to be a place to wait until my class began in Norman, Oklahoma. She was not impressed. I noticed she had not lost her attitude of belligerence. I also noticed she had made sergeant.

"Where were you stationed?" I asked.

"Mohave." She didn't look too happy about that. Evidently the Imperial Valley desert had not been her first choice.

There was a constant flow of WRs moving from their quarters into orientation, and from there out on the streets to face the shock of civilian life. As a result, housing problems developed for those remaining. They left one squad room to double up in another, only to begin emptying that one, creating a need to regroup again. And moving dates seldom coincided with linen change day.

Kilgallen was not subjected to this inconvenience. Having enlisted earlier, she had enough points to be the first to leave our squad room. Before she moved out, Lawson and I talked to her about her plans.

"I'm going home to put my book together, and you're all in it. I've already written the first draft. I'm calling it 'From The Boudoirs Of Montezuma.' It's all down in my diary."

Lawson frowned. "We're not supposed to keep a diary," she said. "It's against wartime regulations."

"Well, the war is over. Besides, I'm not keeping it, my mother is. And it isn't a diary unless you call it that. I call it letters home." She paused. "Almost any regulation can be broken if you think about it creatively."

Lawson asked, "Am I in your book?"

"You're in my book all right. So is Freddy. You're all in my book." She waved her arm in a large circle, to encompass the entire squad room.

Lawson asked, "What did you say about me?"

"If you want to know that, you'll have to buy my book."

Lawson and I joined Kilgallen at evening chow for the week she spent in orientation. "It's asinine," she said. "I sleep through most of it."

That would account for the trouble we had keeping up with her at Victor Hugo's every night.

"An officer talked to us today," she began one evening. "She told us we were the most unique group of women in the world. They had interviewed over 20,000 of us when we enlisted, and not one of us had said we suffered from cramps with our periods."

I remembered hearing Lumpkin moan, "Oh, my achin' ovaries," on a monthly basis. I guessed that was different from having cramps.

"One bride asked her about getting medical benefits for a pregnancy," Kilgallen went on. "The lieutenant said it would depend on whether or not the condition was service incurred."

Her days in orientation passed quickly. The time came, too soon, for her to leave. I was not prepared to say goodbye. When we met with her that last day, a patch, the symbol of discharge, was already sewn on her uniform, above the right breast pocket. It had the figure of an eagle on it, like the one on the pin our returning GIs affectionately referred to as "The ruptured duck."

She seemed troubled. "Freddy," she asked, "do you remember the time Bongiorni and I borrowed some of my sister's civilian clothes to wear to the officer's dance at Camp Pendleton?"

"Boy, do I! The guard at the gate was suspicious because you were bundled in your trench coats on such a warm night."

Kilgallen was constantly breaking regulations but it was the only time she was ever caught. "Did you know I had a summary court-martial for that?"

I nodded.

"Well, they put it on my discharge. It's a part of my permanent record. I'm going to have to explain that every time I apply for a teaching job."

I thought if anyone could explain it Kilgallen could.

She had arranged to ride out on a jeep. It was waiting nearby, and the driver was becoming impatient. We said our goodbyes hurriedly and she climbed aboard, perching on top of some sea bags piled in the back.

The bags were being taken to Irvine. That was a small railroad stop near El Toro, used as a loading dock to ship produce from the neighboring farms. It did not take on passengers. Kilgallen was unclear as to how she would proceed from there.

She held her suitcase in one hand and turned to wave goodbye with the other. I started to move closer. There was so much I wanted to say. But I heard the engine start and the jeep began to move away, taking her out of my life.

"Remember," she called back, "you're all in my book."

I answered simply "Goodbye, Kil."

She repeated "You're all in my book!" and she was gone.

It's too bad she never got around to writing it. "From the Boudoirs of Montezuma" would have been one hell of a book.

*   *   *

CHAPTER 48.
LIFE WITHOUT KILGALLEN

December, 1945

Kilgallen's bunk in the next bay was empty now, but our squad room remained intact throughout the holidays.

As soon as the war ended, Pellier and Jeter had rented a cottage in Laguna Beach and Peters moved into the space below me. I had a new bunky. Ward and Tierney still had the cots on the aisle. In the next bay, Sattler and Roth were still bunkmates and Lawson was alone, by the window, now that Kilgallen was gone.

We seven became much like a family. We chipped in to get a coffee pot and hot plate. Lawson stored them in Kilgallen's empty locker. In the evening we would gather in the head with our coffee and talk.

Peters once brought in a copy of the September, 1945 issue of *The Woman's Home Companion*. An article in it told about a new idea called natural childbirth. Dr. Grantly Dick Reed had written a book on the subject, called *Childbirth Without Fear*.

"It makes a lot of sense to me," said Peters. "This is how I want to have my babies."

She read parts of the article aloud. While I was fascinated with the possibility, I doubted I would ever have a chance to try it. "Who are we kidding?" I asked. "We can't have babies by ourselves."

They laughed. Of course, they were only twenty-two. I would soon be twenty-four, an age that put me well on the way to becoming an old maid.

Men treated us differently after we put on the uniform. We

had joined to free a Marine to fight, but we ended up having to fight with them. It was there, in the head, that the All Men Are Bastards club (AMABs) would gather.

While Sattler often joined us, she did not share our attitude toward men. She often dated the men on the base, and insisted their pet word for us didn't bother her. She said, "If you ignored that, you'd find out they're just regular guys."

Sometimes a couple of us would take the bus into Santa Ana. It dropped us off in front of Mary's, where we could pick up the best hamburgers in the world. Then we'd hop on the next bus back to the base. By then the coffee was ready, and a meeting of the AMABs would begin.

One evening, when Sattler suggested hamburgers would taste good, the rest of us were already in pajamas so she volunteered to go in alone to get them. On the bus she met a sailor she had been dating, who suggested they stop for a drink or two at the Colony.

A little after midnight I felt a tap on my shoulder. "Freddy, wake up. I have your hamburger."

"Not now, Satt. I'm asleep."

"You ordered this. If you don't eat it, I'll have to toss it in the G.I. can."

She knew that would get me up. I followed her into the head. So did Peters, Ward, Tierney, Lawson, and Roth. We ate in silence, and I only vaguely remembered it the next morning. That was the last time we sent Sattler in alone to pick up hamburgers.

Long before the holidays, we started making plans for Christmas Eve. We wanted to spend it here at home, because it would be our last Christmas together.

Roth got permission for us to bring in a small tree. We set it up in the other bay. At first it stood naked on the dresser. We made some decorations, and picked up more at Thrifty's in Santa Ana. It soon took on a personality of its own.

Packages, arriving from home, went under the tree. We drew names for a secret gift exchange. Sattler was going steady now with a sailor stationed on the base. She didn't plan to spend Christmas Eve with us, but she wanted in on the gift exchange.

I drew Tierney's name. She had very conservative taste and therefore could be difficult to buy for. But Tierney was our photographer. She took her camera along wherever she went. I wrapped a photo album for her, along with some of those sticky corners for the pictures, and placed it under the tree when no one was around.

Later I caught Sattler putting a small package there with Ward's name on it. She swore me to secrecy.

One by one the gifts we had for each other appeared, until there were seven of them. The one with my name on it was wrapped in red Santa Claus paper. It was a thin box, measuring about six by nine inches. Light in weight, I figured it was probably a scarf, though I secretly hoped for a pair of nylons. They were still hard to find.

As it turned out, Sattler did spend Christmas Eve with us because her sailor had the duty that night. They met at the slop chute after chow, where he gave her two gifts, a diamond ring and a bottle of Southern Comfort.

Alcohol was not allowed in the barracks, but it was Christmas Eve. She slipped it in.

None of us had ever heard of Southern Comfort. Lawson hid it in Kilgallen's locker behind the Cokes and potato chips. Tierney added a fruitcake her mother had sent, and Peters shared a box of homemade cookies.

Ward scrubbed out a swab bucket and took it to the chow hall to fill it with ice. Roth helped me carry in a coffee table from the upstairs lounge. We put it between the bunks and spread the treats on it.

For a while we sat around and talked, each describing how we had celebrated the holiday back home. Lawson opened a large bottle of Coke. She was about to fill our cups when Sattler stopped her.

"Whoa!" she yelled. "Let's start with just Southern Comfort

first, so we don't dilute it. I wanna know what this stuff tastes like straight."

She poured a small amount for each of us and we sipped on it timidly. "It's so smooooth," said Sattler.

Roth played Santa Claus, handing out the presents from home first. We opened them one at a time. Most were civilian clothes. We were allowed to wear them off duty, now that the war was over.

The first gift I opened was a purse from my sister. A note explained, "This is to match that Navy blue suit you always wanted." I had been wearing forest green so long I forgot I ever wanted a Navy blue suit. But it was a nice purse.

When Sattler's cup was empty, she filled it with Southern Comfort. Then she offered more to us. Smiling, she repeated, "It's so smooooth."

Lawson had already poured the Coke, so we declined.

When there were no more gifts from home to unwrap, we started on the presents we were exchanging with each other. As Ward opened hers, a bottle of perfume, I was careful not to look at Sattler. Three scarves, the photo album, and one lacy slip followed. My gift was last. I began unwrapping it carefully, hoping to save the ribbon.

Lawson said, "Come on, open it!"

Snipping the ribbon, I opened the box. I couldn't believe my eyes. There, beneath layers of neatly folded tissue paper, was a pair of scarlet panties. I held them up. "This can't be for me!"

I glanced around at the group. I knew it wasn't from Sattler. I looked suspiciously at the other five.

"It wasn't from me," said Roth.

"Me neither," said Ward.

Lawson denied it, and Peters looked at me with a half smile, shaking her head. It wasn't from her either. That left Tierney, the quiet, shy girl from Iowa. I had misjudged her.

Sattler sported an impish grin. "I want one of those. Let me see where it came from."

She jumped up quickly, bumping her head on the bunk above,

and spilling most of what remained in her bottle. Then she lost her balance and fell into the dip.

She was out for the night.

Lawson and I washed her and put her to bed. Then we joined the rest mopping up the Southern Comfort on the deck beside her bunk. We wiped up what we could, and left the rest for morning. Tierney placed the near empty bottle on Sattler's pillow, beside her smiling face, and took a picture of it.

After chow Christmas morning, we put on our gym clothes (the ones we called peanut suits) to clean up after the party. Sattler and Roth scrubbed the floor, trying to remove the stain of Southern Comfort, but it was still there. They went to work on it with steel wool. It wasn't coming off. We each took a turn at it, scrubbing until our arms ached, but it was useless. The stain was permanent.

For all I know it remains there still, a tribute to our last Christmas Eve together.

*   *   *

CHAPTER 49.
LAUNDRY DELIVERY

Roth and I were on our way to the coffee shop when she noticed a forlorn dog wandering through the hangar. She called to it, and it came, wagging its tail. Large for a dachshund, and rotund, it looked to me like it hadn't missed many meals.

Roth eyed the dog with suspicion. "She looks like she's going to have puppies."

Picking her up gently, she carried her to the coffee shop, where She bought milk and poured some in a bowl for her. The dog lapped it up quickly, then finished off the rest of it.

Sitting by the door with the dog on her lap, she asked everyone as they came in, "Do you know whose dog this is?"

No one knew, and only a few seemed to care. She followed us out, begging for more. Roth took the dog with her back to the hydraulics department. When it was time to board a cattle car back to the women's area for noon chow, she brought the dog along.

Taking her to the back door of the mess hall, she explained the situation to the cooks. Lumpkin brought out a tray of roast beef, mashed potatoes, and carrots. The dog gulped it all down like she was starving.

Roth watched her thoughtfully. "She must be someone's pet."

"Surely she'll be missed," I said. "I'll ask Lawson to have the art department make some notices. We can post them on the bulletin boards around the base."

The signs were made and posted, but there was no response. Civilians were still working in the hangars. One of them, disapproving of her indiscretion, may have dropped her off. After several days Roth declared, "It looks like we have ourselves a mascot."

She responded to "Shorty," so that became her name. It was nice having a dog around again. Shorty always followed Roth to the chow hall, where the cooks fixed a tray for her and placed it on the back porch. Her appetite was insatiable. We brought snacks back to the barracks to tide her over.

Her waistline quickly expanded to such proportions that walking became difficult. We made a soft bed for her and placed it by the dryers in the laundry room, where it was warm. A WR from Palm Springs who was going home donated the wool lining from her trench coat for padding.

Her belly grew so large it dragged on the floor. Soon her feet couldn't reach to the ground. She took to her bed and had her meals delivered.

Mournful eyes looked up at us pitifully as we watched for a sign that she might be going into labor. When her time came, Hettie Sandfort, a WR from another squad room, stayed with the dog all night assisting in her delivery. By morning there were thirteen puppies. They came in a variety of colors, tumbling over each other in a blind search for that first meal. We fenced off an area in her corner to contain them.

Shorty was able to jump in and out now. Delighted to have her figure back, she began following us to the chow hall again, always eating quickly at the kitchen door, then hurrying back to nurse her young.

There were too many puppies and not enough nipples. The cooks kept us supplied with fresh milk, and someone got some droppers from the dispensary for supplemental feedings. All thirteen survived.

Some WRs took one home when they were discharged. However, when Sandfort's turn came to pack her sea bag, there were several puppies left. She took Shorty and her entire remaining family home with her to her parents' farm.

We returned a washing machine to its former position and

regained use of the corner dryers. The laundry room was back to normal.

Yet, for me, there always seemed to be something missing. I never looked at that corner again without wondering how Shorty and her thirteen puppies were adjusting to civilian life.

*   *   *

Teaford's send-off L to R: Sattler, Ward, Teaford (note ruptured duck patch), Freddy, Roth & Tierney

Saying goodbye to Sattler and Teaford

Roth & Ward not too happy about going home

"I'm going to miss this place"-Tierney

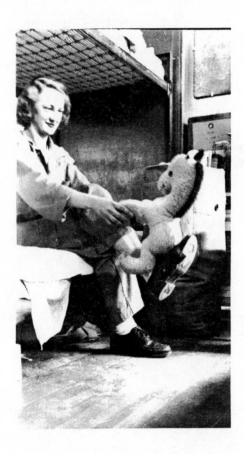

Off to the separation center

CHAPTER 50.

THE LAST CHAPTER

April 18, 1946

My first night as a civilian had been a restless one. The Library Park Guest House in Los Angeles was quiet enough, but my mind was not. The next morning I sat alone at a small table in the USO, contemplating the rest of my life over a doughnut and a cup of coffee.

It was time to make some decisions. I had to find a job, and I still had nothing to wear. Those shopping trips with my buddies had been a waste of time for me. I couldn't believe I had ever decorated myself in those floral prints, flashy colors, and fancy ruffles and bows.

I felt the corporal stripes on my sleeve and remembered that I hardly had time to sew them on before receiving my discharge. The day I enlisted seemed so long ago. Now I was two years older, and not a whole lot wiser.

Sadly, there was no one here to share with me this feeling of emptiness. Most of my buddies were gone. Had they felt this way? Probably not. They seemed so anxious to go home.

Home. My mother was expecting me to return to Portland and live with them. But I knew could never live in the same house with her new husband. How could I tell her I would not be going back? I'd have to think about that.

I had written several letters to Kilgallen in Chicago since her discharge, but she hadn't answered any of them. Was she too busy, writing her book? We had been through so much together. I didn't want to lose touch with her.

The last time I saw Pellier she was heading back to New England, with plans to finish her education and teach.

Lawson and Jeter were both in Laguna Beach. Lawson was living with Stella while she worked at the Sandwich Mill. I heard she had a boy friend now. Jeter worked with a group of civilians who were starting a ceramics business, but in September she would go home to attend college. She had lost most of that charming southern accent.

Pity.

Graves was anxious to get back to Saginaw, Michigan, as soon as she could be discharged, to prepare for Bob's return. But the Marine Corps wouldn't let her go. They made her wait until Bob was discharged.

Kilgallen would say that was asinine.

Whalen had an offer from New York to play with a women's softball team called the Bloomer Girls. As soon as she could get out, she headed there to accept it.

Bongiorni joined the Red Cross to see the world. She would be leaving soon for Europe.

Erickson returned to her home in Michigan to cram for entrance exams to a California University. She would be back in September.

Before Chici was discharged, she spent time at Corona Naval Hospital for surgical removal of her tattoo. She was engaged to a sailor named Bill, and Indian "Joe" had to go.

Too bad. I had grown fond of him.

Peters was in South Dakota, but wrote she planned to join me here later. I wished that she were here now.

Of our class in Norman, only Tierney still remained in the Corps. She said she would stay until the end. Perhaps I should have done the same. It's lonely out here.

For me, there was no place to go back to. Portland was out of the question, and there was little reason to return to Chicago. My brother and sister were both happily settled in their marriages, and Lily and Elsie had their husbands back from the war. I had little in common with any of them, anymore.

I was so changed that I felt uncomfortable around civilians. Their talk of fashion, hair styles, and recipes didn't interest me. What else do they discuss? Husbands? Children? I had neither. All of the men I knew before enlisting had dropped me when I joined the Marines, believing I was a fallen woman. I will never understand that.

I enlisted to free a Marine to fight, though I would have willingly picked up a gun and joined them, had they let me. Now, in my defense, I can only say that I filled a slot in their quota system.

Yet that system was right on target. The atomic bomb was kept so secret that until President Roosevelt's death, even our vice president was not aware of its existence. We had to be ready for a long, drawn out invasion of Japan, with uncounted losses. Our ABG-2 hangars would have been a busy repair center for war torn Marine fighter planes returning from combat in the Pacific Theater for servicing. And I would have helped.

I was proud of my buddies who had accomplished so much more. I remembered Callahan, who rigged the parachute that saved a pilot's life. And there was Elder, my boot camp bunky, helping to get out the payroll for our fighting men.

Graves and others who went to North Island had pulled engines, working directly on planes during wartime in the ABG-2 hangars there. I wished, now, that I had gone.

They were good women, my buddies. I would never forget them.

Several WRs had married Marines while stationed at El Toro. I should have tried harder to understand why so many of them treated us as they did. Except for Mike, I hadn't dated anyone since coming to California. As soon as I heard the word BAM I took it as a personal insult, and I was gone, unable to understand the reason for their crude remarks about the width of my derriere.

Were they simply confused about how to relate to us? Could

the word that shocked me so have been, to them, just an attempt to get my attention?

It got my attention, all right. It also gave them a good look at the part of my anatomy they had described when I stormed off.

At least I still had Mike for a friend. He would not be coming back for a while yet. A latecomer to the Pacific Theater, he had to wait his turn. In his last letter he seemed excited that he had been accepted at the Massachusetts Institute of Technology. He hoped to be discharged in time to start engineering classes there at Cambridge in September.

"Meanwhile," he wrote, "keep those Terry strips coming."

I picked up my paper and found the comics. With my nail file I began, carefully, to remove Terry and the Pirates from the bottom of the page.

"Is this seat saved?"

I looked up. Across the table from me, an Army Air Force sergeant stood lean and tall, gesturing to the empty chair in front of him. He had hazel eyes and a friendly smile that revealed a dimple high on each cheek.

There were plenty of empty tables around, but I welcomed the company. "I guess it was saved for you."

He wore ribbons from both the European and Pacific Theaters, with the familiar ruptured duck perched on the opposite side of his Eisenhower blouse. I was glad I had sewn mine on too. It told us something about each other.

"Would you like your coffee warmed up?"

He filled my cup and took one for himself, bringing a couple doughnuts back to the table. I folded the paper to make room.

"I see you save Terry and the Pirates," he observed. "That's my favorite comic strip, especially now that I've seen China."

"Oh, I don't save it. I mail it overseas. They can't get it there."

"That's the truth. I wish someone had sent it to me."

I looked at this soldier, home from the wars. Perhaps he could tell me stories that would make Terry's adventures seem dull in comparison.

He asked, "Where were you stationed?"

"El Toro."

"You never came to our dances at the Santa Ana Base."

"How do you know?"

"If you did, I would have asked you to dance."

"You would?"

"Yes, I would." He seemed to expect an explanation.

"Well, I belonged to this group that met the same night as the dances." I paused awkwardly. "My buddy, Erickson, told me about them. I probably should have gone with her."

"Kay Erickson? I know her. She's a good dancer. I preferred dancing with the WRs rather than the civilian junior hostesses. They seemed more mature. They had a good sense of humor, and they were a lot easier to talk to."

He called us WRs, not BAMs! I was beginning to like this man. I noted his ribbons. "With all that overseas time, how come you're just now getting out?"

"I was with Air Force Intelligence. When the European war was finished, they sent us to China. We were getting ready to invade Japan from there. I had plenty of points for discharge, but I had a spec my outfit needed, so they asked me to stay until the job was finished."

"What was the spec?"

He grinned. "One of my jobs was to interrogate the pilots after they flew their missions. I wrote the squadron history, and I was the only man in the outfit who could type."

Recalling there were no boys in my typing class, I asked, "Where did you learn that?"

"Well, I'm kind of self-taught. When I worked on the school newspaper at Chapman College I had to type. I used the Columbus method. You know, discover a key and land on it. I can get up to forty-five words a minute that way."

"Chapman College." Pellier had once mentioned it. "That's here in Los Angeles, isn't it? Are you a native Californian?"

"No, I grew up in Kansas," he said. "Hutchinson. But I spent my summers working on my grandfather's farm outside of town. I'm really a farm boy at heart.

"I came out here to finish college. Graduated in '40, and never went home. I like living in California."

"So do I. Just got out yesterday. Don't know where I'll go now. My sea bag is still at El Toro."

"Hey, I left my barracks bag at the Santa Ana base. I borrowed a car from my buddy today to drive out and pick it up. I came in here to see if anybody needed a ride. Why don't you come along, and we can get yours too?"

We stood up to leave. His hand touched my shoulder, gently, as I passed. "By the way," he said, "my name's Milt Ferris."

"Mine's Inga Fredriksen."

Later I would change it to Inga Ferris, because Pellier was right. There were still decent single men around who were not insulting. She didn't get the last one.

I did.

*   *   *

Punchy, our cartoonist